For your e'   love   If
I love y

A PRIVATE WILDERNESS

A PRIVATE WILDERNESS

The Journals of
Sigurd F. Olson

SIGURD F. OLSON

Edited by David Backes

University of Minnesota Press
Minneapolis
London

The publication of this book was assisted by a bequest from Josiah H. Chase to honor his parents, Ellen Rankin Chase and Josiah Hook Chase, Minnesota territorial pioneers.

Frontispiece, page ii: Canoeing on Lac La Croix, Boundary Waters Canoe Area, 1961. Photograph by Roy Dale Sanders, U.S. Forest Service Records, National Archives.

Map on pages vi–vii: Canoe routes into Superior National Forest, Minnesota, and Quetico Provincial Park of Canada, W. A. Fisher Company, 1930. Issued by Border Lakes Outfitting Company, Ely, Minnesota. From the American Geographical Society Library, University of Wisconsin–Milwaukee Libraries.

Published by the University of Minnesota Press
111 Third Avenue South, Suite 290
Minneapolis, MN 55401-2520
http://www.upress.umn.edu

ISBN 978-1-5179-1095-2 (hc/j)

Library of Congress record available at https://lccn.loc.gov/2021058790

Printed in the United States of America on acid-free paper

The University of Minnesota is an equal-opportunity educator and employer.

28 27 26 25 24 23 22 21   10 9 8 7 6 5 4 3 2 1

CONTENTS

ix   Preface

xvii   Introduction: Wild Calling
      David Backes

A PRIVATE WILDERNESS

3   The Winter of Renewal: *January–March 1930*

27   Quiet Desperation: *April–December 1930*

43   Reluctant Ecologist: *April 1931–January 1932*

57   Unsettled in Ely: *September 1932–October 1934*

87   Farewell to Saganaga: *October 1934–August 1935*

109   The Dean: *September 1935–September 1937*

141   Grandmother's Trout: *October 1937–February 1939*

161   We Used to Sing: *March 1939–February 1940*

185   Big Brother's Big Idea: *February–December 1940*

225   America Out of Doors: *January–May 1941*

247   Casualty of War: *May 1941–March 1944*

273   Medium Again: *April 1944–November 1946*

289   A New Life in Conservation: *December 1946–October 1947*

315   The Singing Wilderness: *April 1949–February 1954*

329   Epilogue, 1963–1972

335   Chronology

341   Notes

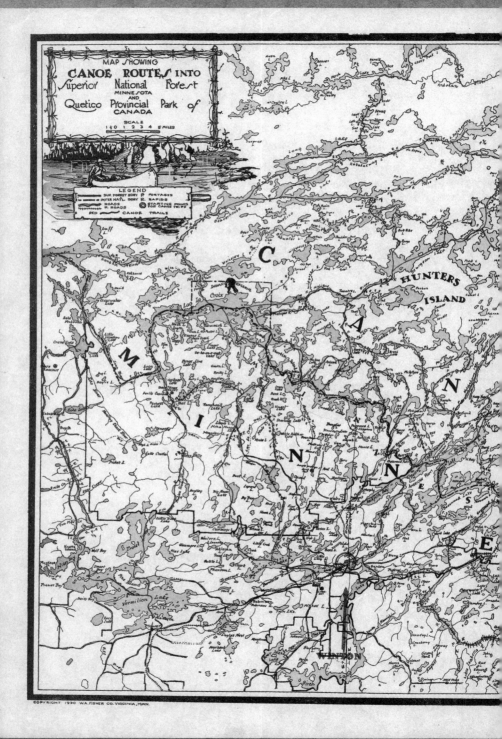

MAP SHOWING
CANOE ROUTES INTO
Superior National Forest
MINNESOTA
AND
Quetico Provincial Park of
CANADA

SCALE
1½ 0 1 2 3 4 5 MILES

LEGEND
SUP. FOREST BDRY ——— P PORTAGES
INTER. NAT. BDRY ——— R RAPIDS
ROADS ——— ⊙ STARTING POINTS FOR CANOE TRIPS
R. ROADS ——————
RED ——— CANOE TRAILS

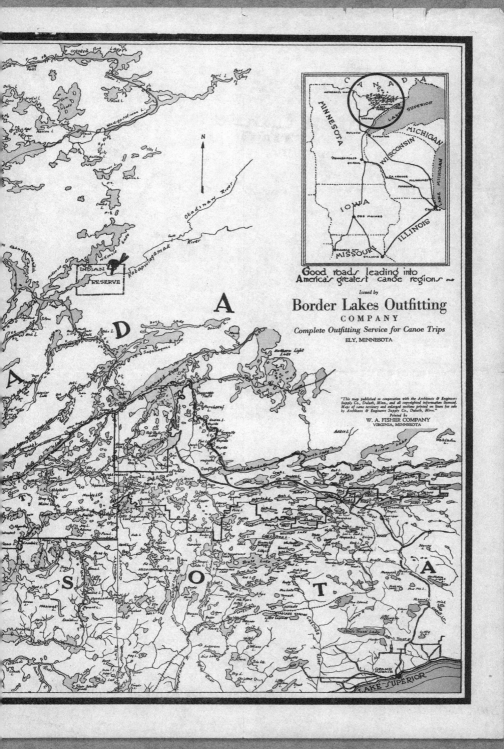

Good roads leading into
America's greatest canoe regions ~

Issued by

Border Lakes Outfitting
COMPANY

Complete Outfitting Service for Canoe Trips
ELY, MINNESOTA

"This map published in cooperation with the Architects & Engineers
Supply Co., Duluth, Minn., and all copyrighted information licensed.
Maps of same territory and enlarged sections printed on linen for sale
by Architects & Engineers Supply Co., Duluth, Minn."

Printed by
W. A. FISHER COMPANY
VIRGINIA, MINNESOTA

Fishing and Canoeing
in the Superior National Forest
and Quetico Provincial Park of Canada.

BORDER LAKES
OUTFITTING
Company

Winton, Minnesota

July 26, 1934

Dr. Bradley just came in and urged me mightily
to go up with him next Tuesday to join the Knowles
party. Said that Syd wanted to perfect the party
and that having me there would do it. Suppose I
should feel somewhat flattered, but that is'nt the
important thing with me. The fact that men of that
caliber want me to go with them, that there is a
common bond between us, that they appreciate the
way I feel and react toward the things of the wild.
that is the most important. That has come through
my writing and it is that that I must strive toward.
Perfection of that bond of enthusiasm which holds us
together, and that can only come by explaining to
the world how I feel about things.

I must have time to myself to do these things and
to write, to consult with the muse as Emerson would say.
That takes leisure and time to think, that takes time
to renew the old acquaintances. Tied in here as I am
all of those things are impossible. I must have the
summer months off to do with as I wish and sooner or
later it will come. I am confident of that. Things will
work out as I want them and getting rid of the Border
Lakes, at least active participation is one of them.

Went trout fishing with Bob and Junior and Bob Mueller
last night and stayed out overnight at the Isabella.
No trout bu I am learing to love those boys of mine.
Jumped young Bob this morning for spilling things
at the breakfast table which I shoul'nt have
done before Bob Mueller. He felt hutt deeply and I must
guard myself and not do it again. I love them entirely
too much I guess. Being with them is just as much fun
as getting a mess every time and in the future I am
going to be with them more and more. That is some of
the compensation of having gone through these years
of preparation.

Must close now and wind this up as someone is coming.
One swirl ths morning, compensation enouhh for all
of the work of getting up there.

The Only Wilderness Canoe Region of its kind in the World.

PREFACE

WHEN I DID MY GRADUATE SCHOOL RESEARCH for my master's and doctoral degrees during the 1980s, I used Sigurd Olson's papers at the Minnesota Historical Society archives and saw a few of his loose-leaf journal entries. Today, his journals are mostly kept at the Northern Great Lakes Visitor Center in Ashland, Wisconsin. But when I started working on his biography in the fall of 1990, roughly 80 percent of these journal entries were still at his home in Ely, most in file cabinets in his writing shack. The earliest entries in the shack dated to 1937, and I was confused to see indications that he had begun keeping a journal in 1930. What happened to the first seven years of entries?

Just as I was about to start writing, his son Bob found them. They were in a cardboard box at the back of an unplugged refrigerator in his parents' basement.

Sigurd may have been a saver, but he was not an organizer. I was thrilled, of course, and those first seven years of journal entries provided invaluable information for the biography, but there is also an important lesson for anyone who wishes to study him in the future: I would not be surprised if there are still other journal entries out there, either squirreled away in unexpected locations among his papers, or elsewhere. In one entry he implied he had kept a journal before 1930, possibly bound volumes. But if they exist, I have not found them or even other references to them.

Contributing to the uncertainty is that his existing journals are not bound. Sigurd Olson's journals consist of entries that he either typed or wrote by hand on individual sheets of paper. On a few occasions he jotted them in spiral-bound notebooks that he was using for other purposes. Often, he wrote on scrap paper, such as the back of memos from Ely Junior College or the back of exam instructions. Sometimes he wrote on letterhead from his Border Lakes Outfitting Company. At other times

Journal entry from July 1934 on Border Lakes Outfitting Company letterhead.
Wisconsin Historical Society Collection.

he used blank typing paper. He didn't always date them, and sometimes wrote the wrong date, so knowing the context of surrounding entries is important for establishing when he wrote a given entry.

After writing, Sigurd may have kept the entry in a folder with others from around the same time, but he often reread them over the years, sometimes jotting down another entry on the reverse side years later. He sometimes referred to them in later journals, too, or in other writings, and so his journal entries didn't always stay together.

His use of whatever paper was available when he wished to write is an indication of the spontaneity that is evident throughout his journals. While any good journal records what the writer is thinking at the time, as well as facts of daily life, many people do their thinking in their head and write down more of a summary and conclusion. Sigurd used his journal as a way of thinking out loud; typically, he wrote *as* he thought, and frequently when his emotions ran high. Entries often approach stream-of-consciousness writing. There are incomplete sentences, phrases jotted down and separated by dashes. Sometimes he wrote in first person, other times in second—even in the same entry. These journals are the top-of-the-head thoughts of someone wrestling with life, talking to himself, encouraging himself, even goading himself, and sometimes falling into despair.

To preserve that immediacy, I only minimally edited the entries. I corrected his spelling, for example, including misspelled names, but I edited grammar and punctuation only when necessary to make clear his meaning.

I underlined passages that he underlined by hand, and I pointed out other passages that he highlighted with a bracket. Understand, however, that because he returned to his journals many times, he may have drawn the lines and brackets long after he wrote the entry. Clearly, though, these passages were especially important to him. When he wrote by hand, he used an ampersand instead of writing out "and"; when you see entries with one or more ampersands, you can be sure Sigurd wrote the originals by hand.

My main editing decision was choosing what to include. What counts as a journal entry, as opposed to an observation or some other form of note, is inherently subjective, all the more so when the entries are not bound and when they are not always grouped together. I largely followed Sigurd's own description. On November 6, 1940, thinking that maybe he would find some writing ideas in his ten years of entries, he wrote, "Your diary might have something but not much except hints inasmuch as it has to do largely with my problem of medium and changing my work. For ten years that went on, paying no attention to the world of affairs at all, merely concerned with myself." My exception to that approach occurs in the final chapter, "The Singing Wilderness." The entries contained there consist mostly of Sigurd's thoughts about what he wanted to do with what would become his first book, and how to do it. Arguably, these aren't even journal entries, but I include them because they help illustrate how much he had changed his focus, and because *The Singing Wilderness* marked the achievement of his dream. He continued to write similar kinds of work-related notes for his other books; I have not included them because they do not add further to the themes that dominated during his years of keeping a regular journal.

There is a lot of repetition in his journals. Sigurd would rehash the same basic issues over and over, especially his need to write, his need to figure out what kind of writing he could do well (what he called his "search for medium"), and his desire to quit his job at Ely Junior College so he could write full time. I have selected around 40 percent of the total content of his journals, eliminating what is mostly repetition or what I believe will be less valuable or interesting to readers. For example, in the many entries expressing his desire to quit Ely Junior College, he often jotted details of family finances that would be impacted, how much he thought he might be able to make up by writing, and so on. Those details are interesting in a broader context of U.S. and regional history but less important to the dominant themes of Sigurd's journals. In cases of repetition, I chose portions that expressed his ideas best and included enough examples to make clear that he frequently returned to them.

What you will read throughout this book, then, is the heart of Sigurd Olson's journals, giving you the immediacy that you cannot get in a biography. His journal entries will open for you a remarkable window into the psyche of someone with a powerful creative drive who was caught in a decades-long struggle to follow what he saw as his true calling. To him, at least at times, it seemed a matter of life and death.

* * * *

I AM GRATEFUL TO MATT BLESSING, who before retiring as state archivist and administrator for the Wisconsin Historical Society encouraged me to take on this project. A large majority of Sigurd's private journals are held by the WHS Division of Library, Archives, and Museum Collections, specifically as the Sigurd F. and Elizabeth Olson Papers, 1916–2003. They are kept at the Northern Great Lakes Visitor Center in Ashland, Wisconsin, and I am grateful for the help of archivist Linda Mittlestadt as well as others with the Wisconsin and Minnesota Historical Societies, the latter of which holds the bulk of Sigurd F. Olson's papers at the Minnesota History Center in St. Paul.

I am grateful to associate editor Kristian Tvedten of the University of Minnesota Press for his enthusiastic support and excellent suggestions, copy editor Mary Keirstead, and the entire production and marketing team of the Press. This is my fourth book with the University of Minnesota Press over nearly a quarter of a century, and I cannot say enough about my experience. There is no better feeling for an author than knowing that your work is going to receive first-class editing, design, and promotion by gifted and genuinely kind people.

I owe so much to the Olson family. Sigurd, Elizabeth, their two sons—Sigurd T. and Robert K.—and their sons' wives are all gone. When Bob died on June 22, 2019, it marked the end of an era not only for the family but for the Listening Point Foundation as well. Bob and his wife, Vonnie, founded it in 1998 to promote Sigurd's philosophy and to preserve and protect the two family properties in and near Ely: the home (complete with Sigurd's writing shack) and the Listening Point property on Burntside Lake. I am grateful to have been involved with the organization since its founding and look forward to the management of Sigurd's legacy by a new generation of devoted, creative, and energetic people.

I have many treasured memories from my decades with the Olsons. There was the time, for example, when Sigurd T. and I were driving south on U.S. Highway 63 toward Hayward, Wisconsin, and he inserted a cassette tape into the dashboard player. Polka music blared from the speakers, and in a moment we were belting out "Roll out the barrel." He was the most happy-go-lucky person I have ever known. I never had the opportunity to meet his wife, Esther, who died in 1983.

I stayed with Bob and Vonnie at their home in Seeley, Wisconsin, many times. It was Elizabeth's childhood home: where she met Sigurd, where they married, and where he almost died of pneumonia in 1931. A place full of stories, but what most warms my memories are their voices, Vonnie's joyful laughter, doing dishes with her, and solving the world's problems over a whiskey nightcap with Bob.

Then there's Sigurd himself. My favorite memory of him is from a November visit in 1979. I was freezing as we sat in his unheated porch. Our breath turned to steam. If the picnic table was gleaming that day, it was probably ice. I had made the mistake of taking off my jacket and wasn't about to put it back on because he—Sigurd Olson!—wasn't wearing one and he didn't seem bothered in the least.

I will share two memories of Elizabeth because, frankly, she deserves it. She was a woman of tremendous spirit and grace, wisdom and intelligence, and no doubt she needed every last bit of it to get through the hard decades to the final twenty-five or so years before Sigurd died, years she loved. I was one of hundreds of people who dropped in on her and Sigurd unannounced. I wasn't trying to be rude; I was too shy to call and ask permission, and finally talked myself into their driveway. It was the summer of 1978. As I approached the house, I saw Sigurd through the window, sitting at that picnic table in the porch room. He was talking to someone, a man. Elizabeth, standing by the screen door, saw me coming up the walk. "Come in, come in," she said, opening the door. "I'm sure you want to meet my husband." And she introduced us (the other man excused himself and left) and went to get some milk and cookies while Sigurd and I got acquainted.

The most common statement I have heard about Elizabeth from dozens of people whom I interviewed for the biography was that "she was a real lady." To me, she was also a grandmother figure, and both of those come together in the final words she ever spoke to me. It was the spring of 1994, and I was about to give a talk about her husband at the Sigurd Olson Environmental Institute at Northland College in Ashland, Wisconsin. I had started writing the biography, and this was my first talk about his life. On the way to Ashland, I stopped at the Hayward nursing home where Elizabeth had been living for a number of months. At the end of a pleasant visit, she apologized to me for not being able to come and hear me speak. I was deeply touched, but then she brought tears to my eyes with this: "Since I can't be there, let me applaud for you now."

And this ninety-six-year-old woman, frail in body but strong in mind and character, lifted her hands and brought them together several times. I got to my car and sobbed.

A couple of months later—twenty-five years ago today—Elizabeth Uhrenholdt Olson died of heart failure. I am more grateful to her and her husband than I can ever fully express. I dedicate this book to them.

South Milwaukee, Wisconsin
August 23, 2019

INTRODUCTION

Wild Calling

DAVID BACKES

THE MOST ICONIC PHOTOGRAPH of Sigurd Olson was taken in 1961 by Alfred Eisenstaedt, often called the father of photojournalism. "It's more important," Eisenstaedt maintained, "to click with people than to click the shutter." And so when he came to Ely, Minnesota, the famous photographer of world leaders and celebrities spent time with his subject at Sigurd's beloved Burntside Lake property known as Listening Point. There Sigurd could be himself.[1]

In the photograph, Sigurd is sitting with his back against the cabin, legs crossed, hands resting on his lap. He is wearing his best outdoor khakis, clean and pressed. His left hand holds a folded map of part of the nearby canoe country wilderness; his right hand, resting on his left forearm, holds his ever-present pipe. A pair of binoculars hangs down at his waist. Eisenstaedt positioned the camera so Sigurd had to turn his weathered face a little to the left and gaze slightly downward. He looks poised, confident, and at peace.

This was Sigurd Olson at the height of his career. He was a best-selling author whose books were read over public radio, a leader of conservation organizations, and an adviser to the Kennedy and Johnson administrations on wilderness and national parks. He played a role in the establishment of a number of national parks, seashores, and historic sites, including Cape Cod and Padre Island National Seashores, Katmai and Wrangell–St. Elias National Parks, and, close to home, Minnesota's Voyageurs National Park. In moments of crisis, such as when a transmountain road was about to be built through Great Smoky Mountains National Park, or when a key section of Olympic National Park was threatened by logging, Sigurd was instrumental in stopping the threat

Sigurd Olson at Listening Point. Photograph by Alfred Eisenstaedt for *Life* magazine, 1961. Copyright LIFE Picture Collection/Getty Images.

because of his influence in the Department of the Interior and its National Park Service. He acted as what one Interior Department official called "an ambassador without portfolio" to Canada, working to get Canadians to preserve five million acres of the Yukon adjoining Alaskan wilderness.[2]

That man in the Eisenstaedt photograph received not only the highest award in nature writing, the John Burroughs Medal, but the highest honors of four of the most important environmental groups in America: the Wilderness Society, the Sierra Club, the National Wildlife Federation, and the Izaak Walton League. No one except John Muir had achieved such recognition in his lifetime as both a nature writer and an environmental leader. As Sierra Club president Edgar Wayburn put it, "To many of us, he is the personification of the wilderness defender."[3]

If Eisenstaedt had come to Ely thirty years earlier, no doubt he would have taken a very different portrait. That poise, confidence, and peace were fleeting qualities in Sigurd then. This was long before the books, long before the beloved Listening Point. Sigurd was barely known beyond the borders of the little mining town of Ely. But Eisenstaedt, clicking with the person rather than the shutter, certainly would have spent time outdoors with Sigurd to get the best photograph. And in doing so, he might have discovered that inner light described decades later by Wilderness Society president George Marshall, who said of Sigurd, "He made wilderness and life sing."[4]

What was the source of that inner light? The wilderness. More broadly, all outdoor places, from little oases in large cities to backyard gardens to rural fields and woods, where he found connectedness and fulfillment by doing simple things in harmony with his surroundings and his deepest nature as a human being. His childhood in Wisconsin was an outdoor immersion school, from the wild Lake Michigan shores of the Door County Peninsula to the patchwork fields and woods of the cutover region to the backwater sloughs along the southern shore of Lake Superior. Each of those locations gave him an education far beyond what he received inside the walls of classrooms. He learned much about the ways of nature, of course, but perhaps more importantly he began intuitively to understand and appreciate intangible values at the heart of human fulfillment. Beauty, for example. Wonder. Awareness. Aliveness. Connectedness. And many more.

These stayed with him his whole life, and when he came to write about them, he found that the best way to capture their essence was through not visual metaphors but aural ones. Recalling a particularly memorable experience at an abandoned stone pier near his childhood home in Sister Bay, Wisconsin, he wrote:

> A school of perch darted in and out of the rocks. They were green and gold and black, and I was fascinated by their beauty. Seagulls wheeled and cried above me. Waves crashed against the pier. I was alone in a wild and lovely place, part of the dark forest through which I had come, and of all the wild sounds and colors and feelings of the place I had found. That day I entered into a life of indescribable beauty and delight. There I believe I heard the singing wilderness for the first time.[5]

The wilderness *sings*. And Sigurd heard it. And that shaped his entire life. *Because* the wilderness sings, Sigurd found a wealth of meaning and wholeness outdoors that he found nowhere else. He needed it. He needed to listen for the stirring, yet sometimes elusive melody that unlocked the map to his own inner wilderness. Days when he heard the wilderness sing were golden; days when he strained to catch the chords were somber. And when he was kept inside? Those days were bleak.

Sigurd's family didn't understand any of this. His father occasionally fished but had no real interest in the outdoors. Neither did his older brother. His younger brother learned to hunt but didn't come close to Sigurd's passion. His mother enjoyed picnics and walks but not exploring the woods. "Nobody in the family understood why on earth I had to be running off in the woods all the time," he recalled decades later. His grandmother did, but she was too old to explore with him. So, he got used to keeping his deep feelings from these experiences largely to himself. "I was in a world of my own," he later wrote, "a free and beautiful world where all was fantasy and adventure." It was his own private wilderness, a meeting place of landscape and mind. And every time he explored the singing wilderness of water and woods, he blazed a little bit more of the trail for his soul.[6]

As he grew, he came to realize that while he was not alone in hearing the wilderness sing, it seemed as though many had gotten so far removed from the outdoors that they had forgotten to listen. Maybe even forgotten *how* to listen. Or worse yet: no longer *knew* that the wilderness sings. His life's calling, then, was to help people recover the ability to listen, to help them experience the emotional and spiritual uplift and healing that comes from listening, and to preserve places where deeper immersion produced more finely tuned listening and an even more profound experience of the intangible values. It was an inherently spiritual calling and an urgent one, for he believed that civilization hung in the balance. *Because* the wilderness sings, humans, who evolved in wilderness, need to hear it to be fully human. If there is not a critical mass of humans who regularly spend time outdoors, listen, and keep alive the intangible values that provide essential emotional and spiritual nourishment, society itself will decay. Without the power of wonder, both individuals and societies grow old and die.

Such a strong sense of calling always causes inner struggle. Those who have it often feel at least somewhat isolated. They don't fit in. Few among their families and friends understand them at more than a superficial level. They have strong creative urges but struggle to use them, and if they have a family, these creative urges and sense of deep calling may conflict with the financial and emotional needs of those who depend on them.

Sigurd Olson experienced all of this along with the awe and wonder of wilderness. Decades before his success and fame he was haunted and driven by a calling, a sense that he *had* to find a means to express the deep emotions he experienced outdoors, and then share his creations with a world he believed was longing for meaning. It drove him to heights of exaltation and to fits of despair. "Only one who has experienced what I have, the longing for creation, can understand how terrible it is to find oneself inadequate," he wrote in his journal on October 19, 1933.

He knew by the time he started his journal in 1930 that he had to write. Unfortunately, editors were not so sure. Much of his journal in those early years shows his struggles in becoming not merely a successful writer but a messenger of the spirit. He could write fishing and hunting articles, and in the 1930s he became reasonably well known among readers of the leading outdoor magazines. But that kind of writing soon bored him. His calling was deeper. So he began to write essays along the lines of what would later fill his books. In fact, some of them were early versions of essays that decades later became reader favorites, such as

"Grandmother's Trout" and "Easter on the Prairie." But all he got for them was an occasional compliment; editors said there was no market for that kind of work.

Writer friends and literary agents encouraged Sigurd to try writing short story fiction for popular magazines such as the *Saturday Evening Post*. If he wanted to be able to support his family with his writing, that's what he needed to do. The outdoor magazines paid a pittance, and he couldn't sell the essays. So he tried. He wrote stories about outlaws and trappers and loggers and rangers, crude pieces full of random action and not much plot or character development. He tried writing them off and on for twenty years, usually receiving scathing rejection letters.

So what was he to do? He had this urgent sense of calling. But how could he live it? He debated the possibilities endlessly. At times he thought he should go into scientific work, either as a university professor or as a field biologist for a federal agency. At least the latter would get him outdoors, in contrast to his teaching and administrative work at Ely Junior College. But every time he tried to push himself in that direction, he hated it. "I hate the very sound of the word Ecology," he wrote on December 14, 1931, while in the middle of earning a master's degree in it. Even so, he couldn't just drop the idea, and it kept returning like some undead lab specimen in a horror film.

He went through a brief phase thinking he should drop writing and become an artist. If his word paintings couldn't sell, maybe oil or water-color ones would. He even tried to persuade himself to enjoy being a junior college professor and dean, knowing he was good at it and that he was making a difference. He told himself he should give up writing, focus on what he was good at, and let go of the angst that came with his sense of calling. However, he asked himself on April 2, 1940, "Could I forget my wanting to write?"

No. His need to write always reasserted itself. That's the thing about callings. Move away from them, and restlessness and despair follow. Move toward them and accept them, and peace and joy follow. Not always, and maybe not even often, but enough to draw you toward their beauty and make it nearly impossible to let them go. To abandon them is to abandon yourself. And that is the one thing Sigurd Olson could not do. Because the wilderness sings, and he heard it: "I am a harp on whose sensitive strings the winds of the world blow and my task is to set to music the strains I alone can hear," he wrote on May 2, 1940. "I must give ear forever to celestial music—each day when I go abroad, I must look for it, try and catch the strange something."

Sigurd wrote or typed journal entries mostly when he was down, worried, or confused. When his writing was going well or when he was preoccupied with other matters, he was far less likely to dash one off. The bulk of his loose-leaf journal runs from 1930 to 1941. That's when he got a contract from Paul Meyers to write a syndicated column called "America Out of Doors." Sigurd thought he was finally about to achieve his dream. World War II would take that dream away, but his column helped prepare him to write books, and meanwhile he found a new career as a leading spokesperson for protecting wilderness and other wild and scenic areas in the United States and Canada. His journal, therefore, tapers off after 1941. It spikes, briefly, from December 1946 through May 1947—a period of anxiety and unhappiness that led to a final break with the junior college and the start of a new life—but then after that, very little. He was finally finding the happiness and fulfillment he had longed for.

When I describe Sigurd's life story to people, I say it's about far more than a beloved nature writer who became an icon in the national wilderness preservation movement. That's like taking a quick glance at the Eisenstaedt photograph version of his life. The more inspiring version is there too, but somewhat hidden. His face is weathered not merely by the thousand suns of his wilderness travels, days marked by aliveness and wonder and physical challenges. The deep lines also contain the more fleeting joys, the days of darkness, and the ultimate peace of a man who explored the far more difficult terrain of the wilderness within. Above all else, it is a story about someone driven by a powerful sense of calling, who enjoyed occasional glimpses of tantalizing success but more often struggled through rejection and occasionally despair for thirty years. Somehow, despite tremendously long odds against him, he never gave up. He found the fulfillment he sought, helped protect beautiful wild areas all around North America, and touched a deep chord in many who read his books and heard him speak. He also paid it forward, helping numerous young people hold on to their dreams when they were close to giving up.

What you are about to read in this collection will help you better understand just how painful was his struggle, how remarkable was his perseverance, and how much hope such a journey can give to anyone today who has a dream.

A Private Wilderness

THE WINTER
OF RENEWAL

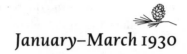

January–March 1930

S IGURD OLSON BEGAN HIS JOURNAL on January 12, 1930, at an abandoned cabin on Grassy Lake, several miles due north of Ely, Minnesota, and east of Fenske Lake. He went there often during this winter of
renewal, making improvements, spending the night, reading, and sometimes writing journal entries with frozen fingers. I have not learned
what became of that cabin; Elizabeth didn't remember it, and Sigurd
mentioned it for the last time in his journal on March 12, 1930. Clearly,
though, it played a vital role in renewing his creative drive and his dream
of writing at the age of thirty.

This chapter reveals his new sense of purpose: "The search for truth
has ended," he writes on January 14. "Now I know where I stand." But
despite this renewal of spirit, bits of tension creep in. He is indebted to
John Burroughs and Henry David Thoreau, authors whose works he
admires, but worries about being compared to them. He begins a years-
long argument with himself about becoming a scientist: he has a talent
for it, and it could give him the kind of recognition and fulfillment he
craves, but he finds it boring and worries it will damage his strong sense
of connectedness to nature. Finally, Elizabeth is worried enough about

Winter in the Superior National Forest, 1940. Photograph by Norton & Peel, Minnesota
Historical Society Collection.

him that she brings up the possibility of divorce. They have been married eight and one-half years and have two sons: Sigurd Thorne Olson, age six, and Robert Keith Olson, age four.

* * * *

January 12, 1930

A beautiful morning after a fresh snowfall. Made it out here in less than an hour and good going.[1]

Coming out I realized as I have many times that the greatest happiness for me is my enjoyment of nature. No matter how much money I accumulate and under what conditions I live there is &[2] always will be one prime source of contentment and that is in the observation of an exhilarating enjoyment of the woods. Think I can be very happy if I get into my writing stride again — My needs are few. If happiness is everyday life, if one makes one's heaven here on earth then I must really be reaping some bit of heaven right now — Sometimes I think my range must be small because it takes so little to satisfy but after all is not the realization of one's wants happiness enough. Above all things desire happiness. I have a wife who I love more than anyone else in the world & two boys both as fine as nature can make them. I have the woods and close contact with the nature I love — Although I do not or imagine I do not care for my work think of the advantages I have over others who have only a short time of the year to enjoy themselves. When I think of the life I would lead if I became ambitious & became annexed to a University job I am sometimes stunned. True happiness comes only to those who realize what they want and attain it. My philosophy makes me content. Research which I should be pursuing were I to obtain a goal as a geologist holds terrors for me. I would much rather dream & write vaguely than pin myself down to the cut & dried realm of classification and analysis. I should forget others' ambitions & pursue to the exclusion of all else the one goal I think will bring happiness, writing. The very thought of writing makes me happy and I am never so happy as when I am putting down my thoughts. Failure to do so gives me always a sense of futility, a sense of loss and wasted time. Creation—individual creation & thoughts are the only dream castles—to me is worth more than putting out weighty tomes of scientific lore. How many scientists are cold analysts, how many of them in their zeal for ambitious work lose sight of the wonder of creation. How often do they fail to see the primary underlying principle of existence. How often do they fail to see the beauty through their microscope and statistical intelligences. In me beauty is all. In me it is far more worthwhile to feel the glory of a sunny morning on the snow than it is to obtain a new specimen, a specimen that hitherto had missed the Linnaean system — That is to me mere bookkeeping —

January 14, 1930

I have long wondered what to do with my life. Since early youth I have been actuated by high ideals, high purposes. Ordinary occupations upon close examination have palled when their mediocrity has become evident. First it was or rather took form as a vague indefinite nothing. Then it took me into the missionary movement and I became a Student Volunteer.[3] How my young heart during those days was bled and torn with indecision. Then when new ideas of religion became mine how shattered was my hope and faith. Nothing left and my once soaring spirit tottered on the edge of the unknown. I remember well how I used to climb to the roof of a high building[4] and there under the stars and with the lights of the city below me I used to pray and battle with my God. Never will I forget the heights to which my exaltation brought me or the depths of despair that were mine. Upon descending from the pinnacle for a time my fancy still carried me along the heights but not for long. Soon I was again in the commonplace and then came a sense of failure and futility. I wanted to know God. I wanted to see him. I could feel his presence but did not know. At last in despair I gave up my dream as a missionary and life's castles crashed around me. Doomed as it seemed to a commonplace existence I gave myself halfheartedly to my work and hung doggedly on. For me life was over. I had not yet developed the philosophy that would have made it possible to override my despair.

For years I went on getting more bitter and disillusioned all of the time. Suicide stalked boldly with me. My only happiness was when I was alone in the wilds. My only hope of existence in any sane form was in the out of doors. My darkest moments were those in which I doubted even that faith as a disillusionment.

Marriage brought me happiness but also misery because I realized only then the extent to which my spirit was bound. About the year 1922

I one day conceived the idea that I should write. I remember it well.
It came to me while hiking back to Nashwauk from Keewatin.[5] I shall
never forget the glory of that walk. It seemed to me that all the problems
were settled and that all of my life had been spent in preparation for it. I
did not realize the years and years of practice that were necessary before
I could do anything worthwhile. However that was the beginning of the
writing urge. Since then it has stayed steadily with me, dying out almost
at times and then again flaring up brightly. It has been through the years
a great comfort to me and has served to give some motivation to my life.

For a while I dabbled and dibbled at this and that thinking that I had
promise. I remember the time the *Milwaukee Journal* bought my first contribution,[6] the story of my canoe trip with Harry and Dan to the border
and back, terrible stuff. I began a number of articles but did not finish.
I had not yet developed regular habits of work and real persistence.
Doubts came again to plague me.

My half year at Madison,[7] a complete failure convinced me that my
mind ran in other channels. I knew as Burroughs did that the very things
that rendered me unfit for business were virtues in the profession that
I choose to follow. In other words my dreaming and imagination had a
function to perform, and in writing they would stand me in good stead.

January 14, 1930

Reading Burroughs and Thoreau has restored to me somewhat my capacity for enjoyment. My daily excursions into the wilds on my skis are
as thrilling to me as they would have been twenty years ago. My mind
is fresh and I see things with the same newness and experience the
same thrill I had as a boy. The trouble with those to whom life has gone
stale is that they have lost their freshness of perception, their naivete.
The world looks old and not even the brightest morning is to them unclouded. The universe is seen as through a glass darkly. The ether of their
understanding is befogged and at no time does the clear sunlight of un-
sullied perception steal through....

This winter has been a revelation to me. It has served to clear up
many of the doubts which assailed me on every hand. Now I know
where I stand. Now I know what I can do and what I am fitted for. Never
again can anyone accuse me of slothfulness, indirection and dissem-
ination of my faculties. From now on my energies will have a single-

ness of purpose that will ultimately bring me to the goal I seek, literary perfection but firstly the expression of my feelings. There is also this satisfaction and it is not one to be scoffed at. Suppose that I never in the popular conception of the term arrive, what then, I will still have the joy of creation for my own pleasure. Thoreau wrote for himself alone and it took the outside world to discover him. I do not propose to leave it to the world but will be my own publicity agent. If I am unsuccessful that is my own fault, but I cannot be totally unsuccessful. My work and my daily life will be compensation in itself. No man loses in life if he has the seeing eye. Life is full for him at all times and his pay is not reckoned in worldly things. A man who has reached the pinnacles of understanding is never ruffled or distraught. Perfect happiness will be attained for me when I have demonstrated to the world that my message can also earn me a comfortable livelihood. Think of the wonder of being able to live on dreams, of being able to do what more than all else in the world you have wanted to do. Think of the wonder of knowing that you have found yourself. It is a spiritual rejuvenation, a conversion as complete at the moment of its conception as the change of light to darkness. Though I live to be a hundred what I have gotten during the past few weeks will never leave me. If I should die tonight the experience of this winter will have been justification enough for the short tenure of my stay. It has all come about so naturally that sometimes I doubt myself and wonder if not after all it is another illusion. In my saner moments, however, I know the wheat from the chaff. This is reality for me. The search for truth has ended. Now I know where I stand.

January 16, 1930

Today I have read the life of John Burroughs and have been impressed with a strange similarity between his life and mine. He found the same inability to resign himself to business and the humdrum existence of commercial life. After teaching school for some ten years and nagged by an ambitious wife to try to put his good brain to some lucrative use, he tries anything that will give him a release but only to find that he cannot devote his mind to it. In the midst of figuring and worry he finds himself slipping away to do some scribbling as his friends called it. Many is the time he was discouraged and hopeless but there was always his out doors to give him renewed strength and vision.

I have been teaching for ten years with the same leisure he had, leisure devoted to rambles in the woods, reading and thinking. I have browsed among the philosophers perhaps more contemporary in their scope but not any more hampering than his. Mine have given me the best of modern thought, explanations of the slow old theories he had but the result has been the same. I have gotten a broader scope and understanding of human nature and of man's relation to the universe than I could have gotten any other way. What has my reading been through the past ten years if not a conscious search for the truth, the truth regarding religion, faith in God and immortality. I have read the beliefs of all the great thinkers of our day and have come to the conclusion that they know no more than I do myself....

I have been my own University. I did not begin to get my education at school. All I learned there was enough to enable me to teach a primary subject and to earn my livelihood. That much I have it to thank for, but for real understanding that I have my own tireless research and unconsciously well-directed efforts to thank. Many is the time I have looked over the reading and thinking I have done during the last years with a pang of regret thinking of all the time wasted. At the time all of the satisfaction I did have was that it gave me pleasure. It brought me slowly to a peace and calmness that will never leave me.

January 16, 1930

Burroughs had a rather hectic time of it even after leaving teaching down at Washington. More comfortable and undoubtedly with a happier home life as a result of it, still he longed for the country. As he expressed it he wanted to get near the soil and to eat it. Ten years at Washington in the Treasury Dept gave him leisure and the chance to keep up with his writing and reading. He made very little off his books, not half enough to keep him alive. He had to depend upon his other means of a livelihood, but that made little difference to him. The joy was in the writing, in expressing his thoughts and in working toward the goal that he felt now was closer and closer, its fulfillment. How serene he must have been to have kept steadfastly toward the objective he so early had set for himself.

As the years roll by I am also convinced that only one happiness is for me and that the steady observance and interpretation of nature and man's relation to it and not scientific research, fascinating as that may seem. That does not interest me, perhaps because I do not know enough about it but I do not think that is it. I know enough from close contact with science to know that it would pall me. I am not interested in seeing a dead mouse or a fine wolf skin. I am interested in knowing how life is lived, how it compares with ours in aim and substance, in interpreting the primitive urge of all breathing things and in studying the beauty of organization rather than the detailed intricacies of analysis and classification.

After reading over "The Free Lance Writer's Handbook" last evening, which I had purchased at the outlay of $5.00 misspent dollars, I was filled with gloom and foreboding. All of my elation of the last few days was dispelled as an illusion. I came back to earth from the heights I had traveled with the natural philosophers and the coming back was anything but pleasant, for all the world like coming back to a disagreeable world after a glorious vacation in the wilds. I am easily moved, permitting the reading a cheap book compiled no doubt by someone with half my understanding and knowledge. Why should his ideas fill me with foreboding as to my future? When I think back over my gloom, I am ashamed at my timidity. I should better be able to sort the wheat from the chaff.

January 16, 1930

My immediate task is to determine how best to do the thing I want to. I cannot follow the Burroughs or Thoreau type of essay without being accused of plagiarism. I must find some other type of work that will stamp my writings with individuality. Success is only accomplished when something is done in a new way. The man who can say in a different way old truths as old as the hills, show old pictures in a different light and do things in a different way will speedily be proclaimed as a genius. I am still groping but someday not so far away if I keep at it the light will come. I should be thankful for knowing that is my problem. Think of the darkness I labored through for many years being unable to analyze my own thoughts and emotions. At least I have been able to do that and it has taken all of ten years to do it.

I feel confident that someday the light will burst upon me as it burst upon Burroughs when his Expression was criticized as being too Emersonian. When he knew at last he was filled with such happiness that no matter what happened he was buoyed up by a feeling of ecstasy. That to me will be the one great moment in my life. I am looking forward to it with more joy than to any event I could possibly imagine. If I keep on thinking and wondering about it, keep up with my reading and philosophying, it will come.

I find that it is a remarkable clarifier of my thoughts to be able to sit down and write them. Thoughts formerly vague crystallize out with remarkable vividness when they are put down on paper and what is more one does not forget them so easily and one can refer to them later on if one so wishes to see where his thoughts left off. What I have jotted down in the past week has been a great help to me. It has helped straighten out a fogginess that would have only gathered more fog if it had not been dispelled. Then too it helps in that it gives me always a sense of being purged and of having accomplished something worthwhile. That must be the eternal writer's itch to be doing something. I am not happiest when I am writing but I am perhaps happiest just after I am through. It is like physical pain, really enjoyable in a sense because of the relief after it is over. So with writing, not so pleasant at the time although one must admit that there is some pleasure to putting down thoughts on paper, but satisfaction afterward that counts most.

What hurt me last night more than anything else was running into the sordidness of writing for money. If it is to be a sheer money-making profession for me then I want nothing of it. My type are scorned by writers of such books but how much literature will they put out. How many of them will be remembered a hundred years from now. They are cheap, commercializing an art that should be reserved for higher things. But at that one must be tolerant. A certain bulk of cheap trash must be ground out for the mob and that is the group the author of the Handbook was talking to, money, money, money, the note sounded all through the book, prating about human understanding stuff he had read in books and did not know, a journeyman's handbook but nothing more. No talk of sounding the note of beauty.

Undated, mid-January 1930

I often wondered how long my enthusiasm would last, whether or not it would wane as my interests grew more variegated — I know now and can see like Walt Whitman "30 years of age & in grand health I now begin." I know that instead of diminishing, my ideal life will have a stronger & stronger hold upon me.

Burroughs kept up his interest until the day he died — He had the same inherent love of the soil I have — sometimes I want to eat the earth it smells so good to me — His last utterance "It looks like it will rain" — How like him — his last written word of the weather — He felt the rain coming, to the last the observer & lover of the earth. Thoreau the same & all the rest — Instead of diminishing it grows on one, the older one gets the surer the hold, the firmer is the foundation upon which our past is built. With myself it will be no different, every day I feel the bond growing stronger. My whole life is colored by it and sometimes I wonder if it is real or illusion —

January 17, 1930

A beautiful winter morning, cold and clear. All of the fogginess and mist has gone and the air is as clear as the bluest ice. It must be forty below at least for on either side of the sun the sundogs are riding like two miniature rainbows, the kind of a morning when I would like to be on my skis skimming along the lake trails. The air alone is enough to make one long for action. Breathing itself is an exhilaration. On mornings such as this in spite of the cold I understand why people will persist in living in the north. South there is never the wild joy of living there is up here. One morning such as this compensates for a dozen others. All one's fears vanish, life and one's dreams assume a rosy hue and ambitions are almost realized. To be abroad with the dawn is compensation enough.

Before me lies search and exploration. I must find the medium of my expression. Needless to say, I cannot plagiarize Burroughs and Thoreau. Their field is unique and without parallel. The more I study them both the more do I recognize a similarity both in text and form. They unconsciously choose the best medium of expression for their particular field. It will be impossible for me to work into the essay without seeming to imitate. There is no excuse for that unless one is absolutely barren of ideas. At that they chose the most natural medium for the thoughts they wanted to bring out. It will be harder for me to pick my field but once I arrive at a definite conclusion nothing will ever stop me until I have made a success of it. I know this about myself, that once I have begun the search for something, I never give up....

A number of writers have gone into the animal story field. In a way this is a very attractive one but rather limited in its human appeal. A man will soon run short of material. I have written a number of stories myself and know. "Snow Wings" sold to *Boys Life* is a good example of this type. There is a limit to this type of experience an animal or group

Sigurd and Elizabeth skiing near Ely, 1920s. Wisconsin Historical Society Collection, 63200.

of animals can have and also to the human characteristics that you can impart to them. I seldom read animal stories because there is usually a false note in them. Samuel Scoville has written some very fine stories but how often have I not recognized a note of insincerity in the repetitions in his frantic endeavor to fill in space.[8] It is a poor field for a man with ideals and broad conceptions regarding the riddle of existence. I am afraid that I would wither up and my spirit die from lack of nourishment were I to adhere strictly to this type. I must have room for my thoughts to take form and that cannot take place in a plain narrative where the main principle is to interest by a succession of events. There is a possibility there but a limited one. I shall no doubt write a few more animal stories and bring in the human interest necessary for them to make an appeal but their number will be limited and are now recognized as a narrow scope of endeavor for my dreams....

You have had a wealth of wilderness experience, roaming around by yourself and guiding parties, you have had far more than the ordinary man and here is a field that may be worked into something unique in its line. Neither Burroughs nor Thoreau or any of the other nature writers ever had any guiding or professional woods experience. Neither were looked upon as real woodsmen. I am considered a woodsman of the first water in this country which is one of the frontiers. To have a guide interpret his experiences in the world, to have him show the beauty of nature through his eyes may be a new slant. My "Reflections of a Guide" in *Field and Stream* met with immediate response.[9] That was something new. No one has tried to imitate it and there are few guides able to express themselves. At least here is an idea as fresh and untainted as the woods themselves. If I can develop a following as a guide philosopher and make my vision beautiful enough I do not think I will be so far off the track of my search. One must write about what he is most interested in in order to be genuine and sincere. I know the woods better than anything else. About my feeling and interpretation of them there is no insincerity. Men want the original thoughts one has [and] if they are truths painted in new colors, they will always listen. Cannot I show human nature and show my love and my joy in that love of the outdoor life. It may be that I can work into the philosophical essay if I do not tread on the toes of the New England philosophers. The essay is by far the most convenient form of expression for this sort of thing and

I know and feel that I can put my whole soul into it. From them may come other things, perhaps better, but at least this will be a start and the beginning of recognition....

Doing some writing every day is a help to rapidity and clarity of thinking. When one first sits down with very little to say it surprises one, the amount of information one can dig up out of one's subconscious. One does not know what one has until one looks for it. If we all explored the hinterlands of our minds we would perhaps be agreeably surprised with the vast fund of material lying there dormant. It is like a man living on the edge of the wilderness but who has never been beyond his own fence. He knows of the wilderness but has no idea of its enormity or of the treasures that lie there until he has gone exploring. Then he wonders why it was that he waited so long to partake of the pleasures that merely awaited him. So it is with us. We discover new interests and create new enthusiasms, the further we go into them the more fascinating they become until they have so absorbed our lives that we wonder how in creation we could have ever existed without them. Many go through life without making an effort to unearth the hidden stores within them and die having lived sterile lives in their own arid deserts. Many go through stifled by the narrowness of their daily affairs little dreaming that at their very doors for the asking is a wilderness to explore, the wilderness of their own understanding.

My task as an explorer is to open up to [the] world a new field of enjoyment, a new wilderness of hitherto hidden desires. I shall endeavor in my own humble way to give understanding I have gotten of the joys not only of simple living but the joys of beauty, nature unadorned (what that term means to me), the joy that I get out of my rambles in the wild, the joys of solitude, the physical joy of action, the interpretation of the primitive impulses that connect us so closely with nature.

January 18, 1930

Last evening after a long session of nothingness, good food & much talk I consoled myself with Burroughs' essay on realism. How true it is that only by combining the spiritual with the real can one hope to touch the hearts of men. Realism for its own sake is merely photographic. The real is well and good & there must be realism but one must infuse in it that spark of genius which gives one a sense of allusion as to the ideal (now I am rambling, come to earth). I have always held that Sherwood Anderson and all of the contemporary school were accomplishing nothing adding nothing to the beauty of life with all of their stark interpretation. In a hundred years their work will be dead. There must be something of the idealistic infused if it is to live. Human beings need to be shown the spiritual as well as the matter of fact. God in literature like science leaves me cold. If one is to write something worthwhile then one must infuse into one's accurate observation of things as they are what Thoreau calls the "effluences of nature." What it is—hard to define but it is that which uplifts one & makes one feel that after all there is a meaning to life....

"Know thyself"—an old adage but how true if you are to make peace with the soul. I feel now that I know where I stand. There are no more illusions. I am quite happy & I know where my happiness comes from.[10] I know my capabilities & I know my failings — Why try to do anything for which one is unfitted when it is so much easier to do well what one likes to do. Writing gives me a sense of accomplishment that nothing else does. I do not believe it is because for the past ten years I have dreamed of writing as a field of endeavor....

I have reached the age of first wisdom. Though only thirty I have done with the first callowness — Years will ripen what I am now beginning to see. My writing will develop it — For the past weeks I have been imbued with the secret of success. It must come — I cannot fail — I must make my stories of outdoor life & nature alive. Others must feel. My work must be beautiful & above it all must run a strain of serenity & poise. Be of good cheer it will come.

Undated, mid-January 1930

I must start at my writing soon or there will be another winter gone. My conscience bothers me when I think of the work I might be doing along Zoological lines. Dr. Cahn's letter to me filled me with dismay.[11] Such energy & such unlimited enthusiasm for natural research. I feel that I will never be able to equal his acumen, his scientific ardor — Burroughs says — No great work of literature will ever come from too close a scientific application. One must have dreams & time for meditation to bring out the bigger finer conception of what is worthwhile in life. I console myself with the philosophies of others — At times however I am filled with doubt & dread. Perhaps all I am is a dreamer. Perhaps all of my meditation is merely an excuse for lack of ambition — at times I accuse myself of mental laziness — I hate detail & routine & am only happy when I am alone with my thoughts. Thoreau I have some of your complex, solitude and happiness for me as well.

What I need more than all else is direction — I know with work being done, stories coming from my pen I could be happy—very happy — I must start, write anything, anything to conquer the desperation that each day becomes stronger & stronger.

Illinois zoologist Dr. Alvin Cahn, 1930s. Listening Point Foundation Archives.

January 20, 1930

In spite of the cold last night I went off on my usual jaunt toward Grassy Lake. It becomes easier and easier to make the run each time I do it until I wonder how it was that I ever became tired making the same run before. My muscles are becoming harder and my wind is getting better. In fact my whole system is getting toned up and my mind becoming more alert. It is surprising the effect that exercise has on one's general attitude toward life. When one sits indoors all day one's mind becomes as sluggish as one's body. An hour or two every day has a stimulating effect on every part of you. It is easy to see why it is that men who do tremendous mental tasks take their recreation seriously. They have to in order to keep up the pace they have set for themselves. Last evening for instance, upon returning I worked for almost three hours writing letters and the whole time I was not afflicted with the ennui that used to attack me about 9:00. I was not tired and was filled with a delicious sense of having done my work well. No other New Year's resolve has been as worthwhile as this and if it is physically possible, I shall try to keep it up in spite of interruptions. There is a great satisfaction in work. Only time wasted gives me the blues. As long as I am profitably employed I am reasonably happy.

The habit of writing every morning has also been the source of particular happiness. I find that my mind is awake then more than at any other time. One hour after breakfast is as good as two or three at any other time. If I had to make writing my source of livelihood, I would write in the mornings, and play in the afternoons. One can, if one's mind is functioning, write two thousand words without any trouble in three hours or four at the most. That done well is plenty of work for one day. Any more and one would accomplish too much. I find also to my great pleasure that this regular habit of writing is making for increased facility in the use of ideas and words. It is possible for me to sit down as I have done this morning without a thought in my head and rattle off a thousand words or so without having to stop to think. Putting down your thoughts is as much a matter of habit as doing anything else. One's brain becomes functional in much the same way that muscles do. It gives me increased confidence in my ability. Often times after long periods of sterility, I would sit down only to find that I did not have a thought in my head, which would plunge me into despair and foreboding as to my future. No wonder I did not have any thoughts, my brain was so benumbed through inactivity that it would indeed have been a wonder had any thoughts come. This I know now, that all writing needs is practice. The more I write the more I am convinced. Of course one must have a modicum of brains or it all avails nothing.

January 20, 1930

Have been reading Hudson's *Far Away and Long Ago*.[12] The more I read of the great naturalist poets the more is my belief vindicated. They are akin to me in every action, every thought. Hudson in his attempt to explain his feeling toward the supernatural in nature tells the feeling he has at certain times, moonlight nights in particular toward trees, horizons, space, a feeling of awe and reverence almost akin as it develops to fear but intensely fascinating and impossible to subdue. How well do I recognize the same in my own reactions. Yesterday while on my skis, pausing on the high ridge north of Grassy Lake and overlooking twenty miles of wilderness valley to the great range to the southward, for a moment I had the sensation of harmony with the infinite. As Hudson expresses it when he climbed a hill to look for the sunset, "I sat down and waited for it to take me." This being taken expresses it so perfectly that any further attempt would be superfluous. One is taken body and soul and while the illusion lasts one is filled with an elation, transported as it were into another world far from the strife of this. It does not last long, can be broken as mine was yesterday by the approach of a truck along the road a quarter mile away. For perhaps a full minute I stood on my skis steeping myself in the glory of the scene before me. All thought of time had flown or of past and subsequent events, for a moment I was transported. Then like an unpleasant memory I was aware of a hostile influence approaching and I began to retrace the way to the matter of fact. It was nothing but the click, click of a chain striking a fender but it was enough to break the spell. It drew closer and closer until the air was filled with the unpleasant clangor of metal upon metal. I looked up in disgust but the truck was hidden by the trees. It grew fainter and fainter and at last was lost entirely. I stayed for a moment to try and recapture what I had lost but although I did for a brief moment, it was impossible to regain the complete beauty of the first. I pushed on my ski sticks and slid down the trail toward the lake. Once more I had had one of the moments for which I go out. Not always am I so successful. Some days I see nothing, hear nothing, on others every view gives me a glimmer of the goal.

On my canoe trips, much to the secret amusement of my parties, I used to steal away for a silent paddle by myself after the others had gone to bed. They used to chide me about my peculiarities in the morning and make inferences as to my poetic leanings. Many of them would understand, however, and I would detect a feeling of understanding and sympathy. Most men would do likewise if they could. Few can or are able to see what I see, very few. One must have a peculiar harmony with the infinite, one must be a mystic to see the supernatural. Most of all would I find what I sought on brilliant starlit nights. I would paddle out swiftly onto the open lake if the moon was shining down its path. It never failed to come to me when going down that brilliant shining highway into space. Most completely of all would I be taken when lying on my back looking at the stars. The gentle motion of the canoe softly swaying, the sense of space and infinity given by the stars, gave me the sensation of being suspended in the ether. My body had no weight, my soul was detached and I careened freely through a delightfulness of infinite distance. All sense of the present would leave me, all responsibility and worry would flee. Sometimes the night cry

An early canoe trip, 1920s. Listening Point Foundation Archives.

of the loon would enhance the illusion. For long periods, I would lay having lost track of time and location. A slap of a wavelet would jerk me back into the present and I would paddle back to the deserted campfire, there to sit gazing into the coals trying to fathom the depths of the experience I had been through.

In the morning I would receive the jibes of my party with good grace. I knew what they thought, "Moon struck, the yearning of calf love." Little did they know and how far removed I had been from them. How much would they not give could they have had one of my moments with me. I laugh with them and let them think I am peculiar. I would not think of quarreling because I have really cheated them out of something which they cannot feel.

I remember a sunset on the top of Robinson Peak, alone as I must always be if I am to receive the vision in its entirety. The sun, a round red ball on the horizon separated from me by leagues and leagues of primitive wilderness. It hung suspended swelling glowing palpitating with energy. For a brief moment I experienced the sensation of feeling the earth move away from the sun. Nothing akin to it had I ever felt. Here was I, an atom of life on the rim of the world, watching it turn. Never before had I experienced anything which placed me so in harmony with the infinite. The play of gorgeous color on water, sky and land no doubt helped to create the setting, but the main sensation, the illusion governing the whole, was a union of myself with the plan of creation. Then more than at any other time did I feel that I was a part of the beautiful life I loved. From that moment on I was a spiritualist. Nothing could ever take from me what I found.[13]

Years passed before I could analyze those moments and know in what their attraction for me lay. Now that I know I can see the explanation of many things I have done....

There are few who see what I see, very few. Even the great writers of nature, many of them have failed. Occasionally there crops out an inkling of it but none of the clearness of perception and depth of feeling that I know. Why I should have it I cannot know, perhaps it is an inherited instinct from some far ancestral mystic. Surely none of my family have it, if they do it is hidden and unrecognizable. In me have been concentrated that natural mysticism of centuries of my race. I have been given the seeing eye. It is my mission to give my vision to the race in return for the beauty that has been shown me. I cannot go through life keeping it to myself. That would be rank ingratitude to the nature I worship.

January 22, 1930

If a man is true to himself and sincere in what he does even though the bulk of his material is common knowledge there will be occasional outcrops of pure metal untarnished by the matrix in which it lies. These veins of high ore will be sufficient warranty for the rest. If one real thought or idea in a chapter occurred in this manner it would have made the work worthwhile. That is the only hope and salvation of the author now. So much has been written upon every conceivable subject that a man has to be clever indeed to have his work original. Remember that mountains of inferior ore are worked over in order to secure a ton of precious metal....

If my outfitting business[14] would only get sufficiently on its feet so that I could devote six months of the year to writing at my own pace and speed, I really think I would accomplish something worthwhile. I know this, that this winter has given me a new insight into the workings of my mind, has given me a new perspective. I feel more confident this winter than at any other time since I began having the illusion that someday I might become a writer. My renewed understanding of nature gained through reading the natural philosophers has been a great help to me. I know now where I am at and have no longer any illusions as to my purpose in life....

I have to smile when I think how intolerable life in town would be for me. The trip I made down to Chicago was interesting but what a relief it was to get back to the woods and quiet. I felt as though I had been in a boiler factory, in a world of incessant noise and confusion, and by the time my week was up I was almost insane with the turmoil of it all. I am insolubly wedded to the wild. There is no cure for it. Ever since I can remember it has been the same and I know now that with almost half of my life gone I will not change. Every year grows more wonderful to me and if it keeps on my life will be too complete to live in anything but ecstasy....

I have broken a new trail along the ridge north of the lake, giving me a half mile of glorious view to the southward. Before this improvement of my domain, I had to be contented with only one view of the valley and that as I emerged from the woods unto the open hillside. This is still the most glorious of them all but is not as continuous as what my new trail affords. There I not only have distance but a variety of scenery. At one point I can look down on the spires of the black spruce trees of the great swamp. At another, I see in addition to my background of spruce glimpses of the lake and the far ranges beyond. My way of making a trail is a slow one but it is the true trail maker's habit. The first time through it is a case of picking out the easiest ground to travel through. The next it is a case of breaking off the branches that might cut across your frozen face. Each time the trail becomes more and more easy to follow until at last when the track is worn well and all the whipping boughs are broken off you have a highway of your own, one that has never been traveled before and one that you can close or abandon as you desire. It is the king's highway, and you are the king. All the life on either side belongs to you. The scenes are yours because you have made them. Each view is of your own making and enjoyed by you alone. The pictures are no lifeless ones of art, but can be remodeled or changed as the spirit dictates. Here you are the arbiter of destiny, the lord of all you survey. How few men have a road all of their own that they alone travel and enjoy, and how few can afford, once they have so expensive a treasure, to abandon it as I can. I am a millionaire of the spirit. My treasure is counted in terms of world exploration.

I am going to take the Sunset Trail tonight, the trail that gives me the sensation of skiing along the rim of the world.[15] What light effects do I get along the edges of those drifts, what eerie shadows and silhouettes. Each day it is different and no time have I found the old trail monotonous. There is nothing similar in nature, two things are never alike. How could two days be alike or two sunsets. They are as different as I am....

I realize that soon my wanderings in the field of exploration must cease. It has been a very pleasant experience and I have learned much about myself and the work I am to do. I know that I will never lose interest in the world about me, that my interest is greater and of a different caliber than that of most men. I know too that sincerity and genuineness as well as accuracy of statement are absolutely essential in order to produce anything worthwhile; that one's style though important will come if one has a message that is worth the telling and one knows

Pines and lakes of the Quetico–Superior wilderness, 1930s. Listening Point Foundation Archives.

what one has to tell. One must interpret nature through one's own eyes, making one's own observations and drawing one's own conclusions. Mimicry is useless and will get a man nowhere. The interpretation of nature is simply the telling of one's feeling for nature. Do not forget that communion with nature is communion with one's own soul. Nature is beautiful only insofar as we can reflect our own beautiful thoughts in her. She acts like a mirror. We see ourselves in nature. Clouds and trees have no universal meaning. Each man sees those things differently and here is where an author's charm comes in. If he can give an interpretation different from most his thoughts will be in demand. If it is the same old story he will go looking long for a buyer of what he had to sell. I may not have an entirely new viewpoint, but at that I think it is unusual enough to make it worth my while to try.

This I know, that I will never be happy unless I can be writing. No matter what my job or how much I am absorbed in it, there will always be the itch to write. I can't get over that. It has been the guiding factor in my life and activities for ten years, the ten most formative years in my life, so do not think that I will quickly get over it. I feel that no matter what else I have to do to earn a living, that alone is my real excuse for existence. In order to preserve my self respect, in order to remain true to my ideals, I must follow that star. If I gave it up, no matter what success I might have I would feel that I had been a traitor to the cause I was born to champion....

An hour has gone by and my college class has begun to dribble in. The time flies when I am writing. Thought it had been only a few minutes. My mind is dry for the time being. I must begin now to think of scorpionidae and the myriapoda, king crabs and what not. Back to earth. Goodbye to dreams for another day.

January 23, 1930

It will be hard for me to write cheap stuff anymore after going through what I have this winter. I can not sacrifice beauty on the altar of commercialism....

I have had faint murmurings of doubt today — Shall I keep on with my journal or not. I say now by all means, no matter what it is you write keep on because only in that way will you ever perfect any sort of style and style is what you need.

I must develop my ability to analyze character because if I go into this thing seriously there will have to be short stories —

Elizabeth keeps worrying about me and my work. I am putting nothing into it, all my energies go in dreams — She spoke of divorce to relieve me of my burden & her of her worries — I smiled — In due time she will see where my energies have gone. I have not been wasting my time. I have been employing every minute to good advantage — Someday soon I shall find the medium of expression for me. It may take years but I will keep at my probings and I am confident that it will not be in vain.

January 24, 1930

Had the most unusual experience coming up from the last ridge toward town. Emerging from the timber following the pole star I first became aware of an unusual glow in the sky, an eerie unnatural light somewhat akin to the aurora but softer and more diffused. As I worked my way up the hill it grew in intensity until the northern sky was a mass of brilliant rolling clouds of light, looking for all the world like the illumined vapor over a giant cauldron. For contrast I turned and looked to the southward over the ridges and valleys I had just come, the sky blue black, brilliant blazing stars, each one a glowing spear point incandescent against the heavens, the trees black and velvety or outlined like frozen lace against a spangled background. Ahead was warmth and civilization, noise and confusion, behind me the wild, frozen and quiet, beautiful in the icy solitude of mid winter. As I topped the ridge the yellow twinkle of the lights burst upon me, first a few of the higher and then all of them, the town lying below like a huge lighted Christmas tree.

February 2, 1930

I have written nothing in my journal for a week or more having been much too absorbed in the writing of "The Pike Pole" to think of anything but that. Started and wrote most of the tale out at the cabin and during the course of the week ran it through five revisions which is where it rests now. Read it to Elizabeth for the first time Saturday night and although I received the criticism I wanted I was greatly encouraged. At least she admitted that it possessed merit and with some more polishing would pass muster in the better class of magazines. It has given me the same old thrill, the writing of this story. Do not think the time will ever come when I will fail to get a great satisfaction out of it.

My work now is to cut down and eliminate unnecessary material. There are many places now that can be cut down. While reading the book *The Author's Art*, I was impressed with this unanimity of opinion by all of them, that work in order to be classed as literature must be brief. Try to say in as few words as possible what you have in mind. If one word will take the place of three or four use the one. Brevity is the soul of art. Simplicity is everything. One does not have to use long encumbered words or sentences, because one's appeal is to the mass and that would be unintelligible to most. Do not cut down however when there is danger of losing one's thought. Do not write unless you are full of your subject and feel deeply what you have to say. Know your subject above all and give the impression that you have much more to say than you really put on paper. Give the idea that what you have has been boiled down. Do not have one extra word or sentence than is for your thought. This idea of brevity is important and is one of the evils you must conquer.

Read over a story by Herbert Ravenel Sass this morning, "Wild Mother" in the *Ladies' Home Journal*. It gives me confidence. I could have written that thing with ease. Someday I will get my stuff taken and will add materially to my livelihood enough so that I can devote all of my time to writing instead of my spare moments. That story is nothing exceptional and could have been compared favorably with my "Snow Wings."[16] I know that someday I will sell everything that I write.

March 12, 1930

I finished "Logs on the Quetico" and sent it to the *Atlantic Monthly* and had it come back with a most complimentary rejection slip. Have not sent it out again, the same old heartaches accompanied it....

The past week it has been warm and I think spring has come. It is hard to believe that the winter has gone and taken with it all of the beauty that is hers. I love the winter, the ski trips and the twilights. Think of the many memories my afternoon jaunts stored up. I was really happier than I knew. I always am in the winter time. There is not the sense of strain and constant struggle there is at any other time of the year. Now the spring is here and all of that is past.

QUIET
DESPERATION

April–December 1930

S IGURD'S HOPES WERE DASHED and his confidence crushed when two national magazines returned a story. This, combined with busyness that kept him from writing, plunged Sigurd into despair.

In these entries and throughout the rest of his journal, a tourist business played a large role in Sigurd's hopes and frustrations. A year earlier, on January 1, 1929, Sigurd and two other men bought J. C. Russell's outfitting company and renamed it the Border Lakes Outfitting Company. In his journals, Sigurd typically called it "the Border Lakes." One of the partners, Walter F. "Wallie" Hansen, worked with the canoes and camping equipment. The other, Mervin W. "Pete" Peterson, worked the books. Sigurd, with half a dozen years of summertime guiding experience, managed the day-to-day operations.

Unfortunately, because of the amount of time needed to run the Border Lakes, Sigurd could no longer spend his summers guiding parties into the canoe country wilderness. He might do one or two trips, but for the most part he had to work at the company's headquarters on Fall Lake in Winton, a tiny town four miles northeast of Ely. Sigurd's hope was that the Border Lakes would become profitable enough that

Palisades on the west end of Arrow Lake, Ontario, 1936. Photograph by Bill Roliff, U.S. Forest Service Records, National Archives.

he could quit his teaching job, giving him a lot of time to write between September and March. In the meantime, though, much of his free time from work during the first several months of the school year he devoted to hunting, so his window of opportunity to write fell between Thanksgiving and late March, when the Border Lakes began receiving a flood of inquiries and summer reservations. Whenever Sigurd's journals mention his "year's output" or "winter's output," he is referring to what he wrote during this four-month period.

But how much income did the Border Lakes need to provide in order to convince Sigurd that quitting teaching (and later, his position of dean at Ely Junior College) wouldn't put his family in jeopardy? That depended on how much Sigurd thought he could make from his writing. If the Border Lakes plus his writing income could come reasonably close to matching his teaching (or later, dean) salary, he thought he could do it. But he would not take the chance until 1947. That means he wrote nearly all of the entries in his journals during the seventeen years when he had just four months a year to prove to himself that he could make a living out of writing. It may be the single greatest cause of his struggles, for when he was not writing or spending a lot of time outdoors, he often was miserable, occasionally panicky, and feared he would never live his true life.

By the end of this chapter, University of Illinois zoologist Alvin Cahn's attempts to persuade Sigurd to come to Champaign for a master's degree were beginning to take hold. But was Sigurd being pulled in that direction more by genuine interest or by quiet desperation?

* * * *

April 1, 1930

It is nearing the end of my 30th year and I hope the end of a gloom which has been withering my spirit for many days. I know what it is all about. I know myself too well not to know. My story has come back from the *Atlantic* and from *Harper's* and there is very little chance of its being taken by any other. I feel that my writing is more or less of an illusion, that there is no use in my going on and that I might as well give it up. But here is the rub. The instant that I come to that decision, foreboding overtakes me. Life becomes purposeless and empty, my ideals are gone and I become instead of the animated naturalist alive to all the beauty in nature, a dead unfeeling automaton.

The instant I stop writing, I am unhappy. I have been out of the harness now for several weeks and how unhappy I have been. Contrast my mood of today with the joyous exuberance that is mine when I am working on a story. It must be that I have it in me. I can't be all wrong all of the time. I know that no sustaining happiness is mine unless I am writing and expressing myself in some way. My whole attitude toward life changes. Everything becomes animated and beautiful and all life and nature is filled with beauty and divine meaning. The instant I stop, it loses all of its glory and life becomes drab. <u>I should know by now that writing is my only salvation</u>.

This morning I feel desperate, suicidal if anything.[1] It is spring but it might as well be spring in a great city as far as I am concerned. Somewhere in the course of the last few days the best part of me died. The only way I can resurrect myself is to start writing again and the tragedy of it is that I haven't time to do anything or think of anything but my business and how that irks me.[2] How I hate it. I never was meant to make money in that way. It is all sordid for me and I can never throw my whole self into it. I will have to carry on and do the best I can. Think of the struggle of Sidney Lanier and brace up.[3] At least I have my health and a robust body. But how the woods call and call.

The Superior National Forest resident naturalist idea is a good one. I really think I might be quite happy if that came true. It would give me plenty of time to write and work out my ideas and would carry me away from the stultifying atmosphere of this school system. Another few years here and I know my soul will shrivel from the dryness within these walls. I must get out or it will be the end. This I know, that I must write and I must live out of doors. That is something. I must write. I cannot live and not write.

April 2, 1930

If the old Border Lakes could only get on a paying basis so that I could put in my whole winter writing, I know that I could accomplish much. I want to write and the only road to happiness for me is to keep on writing until all of the feelings and longings within me have been expressed. No happiness can come until I have told the world how I feel about nature.

Many before me have felt the same and have followed their star through great suffering and privation. Think of the happiness that must have been theirs, however, when at last their dreams have come true. This wanting to write has grown upon me until it is more of an obsession than anything else. It must be satisfied and if I fail in accomplishing that, something within me will be atrophied. Only through arriving at the goal which is still dim to me will I be satisfied that I have not lived in vain....

The day after tomorrow I will be thirty one. I am getting along in years. I am almost middle aged and have accomplished nothing yet. But this I have and that is the open heart and my life has been filled with the experiences that only a lover of nature knows and values. I have a background of material that once I reach the point where I am accepted by the reading world will prove a gold mine to me.

April 7, 1930

At the rate I am going now I will never do anything. Putting in my worst hours on what I love most, stealing time from my work to do what means most is atrophying to say the least. If I could put the best hours of the day doing what I want to do I know I could accomplish something, but this way never.

I think of going away to school. Some days it looks like a fascinating outlet but then again it gives me the sensation of going into a dungeon from which there is no outlet, burying myself a little deeper in the morass from which there is no escaping and which only will prolong the day when I will be able to do what I want. Why not take life by the horns and settle once and for all the problem of existence for me. I do not want to meddle with too much of science at the sacrifice of my soul. I must retain my original freshness of perception. I cannot give it up no matter what the price.

My work — To write more beautifully of nature and life than anyone ever has; to impart to the world my joy in life, my enjoyment and interpretation of nature. If I can do this life will have had imparted to it a new meaning, a new significance. I am as I am for a purpose. If I fail in my dream it is my own fault. The way will be long and hard but I must follow or die. TO WRITE MORE BEAUTIFULLY THAN ANYONE ELSE ABOUT NATURE. If I can picture life through my eyes, what a picture it will be. I must, I cannot give it up.

Sigurd (*right*) with Wallie Hansen, partner in the Border Lakes Outfitting Company, 1929. Listening Point Foundation Archives.

The popular nature writers have never touched the depths whatever. Theirs have been mere frothy descriptions of what they have seen and experienced but they have never given people what they want. That is my task. A new type of story with a touch of the spiritual in it, a deeper understanding and appreciation and I think after a bit the world will be looking for what I have to say. I have faith in myself, a faith that I have what others have not. In that egotism lies my greatest strength.

May 23, 1930

The spring work is piling up heavily and I am drawing closer and closer to the summer and its dreaded work.[4] Someday I am going to approach summer again with glory in my eyes, the glory of great distances and new country to discover. This making money is terrible. It robs a man of so much that is worthwhile....

I am nervous these days, jumpy at slight noises, irritable and on edge. What I need is a long trip. Campfires and distance, night in the old tent, time to read and think. All that would put me back in a hurry. At least I know this, that when the strain gets too great I can always go home.

I may not get another chance to write in my diary. When next I come back to these pages, I may be ruined or wealthy.

September 28, 1930

The summer is over and once again I am back at the old grind. As I look back at my diary it is really amusing to see the change in thought from the idealism of winter to the practicality of coming spring and summer, a transition from the world of Thoreau and Emerson to the factual matter of making money. Now I have before me several months of opportunity if I wish the opportunity of writing and dreaming and it looks good.

Two of my stories came out in the magazines this month and if nothing else it gave me confidence.[5] To tell the truth it has been a long time between appearances but the fact remains that I can still do something with my pen. "Confessions of a Duck Hunter," written on such short notice, nine hours altogether has shown me that under stress I can really do something worthwhile. Queer but I must have some incentive to do work consistently.

Duck hunting with Sig Jr., 1930. Wisconsin Historical Society Collection, 74079.

Sent my story "Logs on the Quetico" to Thomas Uzzell.[6] It will be interesting to see how it fares. I am hoping against hope that his report will be favorable. If it isn't it will hurt but it will not in the least dampen my ardor. I am by now used to rebuffs but they only strengthen my resolve. Chances are his report will be rather detrimental than anything else. He will make me revise it and inject more human interest, probably increase the suspense and make the stakes higher. That I can do and don't forget cutting out the description. That will undoubtedly come.

If nothing is doing on this story, I will next submit "The Gentle Wild One." When I think of the time and effort invested there, I can ill afford to let it lie and rot. There is some really good work in that story and with the proper revising should amount to something. I plan on this winter at least finding out something tangible in regard to my ability. I am through guessing and wondering. It has come to a showdown.

I will determine whether or not I have any talent and whether or not it is worthwhile continuing. If it is I will keep on, if it isn't I think I will let it go if I can. If I can is good. I know from past experience that it will be impossible.

November 5, 1930

There is only one thing for you to do in order to regain the peace of mind you ordinarily have and that is to settle down to writing of some form or other. This terrible inactivity is going to ruin my disposition entirely. Days when I accomplish nothing are barren to me and always leave me with a feeling of futility and all goneness. On the other hand, days when I have put in a good lick of work I am feeling on top of the world, happy and at peace with everybody and everything.

Since hearing from Thomas Uzzell on the last story, "The Gentle Wild One," I have been upset. I know now what the trouble is and it seems to me an insurmountable obstacle. How in the world can I ever put in the necessary amount of human interest to be a really great writer, I do not know. I can patter away for years writing paltry outdoor stuff but nothing at all worth anything or of the type that will warrant putting in years of life doing that and that only. It seems to me that this is the parting of the ways. I will know when it is all over if I have the ability or not. If I decide that I haven't the genius in me for genius it takes contrary to popular opinion then I might just as well devote my time to something else. The awful thing about it is that the instant I decide that writing is all over for me I get panicky and want to commit suicide. Today I have had that feeling. It all started the other night, Tuesday I think it was. I was left all alone in the house, everything all ripe for a good start at my story. I started out bravely enough but at the end of an hour all I was doing was gnawing my fingers in despair. It was terrible and I think it has been a long time since I ever went through such absolute misery. My mind was barren of thought, anything I put down was drivel and I was confronted with the bald truth that it was the end. That impression has stayed with me all week and has grown until with the aid of reading the conservation survey given me by King I have about come to the conclusion that I might as well get into conservation work and call it quits.[7] Some hours I am happy and settled in the thought then again I can't bear it and have to decide that I must give it one more try.

If I could only convince myself or have someone else do it for me that writing isn't my field, think of the energy I would save for something worthwhile. But as long as I keep kidding myself there is nothing for it but to keep on. I feel though that sometime soon the deciding moment is going to come. This can't go on indefinitely. Something must turn someway or the other.

What hurts me most now is that I haven't been able to get back to the creative thinking. I expect to get back the moment I sit down but that is well nigh impossible. I should really give myself some time to get into the new line of thought. Creative thinking is like doing anything else absolutely strange. It takes time to acclimate oneself and get down to the quick of one's mind.

At home I find it very difficult to write. Maybe it is only my imagination, I don't know. At any rate I don't seem to get anything done at all. I will probably have to get some place to write where I will find myself more in the mood to really work. Someplace where there is no distraction whatever. Someplace where the atmosphere is just right. That is more important than it sounds.

It makes me sick when I think of the happiness that has always been mine when I have been busy working on something, and the abject misery when I am inactive. The thing for me to do is to start on something and see it through. That means happiness to me, so why not go at it regardless.

December 4, 1930

These days have been days of darkness to me, days of indecision and doubt when I haven't known for the life of me whether I was going to continue with my writing or go into scientific research. It is queer but the very instant that I decide to give up my writing and go into science I become miserable. Life loses all of its charm and spontaneity and assumes a gray drab appearance. So it's been for a week or two. Ever since the night when my brain went sterile and I was given the scare by reading Uzzell's book it has been that way. I was certain that writing was not for me, encouraged in that resolve by Elizabeth. For a few days I decided to go after my thesis on the wolf and was vaguely happy in having reached a decision but not for long. The old misery soon came back and I found myself in the most perfect state of abject dolefulness possible. It was hard to think of going back to school and grinding away at something that does not interest me in the least. Dr. Cahn's statement to E[8] that this winter he would see just how far my interest in science extended will no doubt give him a shock, for it is really not very far. I love animals and the out of doors simply because that is the natural thing for me to do. I could no more get over my natural love for the creature of the wild than I could get over breathing, but it isn't a scientific interest that enthralls me, it is something different, a deeper feeling of kinship that scientists could not possibly explain. I am afraid that if I do go down that it is going to be the same old story again of more misery and despair.

Why not be courageous, take life by the tail for once and show that you are master. If you make any sort of a profit by your business next season, enough to keep the wolf from the door somewhat, then why not rent a cabin and spend the winter writing. Surely with your outdoor stories you should be able to make enough with the dividend to make both ends meet, and think of the freedom and the glory of the life you will lead. Think if you can of being able to get up with the dawn, going for a brisk walk along the lake perhaps or through the woods, and then home for a good breakfast, see the kids off to school, and then spend the day in writing, five or six hours of it. Think of the work you could get out by doing that and forgetting all about teaching and the miserable days that go into it, the waste of effort and emptiness. There are any number of things you could write about and with the volume that would come from your pen with the time to put on it, it should not be at all impossible to make both ends meet nicely.

At least doing that would give me an opportunity to see if there is really anything there worthwhile. If I couldn't make both ends meet then I would have to do something else, but I am confident that I could.

Well what is the solution — The thing to do in the next two months is to see if you have anything in you that would be worth banking on. Whether or not it would be possible to go into the fiction end of it or not I don't know, but that I think is the thing for me to find out.

As I wrote this morning, there is no job of ambition that I want. I would rather be a warden than Fish and Game commissioner, a ranger than superintendent of Superior National Forest, rather the humblest workman than in a director capacity, for only by so doing and by so keeping close to the earth can one hope to taste of the earth itself, feel the rain and the wind, know the deliciousness of hunger and cold and warmth after exposure. Those who sit behind desks forget that they were anything but automatons. They have the homes and the servants and prestige but have they enduring satisfaction that the others under them have. It is doubtful. They have lost their close touch with the earth. They are the lost. They are the ones who derive their pleasures second hand. When they read they read about men who are doing the things they cannot do anymore due to their positions, when they see a show or play they are seeing men close to the earth, men who are battling with the elements, facing the wind and storm and fighting life's battles with their hands. You never see a show about generals but here the private is in the limelight. Man is only interested in the natural and requires the breath of natural life. Burroughs says that men have more interest in a weapon than in a lathe, more interest in a knife than a plow, more interest in a plow than in a harvester. Man would rather eat his bread of the whole wheat than refined, which brings us to a great truth, that the closer man can keep to nature the happier he is. He cannot lose his contact with the primitive.

Most men, as Thoreau would say it, "lead lives of quiet desperation." He is more than right. Mine the last few weeks has been just that. Come to school in the morning feeling lower than the lowest, home at noon to a falsely happy dinner, play with the youngsters, back and forth once more and when the hour comes around nothing to live for but the empty shell of what existence should be. Life is too short to keep on this way. It is hardly worth living at all and often times the specter of suicide haunts me as it must haunt many who are of the imaginative frame of mind.

Science has its lure, there is no doubt of that, but when I think of the sterility of life in the laboratory when I might be out living life of my own it is positively stifling. If I can once have the courage to grasp life by the tail, swing it around a few times and make it give me what I want then and only then will I be happy. My chief joy comes from traveling out of doors and coming in contact with life in the raw. It is no doubt a rebellion against the artificiality of life as we now live it. After all my best friends and the ones I like best are the rough lumberjacks of the woods. They take to me and I to them. Their loves and hopes and fears are more to me than anything else. Is this true, I do not know.

I have a field here that is untouched. Around me drama is en-
acted every day but I cannot see it, rich soul-filling drama. Here are
the guides, woodsmen, Finns and Austrians and I see nothing. There
should be as much here as say a man could find in any city or town and
here there is local color of a type that hasn't been scratched as yet. If I
could once get started I would not have much to worry about but it is
the getting started that hurts. I cannot see the chaff from the wheat.
I am still lacking in perception. Character analysis is what I need and
that I haven't got.

It would be wonderful to be able to resign and tell the whole world
to go to hell. It would be marvelous. We could live truly an idyllic life if
we only had the courage of our convictions. It would be wonderful to be
able to write and see returns coming in to vindicate my faith. Think of
selling a story for several hundred dollars and know where more were
coming from and most of all to be independent. It would be hard to believe that any such wonderful thing could come to pass. But it might and
now is the test.

December 5, 1930

This morning my outlook on life is different. With the writing I did yesterday came peace and then the visit of Wallie and Pete last night helped
cheer me up by straightening out some of the wrinkles in regard to the
business. Queer how a little bit of writing about nothing in particular
will help put me on my feet. It seems that no sooner do I start putting
words down on paper than I feel as though I were accomplishing something worthwhile. Silly idea I admit because oftentimes the thoughts I
put down are mere drivel. It goes to show that happiness to me is bound
up in putting down my thoughts on paper. A little of that every day and I
think I would be reasonably happy. This one truth has been driven home
so many times that I should know the significance of it fairly well by
now. Even the little bit of writing I have done this morning has helped.
I think it might be the way Robert Louis Stevenson felt when he was
practicing. Practice was to him always a pleasure because he felt that he
was striving toward an ideal of perfection. Days when I have done nothing are days wasted but days when I have written much, whether the
bulk of it be nonsense or not, there is the subconscious realization that
there must have been some improvement.

Mervin "Pete" Peterson, 1920s. Peterson Family Collection. Courtesy of Daryl Peterson.

December 9, 1930

What a morning, wind out of the west soft and balmy as a morning in September or October with just enough of freshness to make one feel like getting out and wallowing in it just for the sheer joy of living. I think of the life of a writer, on a morning like this he could go out for a walk, go where he pleased and for how long he pleases, and then come back brimful of ideas and wade into them for six or seven hours or as long as he wished.

I think and think of my future. If I go ahead and get more biological training there will be a number of opportunities for me that if I do not go I will be out of reach of. There is the survey, there is King's and Austin's[9] idea of a resident biologist for the Superior National. That last would be about what I would want but I must not plan on it because there is really small hope of its ever going through. Then there is the possibility of being sent on investigative work from here to Alaska for the Survey, but what will that do to my home and family. It might be worthwhile doing it for a time because later on that sort of experience is good to cash in on. Then there is always teaching to fall back upon, the old standby and not so bad at that. If I come back here after getting my master's I will outline my doctor's degree and get the bulk of it out of the way before I go back so that I could spend the bulk of my time on study.

There is really nothing to worry about one way or the other. If I write and the business comes along to give me my winters free it will be wonderful. If I go into the Survey or any similar line there is also a good future and I can always come back to writing as I can to teaching. Those two are the last resorts. In the meantime the thing to do is to live happily, getting as much out of life as possible and not permitting the ogres of doubt and misery camp too much on your trail. It will all come out all right in the end, of that I am sure. Just so that I can get out doors once in a while for a good breath of air, I can put up with almost anything.

In a way I am really getting anxious to get back to school just to dispel the feeling of doubt which continually assails me. At least the year will do no harm outside of laying our supply of funds rather low and it will increase my chances for the future if I ever decide to go ahead in biology. For fifteen years I have been undecided, the fifteen most formative years of my life. Only one thing have I found out about myself and that is that my love for the woods will never die. There is one sustained interest that I know now will never be changed. My greatest joy comes from a life in the open and my greatest misery comes from being cooped up for long periods in town. Knowing that should give me my premise. I should know that any work that keeps me out of doors a relatively continuous period will keep me happy, no matter what the work is. This too I have found, that hunting and fishing isn't everything, but just getting out of doors the main thing. Whether or not I have a rod in my hands anymore means nothing, or whether or not I have a gun. The big happiness comes from merely being out of doors. It doesn't make much difference what I am doing just so I am busy, the greatest happiness is given me however by studying wildlife. Wildlife puts me in touch with all the beauties of nature. I am working with an artistic background and the very knowledge that I am dealing with what I love gives me satisfaction and pleasure. A muskrat becomes a thing of beauty because he lives at the mouth of a creek grown with cattails and bulrushes backed with spruce, the scene that always gives me the most. A grouse is synonymous with poplar woods in the fall, a duck with lake and marsh and wild rice, a deer with snow and thousands of hunting trips, wolves with yellow moons, and howling in the fall and winter, small crustacea with the environment of lakes marshes and streams. There is no form of life that does not give me some degree of pleasure because of the associations it brings. To go out in the woods and spend a busy day looking up the habits of some animal and keeping notes on what you have found is to be about as happy as one has a right to be. Of course there must be a certain amount of sedentary work to make one's findings available to the rest of the world but that mustn't be begrudged because it is the price one has to pay for the privilege of doing the other. As King said it is a shame to take pay for doing anything one likes to do but wonderful if one is able to do it. Most men take pay for doing something absolutely distasteful to them and keep on doing it all their lives, the only pleasure being their short and miserable vacations when they try to regain in two short weeks what they have missed in fifty. They lead truly miserable lives. I suppose eventually I will teach but for the best part of my life I want to be in the woods and there only. Despair grips me now when I think how small my chances are for that unless I cut loose and write. Only there is any semblance of freedom. Any other job means being tied down — but and this is a long thought — I cannot and will never be able to picture characters. There is not sympathy there.

Women I do not know —

Men either —

On mornings such as this I want to go out and write finis to it all, on some high hilltop where I can wave goodbye to the world.

RELUCTANT
ECOLOGIST

April 1931–January 1932

AFTER RECOVERING FROM NEAR-FATAL PNEUMONIA, Sigurd decided to shelve his writing dream and go into science. Given his previous graduate school experience at the University of Wisconsin, and the views he expressed about science in his journal before now, it seems as though he was running away from himself. That would be his own conclusion, in the end.

Meanwhile, however, he persuaded Elizabeth to go along with his plan. They used their savings to move with their two young sons and rent a place in Urbana, Illinois, so Sigurd could spend the 1931–32 academic year earning a master's degree in zoology at the University of Illinois. Despite writing the world's first master's thesis on the timber wolf and studying under the founding president of the Ecological Society of America, Victor E. Shelford, whom he liked, Sigurd hated the experience. "I hate the very sound of the word Ecology," he wrote on December 14, 1931. He swore he had learned his lesson, and that never again would he consider a career in science. As he put it on December 9, 1931, "I agree with Thoreau, I am not a scientist and never will be one. I am a mystic and a philosopher. I can never change that in me."

Conservation work for the U.S. Forest Service at Crooked Lake, 1940. Photograph by Leland J. Prater, Forest History Society, Durham, North Carolina.

* * * *

April 8, 1931

Another year has passed and how queer has my outlook become compared with last year's dreams and philosophy. As I glance over the pages of last winter, now only a short year ago I realize that nothing is permanent and last of all dreams and aspirations. Then it was writing, I had found my goal at last, for me there was nothing to do but to interpret my appreciation of nature for the world, let others see my joy in the out of doors. Scathing were my remarks on scientific research and today I am waiting for news of a fellowship at the University of Michigan and for the assistantship at Illinois. My viewpoint has changed and instead of going at fiction I have decided to content myself with an occasional story or article for the outdoor magazines. After all, I believe this is the saner thing, for if I was to give up everything for writing I am afraid there would be nothing but failure ahead. This way if I go ahead and get some more scientific work out of the way I can still write occasionally and have that satisfaction and make a good living too.

King's rumor of a possible moose fellowship is anything but quieting. For three years at about $250 per month would not be so bad with the chance to work off my doctor's degree. King said that Leopold[1] would push it and that they thought I was the logical man for the job. If that materialized I would be made zoologically at least and the outfitting business and the writing would take care of itself.

Since I wrote last I have had pneumonia and to all intents and purposes almost died.[2] I shall never forget certain moments during those hectic days of late December and early January, some pure misery and some joy. I wouldn't have missed it for anything. Those nights when all was peace and quiet, when all my worries were gone and I seemed to be drifting off into space, the gurgling of the oxygen tanks and their likeness to rapids in the dusk, how can I ever forget it. It was the closest I ever came to sheer beauty and peace. And more, death will never again be a fearsome thing or the hereafter—it is all so natural and so welcome when the time has come. It was all worthwhile and was it not for the long tiring aftermath I would go through it regularly when life begins to drag at the traces.

December 9, 1931

Here I am down at the University of Illinois striving toward my master's degree in zoology.[3] What an illusion I continually labor under. Up at Ely, I believed that I would be happy down here doing work that I loved. At the same time doubts assailed me and I knew that if I came it would be the same old struggle. They don't know down here any more what brings happiness than anywhere else. Although they are zoologists and should be working toward the ultimate which is finding happiness through the study of nature, they are as far off as the average business man. Not a one of them care any more for their work outside of the privilege it gives them to make money than so many bookkeepers. It is all cut and dried and I am horribly disappointed. I am beginning to see that my salvation must be worked out by myself alone and that the only way it can be done is to stay up north and do it. Reading Burroughs and Thoreau give me so much comfort. They are always with me and consoling me when the way is dark. How they would smile at it all. Burroughs secret of happiness, "To find some congenial work, in which a man can lose himself"—how false that sentiment rings down here. All a group of automatons. They are not in love with their work, they get little real pleasure out of it. I cannot wait until I get back to the north where again I will have a chance to write and dream.

Write and dream, that is the keynote of happiness for me. I must write. I cannot get away from that. I thought if I came down that I might forget the urge in my scientific pursuits but it is useless. I can no more forget the thrill and satisfaction that I get from writing than I can forget how to eat. My stories coming out this winter, four of them all told, will help get me started in the outdoor writing field. I believe that with the work I have done that it will be possible to enter into the other magazines as well as *Sports Afield*. I already have a pretty good start and if I put in the time, it should not be difficult to make a go of it.

Writing up problems, how they bore me. Will I ever get through my thesis, I wonder. I hate the very sound of it. That sort of thing I simply cannot get joy out of. I must be working in my philosophy and joy in the out of doors. The rest is as mechanical as though I were pasting labels on cans.

Game management—what an empty thing that will be. To get stuck somewhere in the country that I don't care about working out graphs and tables. How I would hate it. Leopold's job I would go crazy on. That sort of thing would ruin what little disposition I have left. No Sig you are beginning to know yourself and should soon reach the age where you could step out and decide exactly what it is that you want for happiness. Elizabeth is no doubt getting tired of the continual feeling around I have been doing and discontent and dissatisfaction and I cannot blame her. She is doing her best to keep up but how she would love to have me finally decide what I wanted to do and stick to it. How I have thought and explored the innermost reaches of my nature and found nothing but confusion. For ten years that has been going on, still I am at sea. However not so much at sea as I was. I am gradually beginning to eliminate and getting down to the quick of my nature, eliminating those things that for a while I thought would give me happiness. For a while I thought that a university job would do it. Down here I would soon go insane as at any other university. It would be the same wherever I go. Tonight I am going to be initiated to Sigma Xi. What a travesty that is. Recommended because of potential possibilities as a research man. I could laugh and wouldn't Thoreau and Burroughs laugh with me. Research, <u>yes into the hearts of men and how best to go fishing and roaming through the woods</u>. I agree with Thoreau, I am not a scientist and never will be one. I am a mystic and a philosopher. I can never change that in me.

What I want is the same old thing, to be able to get out of doors enough to give me the exercise I want and then time to write. I am thirty-three now or soon will be. It is useless to suppose that I will ever forget or get over that. To think that perhaps at the age of forty which is only seven years away I will forget is ridiculous. I will always want to write. During the past ten years I have always had it with me. I think again and again that I went through the same thing at Madison when I went down to do my graduate work. How I hated the routine of study and how I dreamed of writing and how I did write. That was really where I got my start and I have been at it ever since. No, ten years more I will still be at it and getting the same thrill out of it that I always got. It isn't so much the writing itself as the chance it gives me to philosophize and dream that I crave. Of course seeing my stuff come out is a tremendous kick in itself and the financial end is not to be forgotten. I still believe that with the proper time put in I can make the larger magazines and get in on the bigger money, enough so that I will not be scoffed at. Novels, no, I will never try to do that, but short stories and philosophical essays is what I will want.

Go back to Ely, take your old job until your debts are out of the way. Work it with the Border Lakes a few years more. Build yourself the house you want and in the place you want it and I believe that you will be reasonably happy. If the Border Lakes makes enough so that you can quit your teaching job and spend the rest of the year at writing it will be something. There are very few that can promise themselves that. You have a good job waiting for you and with the combination of the business you will be making enough so that you will not have to worry very much at any rate. With the total combination of teaching, outfitting business, and writing I stand to make better than $4,157 (last year's). With good luck in my writing it should not be difficult to make $5,000. Now $5,000 is not to be sneezed at at any time and a man of my type will go a long way before he picks up a job that will pay him better than that. In addition to that you have plenty of time to be in the out of doors that you love more than anything else. By conserving your time you can do a tremendous amount of work. Teaching will never take more than the time between eight and four. From four on you have it all to yourself and the weekends and vacations are not to be forgotten. Adams and Al with their doctor's degrees getting only $3,000 is not so good. Think of the opportunities I have that they haven't got. In the meantime I will be building up my reputation so there is really nothing to worry about greatly.

If I can live through this horrible year which is now almost half gone and get back with my master's degree I will be set for life as far as my job up there is concerned. Why get excited about such a prospect. I have everything I want up there, good financial prospects, a life in a country I love, practically no responsibility outside of the business and that is split three ways, friends I love and admire. For heavens sake Sig cheer up and take stock of the opportunities you have. This year will soon be gone and then nothing ahead but love and adventure. Life is too short to worry greatly about anything. If you have health and strength to do what you want, why worry or fret.

December 14, 1931

I have just returned from a conference with Vestal[4] on my Bass Lake problem and am again low in spirit. What a meaningless thing all of this research is and how I hate it. Detail, dry and musty, Latin names and xeric conditions, how they pall and choke the real me. How familiar it all sounds, the word hate has cropped up again and fits in once more with my scheme of living. When will I ever be doing what I love to do? When will I be able to say that I love what I am working on. I am now thirty-three and still the old battle continues.[5] I am getting tired of it all. When will I have the courage to stop and do what I want. I have half a notion to leave it all, go back and write. The outfitting business will pay expenses and I can write to my heart's content. Will I finish that problem and get it ready for publication? Not if it takes me a thousand years. When I get through with it here, I am Through. I will bury it away someplace and never again as long as I live ever touch it. I hate the very sound of the word Ecology, plant or animal. There is something stifling about it that will never quite make it possible for me to go ahead. Get my doctor's degree, the very name is horrible to me. Write, yes, that is all I want to do and that I can do better than anything else. These devils here will kill every beautiful thought I own. How I long to be back to where I can dream and think and write the philosophy that means more to me than breath. Take pictures and explore.

If I had only known. I should have known myself better than to expose myself once more to this atmosphere. I shall never do it again as long as I live. If I can put up a false front and make them believe I am interested I may get by but what a horrible struggle it will be. All of my life has been a search for happiness. I do not want to go into scientific research, of that I am sure. I hate the sound of it, at least the type of research I have seen here. Nothing could be more terrible than to compile statistics the way these men do. I must deal with something that takes into consideration more than figures. And I must have action, exercise. If I don't get some of that, I shall go insane. I think I may do that before I am through this year. Thoreau and Burroughs help me today, give me some of your strength and poise. Lord God help me. Give me strength.

When I read this next year, I shall smile and grit my teeth and resolve never again to let it happen, as long as I live.

What do I think I want to do. Writing gives me happiness. Roaming the woods gives me more happiness. Having time to philosophize and dream, absence of details and dusty grubbing. Perhaps I am all wrong. Suicide again stalks with me. It would be pleasant to forget it all. A dangerous thought and so easy to achieve. This life has been nothing but unhappiness. If it were not for Lib and the boys I would leave. They have given me all that I have and I love them.

December 26, 1931

Since coming to Ann Arbor, I have been thinking hard and fast.[6] First of all my illusions in regard to ever working at a university or living in a university town have been successfully shattered. Any university town would be the same to me. Crowds, crowds, always the same mob of people, no chance to be alone with my thoughts or with the things that I love best. I am more than ever of the conviction that only in one place can I be happy and that is in the north. I have also been reading as I am wont to do if the books are here to read. Emerson: Be true to the highest in you. Be yourself. The only satisfaction comes through working out your own salvation and that is by expressing yourself, doing the things that you want to do at the cost of everything else. What though you gain the whole world and lose your soul, etc. etc. It all boils down to the old conclusion I have long ago arrived at and that is that the only way that I can be truly happy is by living the sort of life I love. And what is that kind of life. Here might be a solution of it.

When you get back to Ely, buy yourself a piece of land across the lake, build a house of the type you want, have your dogs, perhaps a pony for the kids, ducks and chickens, a garden, canoe and decoys at the mouth of the river and a thousand other things that you can only half dream of in town. Live the sort of a life that Burroughs and Thoreau would have led under similar circumstances. Combine the practical with your dreaming and make of your life the full sort of thing that you have always wanted. Thoreau says that there must be some sort of manual labor if thoughts are to come clearly and forcibly, that the worker in the fields can express himself forcibly because the pettiness has been taken out of his system by the physical exertion he had been through. Did not Burroughs feel the same way about it. Did not he also spend half of his time out in the fields and the rest of the time with his muse. Who was it that walked sixteen miles each day and the many other famous authors who spend so much of their time out of doors. It is the only solution to my problem and the only way that I can be fairly happy....

What is research to me. Nothing but a source of boredom. What does a university professorship mean to me, nothing at all. What do seminars mean to me or teaching at all, nothing but misery. I have seen too much of it. Shelford,[7] Al, and all of the rest, what horribly uneventful and drab lives they lead. It seems so to me and I feel that it will never be different. There are many who would give their eyeteeth for his job and his prestige, but I would not, not for twice the salary. The only teaching man I ever envied was Leith,[8] and if I had to live in Madison, that would also pall. At least there was romance there and that is more than we can say for any of the rest.

In a way I am glad that I broke away this year. What seemed vague and far away has now seemed close and clear. I wonder at my attitude of a few short years ago, how I pondered the Biological Survey, the jobs with the universities, research fellowships and what not. My illusions have been taken away, the fog has been cleared and now I see clearly. I know now that what seemed a short time ago as a delightful possibility would only bring me more misery and discontent. By a gradual process of elimination all of the wild and foolish dreams I have had are disap-

Sigurd (*far left*) travels by dogsled during a wolf research trip, 1927. Wisconsin Historical Society Collection, 74111.

pearing and I am finding out what the source of happiness is for me. To live in the woods, yes, with my loved ones near, a chance to work out of doors, a chance to explore the territory around me and get to know it as intimately as Burroughs knew the country about Woodchuck Lodge or Thoreau Walden Pond. That means more to me than trips of exploration to map a new country or find a new kind of mouse or tree. That makes me smile....

Lib says reproachfully that I have never been happy and why. I know now that it was because I have always been searching and wondering, trying so hard to find the solution to it all. The last ten years or say fifteen has been that only. At times I have moments of doubt but they do not last as long as they used to. I have almost eliminated every possible suggestion that might again side-track me. ("The giant of yourself always camps beside you." One can never run away from one's self.) I know now that no matter where I went I would have the specter of myself dogging my footsteps. The only way to real happiness is by finding contentment and knowing that you have found her. I am close to that ideal now. Explain it to anyone else? No, who would understand what I have been through to reach it?

December 28, 1931

Yesterday I spent at the university[9] seeking for that knowledge that would give me peace. Met Dr. Graham, Dr. Dearborn, English, Pullen, and others and am once more convinced that it is the same old story of dry dusty laboratories, much theory and little practice, not a soul among them with the exception of Dearborn who had a spark of imagination or love for what he is doing. He upon closer acquaintanceship might develop into a real friend. The others were so bound up in their own petty affairs that they hardly had time to talk or visit and far too much upon their dignity to ever smile or get enthusiastic. These men have lived too much indoors and not enough in the field to develop the lovable part of their natures. How few are the men who love the game for its own sake. As Graham said at lunch, "A man might become interested in most any subject which he took the time to investigate." In other words that is how he happened to drift into zoology, just by chance. That is so true of many of them; they might as well have gone into chemistry or engineering.

What did I find? I found that a university position is not for me. The four universities that I have visited, I believe are typical of what a man might find most anywhere in the states. I cannot see how I could possibly be happy in such an atmosphere. The labs are dry and uninteresting, research courses are the same and the men who run them more so. Where are the woodsmen who should be in charge of such work, they are in the woods and it is there that I must go for my future training, what there will be of it. No more will I haunt the labs and lecture rooms, what further information I get will be dug out in the field or by independent reading.

There is this much I have found, that when it comes to teaching and research, Ely will give me as much and more than I could ever hope to get down here. Research does not mean much to me and I know that once I get up there again there will be little of it if any. The only research I will do is research into the thrills and joys a man may find by a life in the wilds. Mine is emotional research, not scientific. I get far more enjoyment out of writing an article for one of the sportsman's magazines than ever working out some scientific treatise. Let those with little imagination do that sort of thing. The other is for me.

December 31, 1931

Sometimes I think seriously of leaving the U and going north to spend the rest of the winter writing. I am afraid that might be misconstrued by the world. At any rate I certainly shall not take my ecology too seriously and put as much time as possible in on my writing. That will be some compensation.

December 31, 1931[10]

I am beginning to see after all what my main interest in the out of doors has been. It is not a scientific interest as I thought for so many years and still thought until this year. What has kept me in the woods all of these years is the love of beauty. And now that I think of it, it all becomes clear. What has left the greatest impression, the scenes which I have encountered and not the specimens collected or run across. What has been always boring, to go into the field with the avowed purpose of collecting some animal or plant or even making an observation. When I analyze my reactions now it seems queer that I did not find out what was behind them all of the time. If I was watching a beaver it was not the beaver and its habits as much as it was the light on the pool, the dark mystery of the forest around the pool, the symmetry of the dam. If I was trailing a deer, it was not so much the habits of the deer as it was the vistas I gained along the ridges and through the trees. If it was ducks, it was more than anything else the view of a flock against the sunset or dawn in the rice rather than the birds themselves. In other words it was the scene as a whole which drew me and that I mistook for a keen interest in natural history for lack of a better explanation. That brought me down this year to Illinois to study ecology and it did not take me long to finally discover what an illusion I have been laboring under. I thought it was queer that I could not whip my interest into the proper receptive mood. Why didn't the figures interest me, why didn't I go into ecstatics over the phenomenon of animal numbers. I thought for a time that I was naturally perverse, that I would never find what it was that I did want to do and that perhaps there was nothing that I could do except dream, and that perhaps I was just another misfit. This trip to Detroit and Ann Arbor has given me a chance to think and mull things over in my mind. It has given me perspective and at last I am beginning to see my true nature.

Two deer above a ridge in the jack pine timber, Superior National Forest, 1934.
Photograph by J. William Trygg, U.S. Forest Service Records, National Archives.

When I think of it, a game warden's job, unless I could write or paint my experiences, would be monotonous. A superintendent of a sanctuary with its administrative duties would be the same. A job on a university staff would kill me as would also any job at a wildlife research station. They are not what I want. What I would be doing all of the time would be longing to paint either in word or color the pictures that have been before me. At last you are beginning to know yourself.

In another hour the new year will be here. Who can tell what changes it will bring. The last hours of the old have been very happy and profitable. If I find out as much about my true self this coming year as I have the past, I should be well on the way to happiness. I feel this moment as though I had really accomplished something. The way is opening up as it always will for the one who persistently tries to find the right course to pursue. Only when one allows himself to stagnate and stops searching does he begin to vegetate. I knew that if I tried hard enough I would find a way out and at last I believe sincerely that I am close to the goal that has eluded me all of these years. Here is a cheer for what the old year has brought and a prayer to the new that I may be constant to my true self and not waver whatever the odds.

January 5, 1932

Back again at my desk and back to reality. It is hard to realize that the days of dreaming and thinking are over and that from now on for five months it will be a steady grind of doing things that I am not interested in, days when I will wake wishing it was nightfall so that I could crawl into the protection and oblivion of sleep. Such is a terrible state of affairs but one which is inevitable to me when I am doing what is outside of my dream.

I must try and forget, however, and ride my impulse to leave this mess in view of what is ahead. If I can bear up under it and get through somehow it won't be so bad. I have this consolation. Any spare time that I do have I shall put in on my writing. That will be a relaxation in itself and make it seems as though my time wasn't entirely wasted.

The evening before we left Ann Arbor, I ran across a passage something like this, "Only by following one's dreams does a man ever approach real greatness." Dreams, dreams, how the philosophers adhere to that one idea. Be true to your self and your highest aspirations. Only in that way can you ever hope to attain true greatness and content. What is my dream, yes what is it. <u>To interpret what is beautiful in nature</u>, to live so that I can be close to it always and bring my vision to the world. How will I do it, by writing, by painting word pictures or by going into the field with brush and color. I have little chance of doing much in the latter because my training has been all the other way. I may try it when I return but I feel that it will be only for my own amusement although one can never tell until one has tried. I do feel that when I return to the country I love that I will embark upon an orgy of writing such as I have never known before.

UNSETTLED
IN ELY

September 1932– October 1934

T HE OLSONS RETURNED TO ELY in June 1932. Sigurd's master's degree allowed him to teach at the Ely Junior College. He began that fall, teaching one course at the high school and three at the junior college. A step-up, career-wise, but he was as unhappy as ever.

A year later, just as he began to convince himself that he was in a good and valuable career at the junior college, he took a civil service exam for a junior park naturalist position with the National Park Service. He was considering opportunities away from Ely. In November came a letter from Aldo Leopold, who had just become the nation's first titled professor in game management and chair of a new department at the University of Wisconsin. Leopold, who would go on to be a founder of the Wilderness Society and author of the landmark book *A Sand County Almanac*, wanted Sigurd to be his first doctoral student.[1]

Leopold's letter began a year of turmoil, as Sigurd weighed once again the possibility of a career in ecology. Job offers of fieldwork added to his angst. He found it agonizing to come to a decision, and in every case delayed as long as possible. Finally, late in 1934—a couple of months after he and the family moved into a new home on the south side of

Cabin 26 at the historic Burntside Lodge near Ely. Historic American Buildings Survey Collection, Library of Congress.

Ely—he seemed to have finally decided to stay put in the north country that he and his family loved.

* * * *

September 16, 1932

Well here I am and still I am unhappy. It seems that I do not know what I want, that no matter where I am, I am unhappy and discontented. I don't know what it is, but as Lib says, she has never seen me contented in any situation. Perhaps I will never be contented. I don't know. Well this much is certain, I am through going to school. I don't want my doctor's degree, that will only mean getting into some university or college and there the grind will be exactly the same as ever....

I have gotten in my teaching very close to where I want to get and that is only college work. Only one high school class this year as against three last year. That will raise my self esteem somewhat although it means more work than ever before.

I think one solution is starting at my writing again, but what will it be. I am sick and tired of writing about hunting and fishing. That material is all repetition. I have written out the best I have in that line. It will have to be short sketches of things I have done and seen. It will have to be different. My little skiing jaunt which I wrote up at Champaign might work for one, short philosophical sketches or something of that order. Not the ducks of Low Lake, deer of the Stoney River, fly fishing for northerns, leave that to someone else. If I could find my medium, which I have been feeling around for in my diary for years, I would be all right. The problem is to find that and then get to work on it....

But why be despondent. Here you are, back in good country with a job and a chance to get out. Make the best of it, <u>but Oh these walls and the wind and the sunlight out of doors.</u>

All of this self analysis should be of some use.

September 22, 1932

Read something interesting last night on how to get what you want in life. This author claimed that if a man outlined a definite program for five years that he could do almost anything he wanted. Said that only 25 percent of the people had any idea of how to get the things they wanted and they were the ones who had formulated a definite method of getting there. If it is financial independence then it means a definite budgeting of one's earnings and sound investment. If it is working on some different line of endeavor then it must be a definite attempt towards that end.

Well how does it work out for me. I am 33 going on 34. How is it going to work out. I want to outfit and write, that is my goal and that is what I am fitted for more than anything else. Alaska, the north expeditions, romance and all the rest, when will it ever come true. I am getting more and more resigned to my fate and am afraid that if it goes on much longer this way that I will soon lose sight of my goal. I have had a taste of fame and authority and want more of it. I must make the break soon. This is not my field, I know it and feel it. Do I wake up in the morning anxious to get at my task? No, I count the hours until the end of the week. Surely no future in that.

December 9, 1932

The last week has been more or less miserable. I am still exploring the depths of my mind, strange as that may seem. As I look back over my diary of other years, it is a wonder that there is anything more to find out. Now I have tumbled to a new idea, painting, and realize (for the time being) that I should have been an artist, an interpreter of nature. As I read about the men who have gone in for landscape painting I know that here are men who feel about the beauties of the out of doors exactly as I do. It is their dream to interpret their impressions, moods, or whatever you want to call it on canvas. After all that is all that I have ever wanted to do. To me beauty is everything, I see it wherever I go and am sick at heart that I cannot take it with me. The printed word is so inadequate, description so terribly discounted, that after all there seems to be little there for me. Of course there are scenes that can be painted with words far better than with picture but in writing you have to give up so much that to you is beautiful for its own sake. The funny part of it is that I never discovered this before. Here I have gone for thirty three years, guessing slightly and groping but never dreaming that this might be it. Last year down at Detroit I had the first inkling of it and I never quite got over it. I resolved then that once I got back to Ely that I would start in. So far all I have done is read and that at least has been pleasant.

What means more to me than anything else in life is mood and feeling. I know that I can see and that I feel with the best of them. The stumbling block is technique. At that Gauguin didn't start until he was 35. If I start in now with my spare time, in a few years I will surely know something about it and by the time I am forty, who knows but that I will be able to at least paint something for myself. If I never accomplish anything worthwhile at least it will lead to a greater appreciation of art and land-scaping and it will give me some pleasure, of that I am certain. Photog-raphy never did appeal to me for as Harrison says, it is nothing but our own visual perception that really is beautiful.

Here I am on a side track again. When will I ever discover the ulti-mate happiness. Once it was writing, now painting. What will actually happen is that I will stay on here teaching, amusing myself with occa-sional painting, writing, fishing trips and hunting expeditions, not to forget the Border Lakes. My teaching has not been half bad this year and next, with final elimination of my high school class, it will be better. What an inconstant devil am I. How I wish I could finally arrive at some definite decision as to where my best faculties lie. It may be that I am not actually interested in anything but roaming the woods and living like a savage, and what is so wrong about that?

December 15, 1932

What a terrible week this has been, day after day of gloom and discour-agement. Each morning I come to work heavy of heart, each noon go home with a forced smile and at night look forward only to sleep and forgetfulness. I try to hide my despondency from Elizabeth and so far think I have been successful and of course the boys never catch on. If they only knew, life around home would take on a blueish tint. The worst part of it is that I have reached a point where it is impossible for me to analyze any longer my desires. The week I spent brooding over the art of painting and regretting the fact that I had not gone into landscape unbalanced me. The more I read the surer I am that it is not for me. I am close to 35, no longer have time for training and years of practice. What is more I never did try painting, and drawing I was never particularly good at or cared about. As E says if I had ever taken to it instinctively and dabbled with it all of my life, it could have been different, but to suddenly decide at 35 that I should have gone in for it, seems a little inconsistent. And she is not so far wrong. On the other hand I was always rather good at writing and if I want to indulge myself along artistic lines I should naturally stick to that.

December 28, 1932

Since the coming of vacation, my mind has been in more of a whirl than usual. For one thing I have been obsessed for the past month or so with the bogey of art, thinking that here after all was the solution to my troubles, that I should have in reality been a painter and nothing else, that my understanding of beauty and love of color could only have one outlet and that painting in oil. I have read half a dozen books on art, Birge Harrison's "Landscape Painting," Walter Sargent on "The Enjoyment and Use of Color," "Lives of Famous Painters" and "The Appreciation of Art and Nature." They have all been extremely interesting and I have all but devoured them because I thought they were giving me the solution to my problem. In reality, instead of strengthening my resolve to give up everything and go in for painting they have knocked the props out completely.

For one thing, I realize that if I had the artist's instinct I should have been painting and sketching long ago, and another, that if I ever were to accomplish anything that I would have to spend years and years of toil developing technique. When I read of chiaroscuro, color, line, light and shadow and all the rest, I realize that I am a mere tyro and no matter how much I love color and scenery, that I will never be able to do anything with it. I am too old now to give up everything and try to start something new. I have the artist's gift of sight and should really content myself with that. The trouble with me is that I feel that I have to create in order to enjoy. As ridiculous as the idea of having to play in order to enjoy music, to sing in order to enjoy song and to write novels in order to read. The idea hardly holds water.

All my life I have enjoyed color and landscape and thought I was one of the few who could. However my reading has shown me that I am only one of the many to whom nature and its moods are an open book. There are others who love the out of doors as much as I and some perhaps more passionately than I. In fact most of the great painters have developed a religion more than anything else from it. I see that I am not the only prophet and that much is good for my soul. Why not let the joy suffice and not let the joy of seeing be dimmed by the reflection that I cannot duplicate. The ogre of possession is what is in reality gripping me, wanting to capture each fleeting bit of beauty that is mine.

When I look back at my boyhood and realize my memories of fall coloring, spring mornings when trout fishing, my impression of oneness in and with nature, I know then that there was no attempt to capture but simply content with things as they were. Animals I loved and all wildlife and perhaps it was that they gave me in them a part of the wild, which was really the shrine at which I worshiped. I was and am in love with the wild and always will be. Any part of it is beauty for me. A savage at heart, a rebel against convention, and still I love the other too. There is where the rub comes in. I have a dual personality and can never be wholly one or the other without reservations.

Tonight there is a vague glimmer of hope. The ease in writing which is mine at times like tonight makes me understand as I have often before that perhaps after all, I can find the unattainable in writing. Perhaps with the power of suggestion I can find a little of the beauty of creation which I long for. Perhaps here I can paint in words, which is a medium I know a little about, some of the pictures which I feel deeply must be preserved. Certainly Burroughs and Emerson, Stevenson and others did not scorn their medium but made the most of it. They painted moods and their impressions of nature and gave them to the world. After all the goal of a painter is not to merely imitate a scene, a camera can do that much better, but to catch a fleeting moment or feeling and transmit that to the canvas. With words that can also be done and if I try perhaps I can do the same thing. I already have some fame, already have made an entrance into the outdoor field. Why not capitalize on that and make the most of it. Writing is easy for me once I get started, certainly much easier than trying to get anywhere painting. The only reason painting might appeal to me more than the other is because I delight in scenes for their own sake and make of beauty a fetish, a shrine at which to worship. With writing scenes are only suggested and action or thought more than the actual picture.

Why cannot I try my hand at sketches, make them so beautiful that there will be no gainsaying them. Once I get in the swing of writing tonight I find the old stream once more beginning to flow and the stagnant water, which has already begun to become foul, becoming again unclouded. And so with my spirit, which is an exact index of my activity.

I think all I have to do is get to work once more and this horrible inertia will leave me.

January 7, 1933

Have just returned from a trip up to Basswood Lake. Enjoyed the long stretches of the lake looking up to my old border country, felt good to swing along on snowshoes, feel the muscles working once more and to rest my eyes on distance, blue horizons. Especially will I remember coming out of Wind Bay with the sun getting low and long, snaky wisps of snow blown by the west wind and writhing over the smooth rippled surface of the snow. What a picture that was, millions of snaky streamers, pink and gray in the fading sun. Then dropping in to Ted's, an invitation to stop for the night, an hour at the woodpile more to escape missing the sunset than anything else. How peaceful it was out there with the dogs sitting on their kennels, the clean snow, silhouettes of pine and spruce and the pink in the west. It was beautiful, and when I had finished my pile and it was dark, I was hungry and still half reluctant to go inside away from the popping stars and the new half moon.

I am not much of a cabin visitor. I do not play cribbage, which I suppose I should learn, and find so little to talk about. The only time I love a cabin is when I am alone. Company, like with Thoreau, bores me after a short time. I am happiest when alone with my thoughts, although I do crave the other at times. What I miss most, however, is the chance to be alone where I can think.

Coming back to Pete's Camp on Basswood was also pleasant.[2] Emil made dinner for me and it did seem good to eat. For once I was ravenous. Had almost forgotten how good it feels to be really hungry again. How my spirits always soar when I have had enough exercise. It tones up my system and my mind acts accordingly. The old lesson which I repeatedly forget.

I still ponder my future. What I want to do is to be on my own, to make enough money to be independent, to live in the woods as much as I like. Up at Ted's, how proud I was of my moccasins and red socks, how symbolical of all that I love, rough things, rough clothes, men, dogs, the outdoors and all the trappings of life in the open. That to me is romance. If somehow I could find my medium, what joy it would be to work at it. For a while I thought I had it, but I must have been wrong. It must be something different, not the old cut and dried adventure stuff,

Peterson Fishing Camp on Basswood Lake, 1930s. Minnesota Historical Society Collection.

not essays, perhaps not animal stuff, what it will be if anything I still am wondering.

Saw a picture the other day of a laboratory in botany, an old man supervising a class, and saw myself twenty years from now, a life gone into it, dead and buried. It is hard to visualize. If I could only think and get this thing settled once and for all. I suppose I can keep on teaching, writing small nature skits from time to time and making of myself a pseudo authority on the wild in these parts, but is that what I want. After all I must work in the human element in order to feel that I am accomplishing something worthwhile. Still the world is full of that sort of thing.

What types of writing are there?

1. Essays, like Emerson's "Forest Essays," but there are no opportunities here for any lucrative work.

2. Animal stories, here too the field is limited. Look what happened to Sass, Scoville, and others.[3] They wrote, repeated and repeated until they overran the gamut of possibilities there. The same would happen to me were I to go into that exclusively. Archibald Rutledge is the same. Right now I can see the beginning of the end with him. He is at the ragged edge and unless he branches off into human nature stuff, he is through.

3. Stories of people in the wilderness setting, Curwood, Poindexter, and others, somehow it doesn't appeal to me.[4] A wonderful girl, a love affair, mounted police and all the rest. It does not appeal greatly to me. What then is left for me to do. Certainly not the novel, that I can never attempt, certainly not poetry, that also is not for me.

What do you like to do — merely describe everyday experiences like Thoreau, Burroughs, weaving in the philosophy of the lover of nature.

January 12, 1933

Yesterday I received two manuscripts, one from Collier's with "En Roulant" and the other from the Atlantic. Of course it left me in the dumps when I realized for the thousandth time that the high class stuff is not for me. I must be positively dumb not to have found that out by this time. Still, I keep on kidding myself. If after all of these years I have produced nothing worthwhile then why worry about it, why kid yourself with rose-colored dreamings of fame and fortune to come. It is not in me, that is certain, and I should not have to be knocked down and dragged out many more times to convince me.

What I should do is concentrate on little nature articles which I know I can do and stuff for the outdoor magazines and try nothing beyond that. The other stuff is not for me. Do what you can do and be content with that. And do not let the happening of yesterday so gloom your spirit that everything seems worthless.

January 15, 1933

Yesterday's experience was enough to finally convince me that I am nearing the end. This cannot go on much longer, no matter what the odds. I believe that this is my last year of teaching. I cannot go on any further. Each day that I put in leaves me so much further in the morass of despondency. Life is too short to carry on much longer this way. I have reached the point where I can no longer drive myself, where the work here and the atmosphere is hateful and beyond me. I feel that the long sought for end is here. The only sad part of it is that I have laid nothing by for the great experiment but must make my way with my writing and with the Border Lakes. Just the same, to have actually found out at last that there is only one thing that I care to do is accomplishment enough. How many men go through life never finding out or, finding out, who never have the courage to go ahead and do what they most want to do.

January 17, 1933

Merely want to record that I began "Let's Go Exploring" last evening, a story that I found among my old papers yesterday and one that will give us some fine advertising this spring.[5] It is in pretty good shape and with a little working over should be all right. Since Sunday, I have been lower than low, and last night driving myself to the task, I found that my spirits immediately perked up and by bedtime I was positively jovial. If writing will do that for me, whether or not it amounts to anything, then it itself is justification enough. If I can pull myself out of the dregs by painting a few word pictures and ideas, that at least is something.

January 20, 1933

The Question of a Medium

Last night as I lay in bed, the old question came up, and for the first time I saw it with some clearness. The medium of expression for me will not be the animal story, the fiction story or the type of article of Samuel Scoville, Jr., Herbert Ravenel Sass, or Archibald Rutledge or the rest. As far as I can see they have gone to pot and are not going to be able to stage a comeback. Scoville is completely played out. There is nothing left for him to do. He has already gone through the agony of repetition and plagiarism and I can well imagine what has happened to the rest. If I follow their example it will be the same for me. What I want is a medium that will not play out, some means of expression that will enable me to keep on as long as I live. What will it be. . . .

Nature Magazine and its various petite animal stories fails to thrill me. Field and Stream and the rest, I can never read with pleasure. Even animal stories of the usual kind bore me. It is rather a false hope to think that I can ever then produce anything of that type that will ever amount to anything. In order to do anything, I must have an ideal, a dream to follow, and if I write stuff that I am not interested in, how can I hope to write anything others will also read or enjoy. No, that is sure, I must write the type of thing that I would enjoy most myself. . . .

A painter who realizes that he is doing something mediocre, a writer who realizes that he is writing something that when he gets done will be dull, is like the man who, building a house, knows that no one will want to live in it because of its ugliness, even if he does get paid for it. Will such a creator, even though he gets paid a prodigious sum for it, find much of the artist's or creator's happiness in his work? I fail to see it. So it must be with me. If I am to do anything really worthwhile, I must find a medium which will take all I can give it something that I can look at with pride and say, "That is my handiwork," the best that I can do. Then and only then will you be doing anything worthwhile and only then will you receive the true artist's reward, the satisfaction of knowing that you have created something substantial and worthwhile.

Thought last night of my name. Sig Olson, though alright in the woods, is not what you might call a distinctive name for the type of article that you are thinking of writing. Your full name—<u>Sigurd Ferdinand Olson</u>—on the other hand has a sort of a swing to it that might easily create and hold a following.

Now that so much is settled, what then will it be?

February 6, 1933

What will it be — here I am again at a loss. My scientific work palls. I see names in the Wisconsin summer catalog that were there 12 years ago— old staid professors, now approaching old age, in the self-same rut. I want something more than just that. Only one life—perhaps I attach entirely too much significance to life—perhaps just the doing is all that is important....

What I want is to be able to do something different so that my friends can point me out as one who has ability of a sort & can make his way by his brains alone. I cannot stand mediocrity — I must know that I am being appreciated. Ego, my vanity must be satisfied — If it is writing then what shall it be — short essays or sketches, hardly, there is no money in that and I must have that — I must do something that pays & pays well....

For an hour have been reading Henry David Thoreau's conclusion to "Walden."

"Explore thy self," the old philosopher's refrain.

"Do something well for its own sake"

"Follow your dream for true happiness"

"Only the truth"

For me, then, there is only one thing to do, write my thoughts & none but mine. My ideas are as different and as unique as Thoreau's or Burroughs'. Certainly no object in repeating their ideas. Mine are sufficient enough — I am different. Like Burroughs—"I am surprised to find what fish I catch, once I sit down to think." — I know I have thoughts, for 30 years I have done nothing but think.

Undated, Autumn 1933

Reading Archibald Rutledge's article last night was helpful. He brought out something that I needed, a realization of the opportunity and dignity of my profession — dealing with youth, human contacts, the most beautiful & intangible thing in life. The artist, creation, here it is — beautiful living. Sincerity, no show, human nature — after all nature is life and here is its most beautiful conception, ideals, love, life & hope. Here I have something and don't know it. Contacts with human values, a cultural development.

I am already something of an ideal to these kids — my manner of living. A light in a girl's eyes, a boy's smile and understanding — love and hopes, fears, joys — sympathy — Botany, Zoology, Geology. There will always be a crop and through it all I will always be learning and understanding — Next year, I will teach geology and add one more facet to my interests and we will build a home and I will keep on with my writing and my outfitting and have a chance to do what I want which is to create. Weekends if I want will give me everything I want. If I can teach the <u>mystery</u> of life and see the joy that such knowledge can give, then I will have done something wonderful. I can have a life of gentleness and understanding and above all get away from the old cut & dried idea that teaching is drudgery. It is really a luxury to be in a position to make such contacts. It is perhaps the noblest of all professions.

And if I can develop a knowledge of trees, birds, and rocks, show the mystery of creation to these boys and girls, think what an opportunity. There are compensations, many of them if I only let myself realize it. Those smiles, how I love those youngsters, their hopes & fears, knowledge for its own sake is everything. I always want to be a teacher, always, nothing is bigger or finer. The days will always be glorious and full. True the salary now is low, but it will come up to a couple of hundred and that is enough to live on. To roam these hills & rocks with groups of boys &

girls is enough for anyone's happiness — A nature trail perhaps, idealization. I have the Junior College now, that is what I want and there is every possibility of our keeping it indefinitely.…

Life, life, what a mistake I have been making, life in the raw, it is in Bob & Jr., in the homely little rat in front of me, just as much as it is in a tree, frog, deer, or moose. Beauty is in a smile, a glance, a hope, a fear, where have I been looking, everywhere but in the right place.

I will never get rich but I will always be comfortable and I have beauty always around me. Happiness has been at the end of my nose & I never knew it or could never see it. I have thought that only outdoors could it be found, but actually there is as much here in front of me as elsewhere.

Research is not my life to be sure & here research means nothing. Leave that for the plodder, the unimaginative soul. But teaching, opening the way to understanding, leave that to the born teacher or guide. "You are dealing with the intangible always," the most beautiful elastic substance in nature, a human soul. I am an artist. My life is a model, I must keep it so, always beautiful and filled with satisfaction.

Sigurd with a group of students from Ely Junior College, 1930s. Ely–Winton Historical Society Collection.

September 14, 1933

The question now confronting me is again the changing of occupation. On Oct. 4th I will take a civil service examination for the position of Junior Park Naturalist with the National Park Service. It will take me away from this country and I am afraid that it will mean the severing of my relations with the Border Lakes Outfitting Co., the giving up of my dream to spend the winters writing. Of course it may also mean getting into a line of work that will give me just the sort of life I want, a chance to be out of doors most of the time, time to write and study and freedom from the classroom....

In the last analysis, what I want is a working-writing combination, ala Thoreau and Burroughs. I do not think that I will be ever quite satisfied until I work out something like that. I am close to it now and perhaps don't know it.

September 15, 1933

Last evening as I thought of the opportunity for work with the park service, I found myself wondering when I would find time for writing. The happy moments that writing has given me, have burned themselves indelibly into my makeup. I don't suppose that I can ever get over it. No matter what I do, I am longing for the other. The only really worthwhile activity, putting my thoughts down on paper, the sort of existence that Burroughs might have lived. I tasted that once and cannot forget it....

Nothing seems actually to be worthwhile but that, that is the pitiful part of it. All other activity seems to be wasted. To produce something beautiful, that is the final end. Making money is sordid, even scientific research is dry. All I look forward to is the chance to create. Only then do I find myself upon the heights. But how can I live. I must find a medium there too as we must eat.[6]

October 11, 1933

On returning from the meeting of the International Joint Commission at Minneapolis.[7]

I went down to the hearing with little knowledge of what I wanted to say and up to the time I took the stand, I knew nothing. Right now I do not remember just what I did say but I believe, judging by the many compliments I received, that whatever I did say was pertinent. I forget how many came around, but among them was the attorney general for Minnesota, Frank Warren of Minneapolis, Oberholtzer, Kaupanger and others. All of them said that I had made a wonderful impression on the commission. The fact that the commission itself was interested enough to talk things over with me was of importance.[8]

All of this left me with one concrete impression and that was that somehow I have the power of conveying my enthusiasm to others, particularly men. I can make them see and feel what I see and feel of the out of doors. Of all the witnesses I alone brought out this which explains no doubt that I alone received applause.

October 16, 1933

As the years go on, as they slip by one after the other, I find myself getting increasingly desperate. If I am going to make the break and do what I want then now is the time. However all of my life I have done so many things that are against the achieving of this liberty, one of the last going away for my master's degree and spending all of the money I had as well as tying me up for many years to come. Is that achieving independence and freedom. The trouble with me is that I do not know what it is I do want, and so I squander the precious time and money that I have, wallowing around, stumbling first here and then there trying to find a solution....

Do you really suppose that if you had the courage to break away that you could really make enough to make both ends meet. If I was single, it would be the simplest thing in the world. I could make enough guiding in the summer time to take care of me nicely, the rest of the year. But now it is too late to think about that.

October 19, 1933

Since my last trip, I have been beset with the old doubts. Can I really write or is it just an illusion on my part. When I feel that way, I lose all my joy in living. Nothing seems worthwhile. As long as I am working at something, I am happy and buoyed up, but let the ogre of doubt enter my soul and it is all off. If I could only be working at something all of the time, I would be reasonably happy. I think that is the salvation of my peace of mind. No matter what it is, just so I am pounding off something. What hurts me is the indecision and the doubt all of the time wearing me down.

Sometimes the struggle gets too much and I am tempted to end it all and just let things slide. I don't know whether this is the real thing or if it is just an illusion on my part built up by years of constant thinking and wondering about it. Have I the stuff or have I been kidding myself all of these years. I don't know and I suppose I will keep on this way indefinitely wondering and wondering and letting my indecision get worse and worse. It is hard to say what to do....

I wish I had time to write and still when I do sit down I cannot do a thing. Only one who has experienced what I have, the longing for creation, can understand how terrible it is to find oneself inadequate.

October 25, 1933

I am of the peculiar makeup that requires a fanatical absorption in something. I have been going along all of these years wondering what it shall be and have reached a point of desperation where to decide becomes the most important thing in life. To go along with indecision will sooner or later be ruinous....

The real truth is that I am no longer interested in zoology and botany as a science. It all bores me half to death. I must deal with the intangible, idealism, the artistic, emotions, and there is none of that in what I am doing. I also crave recognition and I must create. What after all gives me greater joy than writing. The very thought of it makes me happy....

The Border Lakes will give me enough with five months of full-time pay, a chance for a dividend and with my writing, I should be able to make it. The very thought that by taking a chance, I can do the life's work that I have wanted to do all of these years is enough to drive all of the gloom and foreboding away....

As I look back over my diary, I smile at the pondering and gradual sifting. It has been an interesting analysis but now it is finished. Your life then will be outfitting and writing. Zoology and botany will merely be a hobby, nothing more and I will forget about the classroom forever. Freedom at last.

November 7, 1933

The other day came an offer from Leopold of Wisconsin asking me if I would consider taking my doctor's degree at Wisconsin. I am going to

Headquarters of Border Lakes Outfitting Company at Winton, circa 1930. Olson Family Collection. Courtesy of David Backes.

write I suppose that I am much interested although in my heart it frightens me. If I was a research man I would have done the Mammals of the Quetico and a thousand other problems here at my back door. Now Dr. Cahn has done them and the glory is his, what little there is. If I was interested I would have attacked the moose problem, but what have I done. I am not interested at all. I let others go ahead while I dream and wonder. After all what does this indicate about my capabilities. Merely that I am not fitted for the role of a game expert. There is something else that I need but not that. The only thing that will give me real joy is the painting of word pictures, moods, and emotions. To describe a hillside covered with snow so that my reader could feel what I feel, there is something worthwhile. To enumerate a list of mammals of the Quetico is boring. Why not do what I know I want. Because doing so means the possible chance of starvation and want for my family. If I were alone, it would not take me long to find myself.

November 8, 1933
If I accept Leopold's offer, there it will be again, research and more research. My only hope there is to have a broad enough vision so that it will override the immediate drudgery. Otherwise I will be miserable there too. However, I am not going to think about that.

In the end, it will simmer down to this. By writing in the wintertime I will build up a considerable clientele, which will mean a dual compensation. Oh the ogre of doubt that assails me. Where is my self-confidence. If I only knew.

November 13, 1933

The past hour I have spent reading over my notes of the past three or four years. Yes they are consistent, so consistent that anyone half blind would be able to see that there is no use trying to analyze myself further. If I do not know now after all of that introspection then I will never know. I can see my diary ten years hence and picture myself reading it. What change will there be. I am sure none whatever....

What will I do if Leopold comes through with an offer. I do not know, but I feel that knowing myself as I do, I should turn him down flat and not consider it for a moment. That is what I should have done with Champaign.

I have many regrets, but as I look back over them, there is some joy in knowing that each mistake has been a definite elimination and without them I would still be wondering....

Know then today that self analysis is over. You must write to be happy. That is as set and stone-hewn as any truth could ever be. Accept it, do not fight it or wonder any more. This much is definite, concrete, clear. Do not argue with yourself any further. Admit it, know that you have found what you have searched for and knowing it, do what you should do, actually sit down and begin work on something. Adopt a fatalist's attitude, if this is it, then this is it, and there is no use quarreling with it any further. ACCEPT, ACCEPT, ACCEPT, ADMIT THE WISDOM OF YOUR CHOICE AND FORGET FOR THE REST OF YOUR LIFE THAT THERE IS SUCH A THING AS DOUBT. FACE THE ISSUE SQUARELY. YOU HAVE WON.

November 14, 1933

Yesterday I received a letter from Aldo Leopold asking me if I would accept a sort of fellowship for a study of deer in Wisconsin. How much would I need, perhaps $3000 a year, I suppose an exorbitant sum. Do I want to do that sort of thing again, and tie up another three years of my life, hunting the unattainable. I am now 35 and as I said to Elizabeth this morning, this will be a final decision.[9] Failure to take advantage of

Aldo Leopold, circa 1940. Courtesy of the Aldo Leopold Foundation and University of Wisconsin–Madison Archives.

this and I will be on the blacklist forever. Aldo Leopold is one of the big men, in fact perhaps the biggest man in game conservation and research today. To turn him down would forever damn me in his eyes and in the eyes of all those who are interested in game....

However, if I take up Leopold's proposition, in three years I will be through, perhaps with my degree. I may get a position with some university or with some state department as a game expert. It is hard to tell where I will be or what will happen. True, this is my big opportunity and this time if I refuse, I am through FOREVER. If this is what I want to do with my life, then here is my big chance. Perhaps in the end it will mean travel and fame and a chance to do a tremendous amount of good. This field is opening up; if a man has ambitions along that line, here is opportunity.

It will mean of course that our home life is to be forgotten for a long time and that I must forget my dreams and my writing. Both choices have possibilities. Which will make me happier. Lib hesitates to advise me because as she says she wants me to do whatever will make me happy. She is unselfish enough to feel that anything will be all right if I am satisfied. I suppose what I want to do more than anything is to write. Then the thing to do is to spend the rest of this winter convincing yourself that you can and will write. If you can do something worthwhile then all right go ahead. This is your last chance, and I feel that next spring something is going to pop. Will I be ready to make my final decision.

November 15, 1933

The more I think of Leopold's offer the more it frightens me, just another blind alley for me. It is no more what I want to do than flying.

November 28, 1933

Now I am confronted again with another letter from Leopold. When will this thing be settled. He gives me my choice of a deer or duck problem....

What will it mean eventually, a professorship at Wisconsin, Michigan or Illinois, finding myself in the same boat as King, Fenstermacher, Dwight or Leopold, impossible, life holds more than that for me. I want romance, joy and life, the joy of creation, the weaving together of beautiful ideas, words are wonderful things to me and a lovely sentence more than any amount of scientific truth. I love words and ideas and there will I be happiest and there only. Of course, I will have my moments of doubt and despair.

November 30, 1933

Sigurd Ferdinand Olson, the name at least has a lilt to it and a swing. Ferdinand at second glance has a note of Spanish romance and so for that matter has Sigurd. My ideal is to make that name above all else something to conjure with. Sig Olson is common, Sig is bad but Sigurd Ferdinand is something different again. It needs the Ferdinand to take it out of the realm of mediocrity, and to give it euphony. That name can be made a power by the sheer beauty of my writing, by my insight into human emotions. As I develop, it will become increasingly well known and respected.

I ponder and ponder Leopold's offer. Other callings have their romantic sides also, that I will admit. Would I care however to be a geologist, would I care to be sent off to Tibet collecting mice for the Field Museum. The killing, measuring and stuffing side of that job would ruin me. In any of those jobs I would have no time for reading and reflection and that for me would be stagnation. How often has the vision of being left alone in a cabin haunted me. That is what I want more than anything else, and then the joy in the appearance of an article of mine well written.

December 2, 1933

I have the terrible urge for self-expression. I can't do anything without having it ride me. If I go anywhere, I fret away the time because I have no opportunity to write. If I go out with other people, I will sit in a corner and read, letting them play cards. I act like a neurotic and the waste of time is terrible to me. Perhaps it is a form of neurasthenia that I have worked myself into. Whatever it is, days and nights in which I am not writing are nightmares. If I could spend the best time of the day working at what I think I should do, then I could feel free to play the rest of the time and play with abandon. This way, I feel my evenings are wasted unless I try and do what I want, and what a miserable failure most of them have been due to the fact that I am on edge and over-nervous.

December 12, 1933

If I get on with the Forest Service on Leopold's new offer with the P.W.A., I am afraid it will be the same old thing again. I can see myself back in a room at night, trying to get some small comfort out of pounding off some little article. All the time I will be wondering when I will be able to get in a little time by myself to think in and to work in. If I am to get anywhere, I must be enthusiastic and I cannot imagine myself getting enthusiastic even about that.

The secret of my discontent with all scientific research is that at heart I am not a scientist, although I am rated as one. I am not interested in any work that has a purely scientific trend. It bores me to death and always will.

December 14, 1933

Today I have a letter to write to Aldo Leopold. Lib tells me that I have no power of decision and I guess she is right. If it wasn't for the fact that I feel I want to write it would be easy, but to make a decision that will take me away from the leisure I need and put me in something else that will be entirely foreign to my interests is a step that takes thought and consideration. I do not know yet what I will tell him, but as usual suppose it will be a half conciliatory promise.

December 15, 1933

Last night I wrote or rather retyped and revised "En Roulant" until eleven o'clock, the night before until almost one. This morning, the old gloom has left and I am feeling fresh and in good humor. It does me good to see a manuscript taking final form on clean fresh linen paper. There is something final and complete about a last revision that is balm to the soul after days and weeks of yellow paper, changes and revisions. "En Roulant" really looks good to me now. Every time I work it over, it seems better and better and I am sure it will find a market if only *Sports Afield* will release it which I am confident they will. Even if they don't it will now appear in a form that I am not ashamed of.

All I need to keep up my spirits is plenty of work and creative work. As long as I am feverishly pounding away at something, my soul is at peace. Let me falter for a day and I am moody and distraught. I cannot stand idleness and writing has become such an obsession with me that only through its medium can I be at all happy. Knowing that, then why ever let yourself get into a state of mind such as has been plaguing you. Why not keep forever at something and getting ideas out of the way. Only in that way can you keep from stagnation. A peculiar complex I have, but a good one at that, realizing what it is. This morning, I am a different man and I marvel at the change.

February 9, 1934

During the past couple of weeks I have done considerable writing, and with it comes the feeling I have accomplished something. I have a series of articles underway now, one which I finished last night for the *Minnesota Conservationist*, "A New Policy for the Superior," another for the *Minnesota Waltonian*, "Roads or Airplanes," one for *Outdoor Life*, "Let's Go Exploring," one for *Outdoors*, title not decided on and a number of short sketches of trips for the *Minneapolis Tribune*.[10] This material will not net me much if anything but it is keeping my hand in and will lead to some

The Gunflint Trail road, 1932. Photograph by Monroe P. Killy, Minnesota Historical Society Collection.

end, particularly if I stir up some sentiment on the Superior. During the next three days, which we have off, I am going to try and get most of this material out of the way. I could easily take a week at it and then need more time. This morning after working over the Superior article, I feel as though life is worthwhile. Queer the feeling that working two or three hours gives me invariably. No day is quite lost in which I pound off something or work on something. I note too that writing is becoming easier the longer I do it....

Finally sent "En Roulant" to *Sports Afield* and it was received with open arms. Whipple, editor said that it was major league material and that it would be featured in the June and July numbers. "May We Come Along?" is coming out in September or October so by the time I get through I will have quite a bit of material about to be published.[11]

Border Lakes stuff is coming in rapidly and I begin to see the end of my dreaming once more. However, I do seem to have more energy than ever before and if I can keep to my working schedule, I will still be able to accomplish something worthwhile. What I would like to do is get all of the above done, particularly the last story and then I will rest on my laurels for this winter.

February 19, 1934

As spring approaches with the multifarious businesses of getting ready for the coming season, I find myself more and more weaned away from my dreams. So it is at the end of every winter. Coming activity absorbs my interests and makes me doubt if I ever had thought for dreaming and writing.

March 2, 1934

I have reached an important conclusion, the result of years of searching and indecision and probing of my capabilities and that is the truth that fiction writing is not for me....

And what is more, I realize now that my sole interest in life is nature. Of course I have always known that but I mean the study of nature, scientifically. There is where I will get my kick and as far as my writing goes, it will come in very handy here. Writing, after all, is a source of power and the practice I have had will stand me in good stead in the years to come. I will have plenty of opportunity to use what knowledge I have and can work in many a small paragraph to salve the wound that this apparent abandonment of my old dream will leave.

What makes me particularly happy is the fact that all of my study of wildlife and the outdoors will not have been wasted. My year at Illinois will now be a splendid investment and so will all of the years I have been at this game. I have now some sort of a reputation, one that has been growing steadily, and now have the opportunity of building on it. The reason the last few years have been wasted is that I have thought that my talents lay in other channels, that scientific interest was only secondary and anything that took me away from purely aesthetic writing was a waste. That is the reason that I have not applied myself. From now on, it will be purely science. I know where I stand and am at last happy knowing. This is the long-sought medium. At last I am down to earth and though I will not plan on my writing ever bringing me anything financially that is direct sale, it will bring me far more, prestige and position and authority....

What I want to do is make myself an authority on wildlife and get my satisfaction out of the study of it. The instant that I plan on making my living from writing like any other scribbler, then I am unhappy. I know my wildlife and others know that I know it. Why try to do something for which you are not fitted at all. Why not stick to your own field and make the most of it, rather than try and infringe somewhere where others are twice as competent. Be yourself and make use of your own talents. And remember that true contentment comes only through the development of one's own genius, from and through yourself, and he that loses his dream loses all. Do not misinterpret this for the old dream was an illusion which the new dream is not. For once you are down to earth and may you never again lose the vision that is yours today.

April 25, 1934

I deal with the intangibles—not the scientific. My field is not in figures and data, my field is in things of the soul— futuristic—That is my field— and mission to create a bond of understanding between men, to work for the realization of what we love & the conservation of our lakes and streams and woods. That is enough for any man and it should be enough for me — That is my opportunity for an outlet — That is where I will get my real satisfaction out of life through that wisdom. Teaching and outfitting will give me my living, but the other will be my field of expression and connection with the rest of the world —

June 28, 1934

This is the first entry in my journal since school let out now over a month ago and as usual it is amusing to see where this month has taken me. The soil erosion proposition is all through. Holt wrote me the other day that game management work had been discontinued so that is that. I turned down the National Park Service, so that is that. Now Swenson and Willard are thinking of putting in a department of game propagation in the State Office Building and are thinking of me. Do I want it or not.

For one thing, it will mean living in St. Paul or Minneapolis. It is hard to conceive of and the boys, I know, will be heart-broken to leave the woods and the open....

I will be constantly on the move and will be gone most of the time, at least three or four days a week, days in which Lib will have to sit home. I will be in touch with Leopold and King and the rest and will make a mark for myself in the field of game management. It is an opportunity all right and it might lead into supervision of some federal refuge someday or something of that nature. It will no doubt be my one big chance to make good in this particular field. And if it comes through, I should take it from that angle alone....

What I need is a job where I have an income that will make writing only secondary as a means of livelihood. Then it will sort of be like the frosting on a cake, something extra and worthwhile, an addition to the rest. And the job should preferably be one that did not take too much mental energy so that I could spend my best on writing and just sort of cruise around getting material....

Lib is so miserable the way things are and I don't blame her. If I could only work things out the way I want them, how happy I would be. It does seem impossible, however. After all her happiness means more to me than my own. If I was not so selfish I would make her believe that I am all set and want nothing more than I have.

September 4, 1934

Here I am back at my old job and it isn't half as bad as I thought it would be. I am doing entirely Junior College work now and as usual have a nice bunch of youngsters ready to start work.

Elizabeth Olson, 1930s. Listening Point Foundation Archives.

When I think of other jobs I might have, I wonder if this is as terrible as it might be. In the Forest Service I would be gone so much of the time and I am afraid that I would miss Elizabeth and the boys. Lib is developing into the most charming creature in the world, more and more the beautiful woman. I wonder if I could bear to be gone from her that much. I am afraid it would be hard. Then too there is a lack of responsibility in this job and a certain freedom that I would get in nothing else. When I think of the Soil Erosion Service and its mess, I am glad I didn't make the move. I have something pretty nice here and perhaps don't know it.

September 21, 1934

Now comes Holt with another offer, Soil Erosion Service, in charge of 150,000 acres—$3200 per year. I am tired.

September 27, 1934

The scene last night, late afternoon toward evening, heavy mist covering the river, the aspens & birches suddenly turned to deep yellow and orange, sedges & willows brown & sere, slate smooth [word?],[12] a rapids, black rocks, framed perfectly between two clumps of birch, the dark spruces velvet black columns against the yellow of the hill. Quiet — peace, serenity — a lull — a benediction to summer.

I would like to paint that—capture it some way—would like to spend my life doing nothing but catch scenes of such sheer loveliness & charm. I know that I will never do it and it hurts me terribly. There is a sense of futility and unreachableness that only those can know who know the unattainable.

Last evening it was almost more than I could bear — it hurt me — I wanted to run away and sob — it hurts me today. Why should it — it should make me happy — Is it because I am over sensitive or that I realize that I can never attain or hold such beauty. But I must if I am not to go insane. I must capture some of that somehow—create something durable.

Always it is that, never satisfied, the soul of me always is yearning for what it hasn't got. It is not enough to possess or see, not enough for the senses to enjoy. I must possess — own — create my own.

September 28, 1934

Spent last evening talking over the Soil Erosion work with E. It is hard to come to any conclusion. It is such a momentous step, one that cannot be passed over lightly. What will it lead into, where will it put me. Will it as E says give me work which I like to do. That is by far the most important consideration. Can I lose myself in this work, wrap my entire being up in it. Will the nights seem too long and the days too short. In other words, will it be what I want, or will it be just another job again.

October 1, 1934

I am supposed this noon to write Holt and cancel forever my chances with the Soil Erosion Service. Ober[13] thinks it is the thing to do. I wonder. Yesterday I was sure. Today, I am a little uncertain. In fact I have a faint feeling at the pit of my stomach. Is it right or wrong, $3200 per annum, Spring Valley, going all of the time, moving from place to place, never at peace or at home. Still perhaps a step in the right direction. Perhaps I could come back here and get further with that training behind me. On the other hand my job is the interpretation of the beauty and the meaning of this country, by means of articles and essays. In that way,

Ernest Oberholtzer at Rainy Lake, 1938. Ernest C. Oberholtzer Foundation Archives.

I can build myself up, keeping hold on the recreational aspects as well. Ober says, your fortune is in this country, don't leave it.

October 11, 1934

This morning is quite different. It is all decided and we are going to stay. I did not realize how much my life here meant to me until there was danger of its being terminated. Like many things we do not appreciate until they are taken from us. Last evening I took the boys off on a little paddle and I was more than ever convinced that the thing for me to do is stay on here. There is so much of loveliness and so little of the drab that it is worthwhile no matter what the odds....

I do not think ever again that I will be in the depths of despondency and despair. I will not give up what I have but will work things out with what I have so that everything will work out for the best. My writing must not be a commercial thing, but an art and for that I must have a livelihood to take the edge off the demands ulterior. If I can be happy in my teaching and outfitting and work in my writing too, then why should I worry ever about anything.

FAREWELL TO
SAGANAGA

October 1934–August 1935

I N 1935 SIGURD ENTERTAINED one more outside job possibility, supervising wildlife research in White Mountain National Forest in New
Hampshire. It was just a one-year position, but he agonized over it. In
the end, he stayed put, and the Olsons would remain at their new home
on East Wilson Street for nearly sixty years.

At the heart of this chapter is the continuing drama of Sigurd's difficult and sometimes desperate search for the kind of writing he could
best do that also would pay enough to allow him to quit the junior college, where by now he was teaching full time. The 1935 New Year began
with a writing experiment that went terribly wrong, but then in February inspiration hit, and he wrote a draft of his first wilderness essay in
the narrative style that became his hallmark.

"Farewell to Saganaga" is one of Sigurd's best-known essays, published in his first book, *The Singing Wilderness*. But as the 1930s approached
their midpoint, when Sigurd first worked on the essay, it brought him
both elation and crushing despair. "'Farewell to Saganaga' may mean
farewell to all of my dreams, farewell to all that I thought worthwhile,"
he wrote on March 12, 1935. The kind words of a canoe trip client would
come at an opportune time to keep his hopes alive.

A winter hike, 1941. Wisconsin Historical Society Collection, 74112.

* * * *

October 18, 1934

It is something to know finally what it is I want to do. I am 35 and like Whitman in good health and ready to begin. All I want to do is to be left alone to live my life as I want, cruise around and write about it. E asked me if I didn't think I would run out of material. There is no end to material unless my mind becomes sterile. Like Thoreau, I want to give my vision to the world. I am a writer, not a scientist, even though the world may think so....

The greatest source of contentment is to do something so good, so much in demand that the world will take care of you. I am different, that I know, and I feel that I have something definite to report. I am the spokesman of the wild, not only of nature but what is within us.

I will read Hegel, Morris, Schopenhauer and the rest, steep myself more and more in the old philosophies until when I write and when I live I will be more and more the philosopher and the mystic. That is what I want from life.

Being out is not enough. I must record and write. I cannot just enjoy but must feel at all times that I am working toward my goal. It will probably be both stories[1] and essays and articles, material and ideas will come to you once you get under way. This winter, I feel, will be the beginning of my race toward my goal.

October 21, 1934

If I can find my medium and get things to working, I will feel fairly happy. That is the one rub now. I am going somehow to work it out this winter....

I long to find a sphere in which I can absolutely sink all of my energies, tire myself out, use every iota of nervous and physical energy I possess, lose myself body and soul in whatever I do, wear myself down to bone and raw nerve, for such is my nature and such is intensity. I have reached the stage where the commonplace will not satisfy, where it becomes imperative that I go the limit. I should regret every moment taken away from my work, be so anxious to accomplish which I have set for myself that exhausting labor will be my joy. Only then will I be happy and content.

October 22, 1934

I must start something immediately, the sooner the better and keep working on it. Only in that way will I attain any peace of mind. Philosophical essays are all right but there is no compensation for them but in the writing. I cannot write of women and children for they are strangers to me.[2] I must write of something I know and only that. I think too of writing about men, but the only man I know is myself. Still I am a mirror of the wild and any man could be myself, in fact any man would have to be myself.

October 23, 1934

I might write hundreds of stories and articles which might be accepted, but not until I contribute something new to the world, help others get some new slant on life, will my stuff be worthwhile.

What then will it be. Prove to yourself that you have something different, show men that what you have is worthwhile. Thoreau developed an unusual philosophy, an independence and aloofness that was refreshing. Burroughs, a homely philosophy of the husbandman and lover of the soil. Spinoza, that the world lies locked up within the doors of the spirit. Emerson, the joys of intellectual analysis. Plato, group philosophy. Whitman, a breadth of vision covering a continent. Mine—still a blank—I am groping and searching and hoping that it will come.

November 5, 1934

On returning from Minneapolis

I went down to the city to settle an important question, whether or not I could stand to leave this country. I believe the past four days of rushing around have done me a great deal of good. For one thing, I would never be happy in the city, no matter what the salary, and although I did not get down in the La Crosse country, I got enough of the feeling of the life down there and the country as a whole to know that it is not for me.

As I stood on Hennepin Ave and watched the great crowds, masses of people rushing from store to store, from work to work, milling and jostling one another, pushing, and hurrying, as I watched their faces knowing that their whole life is lived without the strengthening influence of the earth, without the stimulation of living close to nature, that their sole recreation is the theater, the Sunday paper, dancing and drinking and the influence of home and family, I could not help but see how much fuller a life a man can live up here and how much those people, who after all are my audience, need someone to give them the fresh primitive perceptions. I am working for them, to show them through my eyes what they are missing. I know that inherently they crave what I have, that perhaps it is dormant now and they do not know what they miss, still I know that way down deep there is the old longing for quiet and peace and closeness with things of the spirit. In a city, there is little of that, there is too much crowding and milling around, too little time for reflection. Of course there are advantages, but not of the type I wish. My pleasure is more elemental, more rooted in the soil, there is no definite satisfaction with the other.

November 21, 1934

I am beginning to find out that my mission in life is to develop the philosophy of wildness, the longing of men for the wild and all that it means. I read and reread Thoreau and the more I read, the more I recognize a similarity in spirit. No one has as yet developed a philosophy of the wilderness. That is up to me....

My work must be strong and hard and masculine, the love of men for the wild, its truth, its unvarnished joy, its compensations, the feeling of being alone.

November 22, 1934

My only excuse for the life I am living or rather the position I am keeping in the Junior College and at Ely is in the hope that someday I will produce something worthwhile. It is hard for me to believe that my life itself is enough. I crave some higher form of expression than just living and I feel that writing something worthwhile will take care of that for me. If just occasionally, I could bring out some of the longing that is mine, some of the great and long thoughts that come when I am out, some of the joy that is also mine and the beauty I see, that will be justification enough.

It is snowing today, out of the north and I look at it and dream. How I love the first real snow, cold drifting flakes on the forefront of the north wind, how peaceful and quiet it all is and how the quiet penetrates my soul. How I love quiet and peace. That more than anything else do I crave and need and always is the old dream, have yourself a cabin alone in the wild where you can dream and write and think long thoughts. The first snow is like a benediction, soft and soothing, a balm to the spirit after months of hustle and confusion. Now is the time for rest and thoughts, thoughts on the meaning and mystery of life, life trimmed down to its very core, stripped of all its superficiality. I will now have time to reason it all out to decide what after all are the most worthwhile things, what is the basis of satisfaction and contentment. I know that once I begin, I will find what I am looking for.

Today I am strangely happy and at ease — I am filled with wonder at the sight of new snow and perhaps the prospect of spending three full days on the Stoney River.

December 10, 1934

Thought some of my next article "The Wilderness Idea" or "The Need of Wilderness" or "The Passing of a Wilderness" "Farewell to Saganaga." Sydney seems to think that I will do something wonderful this winter and I certainly am going to try. If I can turn out one good thing, it should be enough. I think it will be on the wilderness idea, at least I am infused with that right now and I should strike while the ideas are with me.

Start out with a picture of Saganaga as it was, follow with a picture of Saganaga as it is, paint a perfect picture of the feeling a man gets seeing it for the first time, a wilderness lake of which he has heard for years was inaccessible. Perhaps the wilderness makes you feel entirely different than anyone else. Perhaps you can interpret the wild as no one has ever done before you, the real wilderness. Surely no one has ever done it before and surely no one has ever had the same feeling toward it that you have. Make your theme song always the wild, make it always sing of the joy of men in the unspoiled, perfection and naturalness. You are different, in the wilderness idea you have something untouched, unusual. Thoreau told of Concord and his little wilderness, why cannot I speak of a larger wilderness such as the Superior-Quetico, the joy of men in exploration and wilderness travel.

I feel of course that what I say will only ring true when I live again as I did. To try and remember all I have seen and experienced is already second hand and tame. Still, why shouldn't my imagination be sufficient to do what I want. Perhaps in this way I will get a start....

Saganaga Lake, 1950s. Photograph by Norton & Peel, Minnesota Historical Society Collection.

Yesterday in church I was sure that no man could feel more deeply the passion I feel for the wild. Why cannot I transfer that passion to the written word, why cannot I give out the intensity of my feeling. For a moment yesterday I felt positively ill with the strength of my desire. I felt it had to come out, that I couldn't hold it a moment longer. Strangely I felt like I suppose a woman feels in travail, succumbed to an almost overwhelming desire to give birth to any idea, to produce something worthwhile. I suppose that after all is the secret of the creative desire. When it becomes strong enough, nothing can prevent its being accomplished. It would be impossible not to do it. To do this one thing becomes then the most important thing in life for me. What is within me hurts me and to receive any peace of mind, I must work it out of my system.

December 14, 1934
"He who can so arrange his life that he can live as he wishes is a genius."

If I can arrange my own life so that I can live as I want then I will be content. I imagine that what I want to do is write and will no doubt keep the job I have to do that. Build me a cabin over on the edge of the woods so that I can have the solitude I wish, so that I can retire on my own at least 2 hours every day, which will mean much to me. How I crave solitude, how happy I am when I feel that I am absolutely alone. When thoughts come, then and only then can I accomplish what I want most of all.

I believe that if I could make some such arrangement that I would be quite happy. I know that what I need is time & opportunity to write & that only writing will make me happy. If that will make it possible why then that is enough — Burroughs could not write with people around, neither could any of the rest.

Sell your interest in the Border Lakes, buy the house you are in, build the cabin for writing and have those precious summers free to do with as you like. I should get enough to pay for it in cash easily —

My school work is not half bad — it gives me time to dream & think and write — freedom from the distraction of business and its worries — $2000 is enough to live on and we could get along if the house was paid for.

An ordinary year nets me $1300 to $1500, almost as much as my teaching. Why not give that up & have from October to May to write, several full months instead of two. Still with the boys' teeth to be straightened and a number of other things coming on why not keep both jobs — build your cabin across the way — and write steadily as a third occupation — you will be busy enough that is sure —

Reduce life to its lowest terms and hold it there — the lowest terms for me are writing & writing — you must have that solitude you need.

Undated, 1935

Write as though you were writing for yourself, as though you were writing a book that you would always want to carry with you—a book that men on canoe trips & other wilderness journeys would want to carry with them & read & reread over their campfire, nothing sentimental but something appealing, something heartfelt & sincere, denoting men's love for the heartfelt & the primitive, something so beautiful, so elemental that they could not get along without it. It must be strong—masculine—short essays beautifully done, weaving in the meaning I get from the life I love—& leaving them with a sense of strength & the nobility of the life—the bond that holds men together.

January 2, 1935

Bear Island Lake[3]

Coming out here is more or less of an experiment to determine if after all I have anything to contribute. I wanted to get away to a spot where I could think, where no one would disturb me and where I could think thoughts through from the very first inkling of an idea to the final finishing touch. Here I am all alone in a cabin in the north far away from town, warm and comfortable, with no one to disturb me whatever. This is what I have longed for for years. I feel if I could do this regularly then I would be happy, then there would be no reason for my discontent. All during the holidays, happy though they have been, has run a thread of discontent, a wish to get away to some spot where I could think and be alone.

One of the things I must have is this, I must find it possible to get away whenever I want to, some place where I will be completely cut off. I need very little for happiness. Food and clothing, my home, and a chance to get away. That is all I need. My recipe for happiness is getting more and more simplified, more and more run down to the bare essentials of things. I am finding out that what I need is a chance to do the things that will give me the feeling of satisfaction. I do not crave crowds, I do not crave society, all I do crave is a chance to get out in the woods, a chance to write and think and dream.

I have been reading much of Thoreau, have steeped myself in his philosophy, and how I love it all. I feel that I have a philosophy of my own and that I have captured a few things that should be worthwhile. Yesterday while snowshoeing down Bear Island Lake, the thought came to me. This is important. This gives me happiness, this is worth all of the show, worth more than any show. This is real, it is not artificial and as long as I know what gives me happiness, then that should be enough. It gave me distinct pleasure to see the snow wraiths twisting and squirming over the ice, it felt good to feel the north wind cutting my face, it felt good to feel the old muscles rippling and the blood circulating. It felt good to look across to a big cliff on the west shore and to get the old feeling of wilderness again. These things give me pleasure, and knowing that I should not have to look around much more. I am pinning my desires down to a point where I know where I stand. I know what gives me satisfaction and that should be enough.

The old question of a medium again—what will it be. I know it will not be fiction, there are others that can do that. It will be something on the order of a philosophical essay, something that will appear in the *Atlantic* or *Harper's* or that group. I do not plan on writing much, but what I do write I want to be good. If I can give others something of the thrill that is mine on my walks, if I can make them see that my way of life is good, that I see through the sham of things and get down to the real earth, then I will strike, I know, a responsive chord. There is so much sham, so much make-believe, people watch parades, they watch shows, they watch panoramas, they are spectators at this and that. They are always in the role of spectators. Why do not they ever settle down to living actually. Why do they not realize that what they need is reality, something that they can place their fingers on. What they want and do not know is first-hand experience, first-hand knowledge of what by watching others they only get a smattering.

The silence seems good—how I have longed for it. I stepped out on the porch just now to drink it in.

January 2, 1935

Bear Island Lake

I am getting discouraged—3 hours out here & nothing done but I should know better. It may take me a week to come down to earth — surely if I do anything worthwhile it will be by the purest accident.

Burroughs or Thoreau write that their subjects seem to write themselves, that it is no effort for them to set down & pound out an article. The only thing that seems to write itself with me is my thoughts & they so often are just ramblings that I am quite nonplussed. The wonderful thing would be if I could really use the thoughts I have, if they were actually worthwhile & good enough to publish. That would be the mark of genius. The next best thing is to write down your thoughts on some particular subject — When I try to compose I find myself clumsy & awkward and it is only when thoughts do flow easily that my diction is anything worthwhile.

In order to have any peace of mind I must write and it must perforce be something worthwhile. That & that alone is an antidote for suicide. I know I want to write & I know it will be outdoor stuff — then your only salvation is to write --

Trees — a treatise on the uses of trees — aesthetic & practical —
I am out here to write & find absolutely nothing to write about.

I have come a long way to a lonely cabin with the avowed purpose of spending a couple of days writing. Here I am—it is true—here is the quiet which in town I thought I craved. From where I sit I can look over miles of wilderness lake, dotted with rocky pine-covered islands — yes there is the woods. And I am out here to write something. Here is the place where I can think a thought through to its minutest ramifications — here there will be no one to interrupt me —

January 2, 1935

Bear Island Lake

Perhaps the trouble is that I have not started on any one particular idea, that my thoughts are scattered.

No the big thing is finding my medium. Once I do that and it may never be, then I feel that I can go on indefinitely, working always working toward the end I have in mind, world-wide recognition, justification for my stand and my staying here. In the essay on neurosis, it said that unless the neurotic finds some outlet for his peculiar temperament then he is lost. He cannot allow it to become ingrown. For ten years I have filled notebooks with my ramblings and I am beginning to wonder if after all I have not been disillusioning myself and that I have nothing in me what-ever. Still my stories were well-accepted, the touch of Kipling, poetry in prose and all that sort of thing. Still there was very little emotional appeal, no letters from the outside or appreciation and love.

Travel will not help, for I cannot escape myself. Unless I have the elements of making happiness right here then it is useless to try to go anywhere else to find it. Here is where I must work out my problem. If I can solve the problem here and like Thoreau decide that my mission in life is the recording of my ideas then it is useless. The important thing is not to try and decide what to do if I give up the idea of writing but to start out on some definite vein and work it.

January 2, 1935

Bear Island Lake

Somehow in town, I had the idea that if I just came out here, every-thing would be all right, and here I am with the setting perfect and not a thought or idea in my head. What on earth is the matter with me. At least I will get down to bedrock soon. Either find out that I have something or else decide that I have nothing at all and that my whole dream is poppycock. It will help I know to shatter this idea of mine definitely once and for all. I spend entirely too much time mooning over what I might do, neglecting the opportunities at my disposal for good and happiness.

I probably should have a couple of weeks for me to find myself in before I begin to get despondent, not just a short day. How in creation can I find out what I want by forcing myself. I dream at home of getting out to a cabin by myself and this morning I was positively thrilled to know that for two whole days I was going to be all alone. Here I am all alone and the thrill is gone. If I could look forward to a couple of weeks of this sort of thing, I don't know whether I would accomplish anything or not. Look at all of this scribbling as merely a set of setting up exercises. Tomorrow morning I may be feeling differently and be able to do something worthwhile. At least I can pound the typewriter with ease and I have written other things in other years, so I know that it is in me.

What do Laura and Oliver expect, what does Esther expect, Dr. Cahn, Ben Mizzen and the rest. What do they expect from me, the embodiment of the north country, what would E expect, what do I want them to expect, what would all of the friends of the north country expect from me and more what do I want them to expect. Whatever I do, I want to be proud of it. I want to receive sympathy and understanding. I want my friends to receive what I give with expectation and joy. I want them to look to me with affection and love as interpreting what they feel but cannot say. I want them to carry my work with them wherever they go, I want them to remember me with love always. For after all, all I care about is my interpretation of this country and hitting that kindred chord of love for it which all of those have who have traveled through it and lived in it. I do not want to write a great deal, but what I do write, I want to be good and of universal acceptance. I want to be proud of what I am doing. I want my friends to feel that I have made the country mean more to them. Whatever I write must be beautiful, the thought in it must be sincere and worth reading and rereading.

Undated, January 2 or 3, 1935

Bear Island Lake

If I can write one good paragraph while I am here it will be enough, get one clear thought — I feel I am different, not of the common run, & now prove it. E is waiting for you, watching, hoping you will do something — You must write for the satisfaction & happiness it will bring you, not for monetary reward. Think of the terrible mistake of thinking that I might make a living writing. It would have been pure suicide — Much better to have things as they are — If I can settle this once & for all I feel I will be quite happy —

I do not need to be a warden plowing through the snow, day after day—nor a ranger, nor a lone trapper in a cabin — my teaching gives me leisure & time to dream & contacts — I might be quite content if I could only find my medium.

January 3, 1935

It is quite hopeless to try and do what Thoreau did, quite hopeless to try and do what Burroughs did. I have not got it within me—I have the feelings, perhaps, but not the ability to put them down. All I can write about is natural history—the wolf situation, the duck situation, the habits of the deer, the habits of the beaver, semi-scientific stuff.

January 18, 1935

My visit to Minneapolis convinced me again that I can talk, much better before an audience than the ordinary man. In fact at any of the programs of the fall & winter, I have been by far the outstanding speaker. Here is something I can do better than others. I can think on my feet—good voice, fine delivery. How can I make use of it — That is the question — certainly not by running a resort — or by being a woodsman — I can as a lecturer in a university do something with it — politics — the stage — conservation meetings — Here is an example of the old adage — "Only by the development of his own particular genius can a man be happy." Well this seems to be my own particular genius — At least here I am supreme and only here —

February 18, 1935

I do not believe that I shall ever settle the question of a writing medium. It seems further from me now than ever. I started "Farewell

Game warden's cabin on Saganaga Lake, 1938. Photograph by Walter Breckenridge. Courtesy of University of Minnesota Archives.

to Saganaga" but it lies on my desk half-finished, the outpouring of a soul which no one will understand except myself, perhaps a little too sentimental....

One thing, I shall never write a book on birds, or mammals or insects, or plants. I am interested in their identification, true enough, but for me there would be no joy in sitting down and pounding off a treatise on such a field. My book, if it ever comes, will be a philosophical work on the joy of living in the woods, of enjoyment of nature. Perhaps I am not profound enough, I do not know, but think of the joy that would be mine if I could actually do such a thing. I want to create something beautiful. If I need broad distances for it, if I need more than I can find here, then I will never do it anywhere. If I were sitting in a lonely cabin up in Alaska, I would die of lonesomeness first of all and my thoughts would be not better than they are right here. Here is where I should work as well as anywhere.

February 20, 1935

A beautiful morning and more beautiful because last night I finished "Farewell to Saganaga." Although E thinks it is far too emotional, she still admits it is well written. The important thing to me is not the fact that it may be good or bad, but the reaction I get out of it personally. Again comes the uplift of spirit, the joy of creation, the sense of fulfillment and completion that I seem to get in no other way. I have proved this to myself a thousand times, yet I go along through periods of absolute blackness and despair when I wish I could walk out of the picture and end it all. Knowing this, why oh why do not I adhere to a definite schedule of writing and so maintain my sanity. It makes no difference much what I write, just so that I keep on working on something. That is the solution and knowing it I actually have the key to happiness for me and one that I can invoke any time I wish.

February 25, 1935

Finished for the *Atlantic Monthly* "Farewell to Saganaga" and with it comes the old sense of accomplishment that is always here with the finishing of any written project. Now I must get going on something else immediately, for if I don't, I will know again the old feeling of futility and wretchedness. I will either start in with the article for *Field and Stream* or begin something entirely different for the better magazines.

I suppose Saganaga will return as have the others but there is always hope and as long as that is true I might as well go on.

Yesterday I worked as I dreamed of working. Got up in the morning and snowshoed for eight miles or so, then back at my typewriter until five in the afternoon. Got much done and was fairly happy.

February 28, 1935

Again comes a proposition, this time from the Forest Service, in charge of wildlife investigation in the White Mountain National Forest of New Hampshire and Maine. Will I take it or not. The same old question of leaving this country or breaking into wildlife work. I must be somewhat of an authority on wildlife or I wouldn't get offers of this type. On the other hand does it not seem as though I am running a gigantic bluff. If I really wanted this job then it would be simple. I would take it without any hesitation. Do I want it or not. That is the big question. The effort of getting away seems almost insurmountable—leave of absence, school and Border Lakes. There is almost too much to fight with to make the move. Of course a year away would be rather interesting for all of us. After all it is just a year and to spend it in New England away from this atmosphere would be an education in itself.

Perhaps I had better take it and see what happens. Then come back here, content to settle down for the rest of my life. Would I be content, that is the question. Wouldn't it mean that I would want to go on with my wildlife work in some capacity. Perhaps there would come something in the state or the university, perhaps with the Forest Service or the National Park Service. I don't know. One thing is sure, that is that it would prepare me for something along that line, a preparation that I haven't got right now.

March 4, 1935

Why not take the out east job and then next summer take the Yosemite proposition,[4] killing two birds with one stone. That would give me some real prestige, a year's work in charge of wildlife surveys, a summer's study with the National Park Service. By that time, I should have a fairly good idea of what wildlife work is....

I have stood on top of a wind-swept hill, waved my hat at the breeze, shouted to the skies that I was alive and I have fought the waves on gigantic lakes and enjoyed the slap of every one. I love the rain, the snow, the thunder, storms, quiet, every change of the weather. That is all part of the picture. Outdoors everything has its place, everything contributes toward the sum total of enjoyment.

I must not forget the silly habit if it can be called that of doffing my hat and waving goodbye to some lake or valley. Doing that gives me a sense of romance that I get in no other way. Goodbye to the country, greet it as you see it. Walk on air. Here is romance and greatness, a substance to fill up the void of too much artificiality.

March 9, 1935

A perfectly gorgeous morning after the storm, wind in the south, frost crystals hanging on every bush and twig, a hard crust and over all the brilliant northern sunlight of March. What a morning to hit the trail and take great strides over the country. Valleys would disappear beneath my snowshoes, rivers flow under me, hills seem nothing but molehills, the kind of a morning when distance counts for nothing and one's muscles seem tireless, the kind of day when romance lurks around every corner and it seems good just to be alive and moving.

March 11, 1935

Coming back down the long portage yesterday afternoon, I was happy with the knowledge that I had found my medium; repeating over some of the passages of "Farewell to Saganaga" convinced me that they had merit and beauty. In fact I was almost transported with the joy of knowing that I had created something beautiful and like Burroughs I almost marveled at where it had all come from. It is now nineteen days since I sent in "Farewell to Saganaga" and the *Atlantic* usually answers in ten days or so. It surely must be getting a reading and even if it does come back, I will know that it was considered....

Burroughs appeals to me more than Thoreau. More of my type, more human and understanding, more lovable human qualities. He picks a subject, thinks about it a long time and then sits down with only a vague idea of what he is going to do and picks out of his subconscious all of the material his article will show. So it was with "Farewell to Saganaga" and so it will be with "Red Socks and Moccasins." I must get at that right away.

What about Hudson's Bay — The Dream of Hudson's Bay, there is an idea.

March 12, 1935

And yesterday "Farewell" came back to me. And though I knew it might come still I was quite unprepared for what it did to me. Today I am sick at heart and tired and almost bitter.

Sigurd takes notes while snowshoeing, 1930s. Peterson Family Collection. Courtesy of Daryl Peterson.

Why do I not leave it all & do something I can do — I have fought for this so long, however, that nothing else seems worthwhile. Another winter gone with nothing accomplished.

I suppose I will try it again but I am growing fast toward a state of speechlessness — I feel deeply but can find no words —

"Farewell to Saganaga" may mean farewell to all of my dreams, farewell to all that I thought worthwhile. I cannot give in, I must go on or die. This cannot be the end — there must be some way out — — Oh Lord help me do what I want to or it will be the end of everything for me.

April 9, 1935

This morning not able to stand it a moment longer, I started out over the old hills I know so well. It was dry enough so that I could go through the woods, and through the woods I went following all the dry ridges, stepping gingerly over still deep snowbanks and treading on the newly exposed ground as though I were stealing up on the spring itself. All along I had the sensation of a Sunday morning, everything quiet and fresh, almost a cathedral hush over the country. I did not dare to speak and stole along as stealthily as though I were being followed. I hardly dared think, it was so quiet. It was balm to my shattered nerves and it did me good. How wonderful it was lying under that big spruce to hear the spring song of the first robins. What memories it brought back to me of boyhood days, fishing on the Tobatik[5] and on other streams and what thoughts it brought back to me of a forgotten past when there was nothing to worry about, nothing to think and fret over. What gorgeous days and how pleasant a place the world to live in.

I tried to think out my problem but all I could think of was the beauty of the sunlight, the sound of the wind through my spruce and the silhouettes of the birches over the hill to the west. The more I tried to think the more soothing grew the influences around me. This was no place to think, this was a place to enjoy. How true that has been all of the time. Great thoughts do not come to me when I am out, but only after I get back and start thinking things over with four insulating walls around me. When I am out I am too receptive, too liable to see only and feel. I become entirely sensuous, an animal soaking up the impressions of color and light and smell and sound.

April 9, 1935

This morning I thought again how much fun it would be to be able to devote all of my day particularly in the morning to writing. The waste of time here at school, hours and days and weeks when I know I could be doing something worthwhile is what is appalling. The time is so precious, and there is such a waste of it every day. To actually feel that I am working hard, doing something with my hours, to know that I am stifling that restlessness, the eternal fire which keeps me going accomplishing something, that will be what will count. What it will be, I do not know, but surely something will come of it. If I don't sell a single thing but find out the answer to the old question, that will be enough for me.

Sent in "The Evolution of a Canoe Country" last night.[6] E says it is the best I have ever written. Perhaps. That makes three this year. I seem to average about three articles or stories every year no matter how hard I try not to do anything.

April 25, 1935

Sent a wire to Laconia, N.H. last night refusing the offer of the wild-life position on the White Mountain National Forest. I have refused a chance to spend a year in the east in the country of Burroughs, Thoreau, Emerson and Whitman. Today I am relieved and somewhat sick at heart, weak from the effort of the decision.

May 8, 1935

My field then is description of a new type. I must cast around for an emotional outlet, a type of story showing the love of a man for the earth, for trees and sunlight, for action and running water, the powerful stimulus behind everything that has made me what I am.

If I can do that then I will be content, but it will be hard and perhaps I will fail. If I can do that then it will make no difference what sort of a job I hold, the big thing in life will be bringing out what I feel more deeply than anything else. I feel deeply about a few things, the rocks, the trees, sunsets, water, quiet on a pond, the wilderness, life out of doors, trees, vistas, views, dogs, rain, thunder, roads, running waters, in fact everything which is natural and unspoiled.

August 2, 1935

Yellowstone River[7] — below upper falls —

If nothing else, this western trip has given me peace of mind. No longer will travel loom as the impossible — no longer will my life seem thwarted or hemmed in. I have seen half a dozen new states, mountains, new country, and I think our own little house and my job at Ely will [word?][8] pretty good. What I needed was contrast & change and this has given it to me. Like Thoreau & Burroughs however, I find that one cannot escape one's self, no matter how far one travels. Here on the banks of the beautiful Yellowstone a thousand miles away I find the same old longings and desires are still with me. I do not care to write of my experiences, fishing and mountain climbing except insofar as I can interpret through them my own feelings and the intangible deeper meaning of the country itself. Looking at an etching of a cowboy on a horse in the Buffalo Bill museum in Cody, for a fleeting instant I caught the old feeling and I knew then that what I wanted to do was <u>write deeply of man's love of the earth</u> & its beauty. If I cannot do that for the West not knowing it I can do it up north where I do know it. Which brings me back again to my old medium question, the problem that has been haunting me for years. It is the same here as home. Unless I can find that I can <u>do nothing</u>.

Rangers & Ranger Naturalist. How little I know of the whole naturalist's proposition when I first met up with the idea.[9] I had no idea of the crowds they must handle or the stereotyped work that is theirs. I could learn to love the park, by being alone in it away from the crowds — I see a few across the river now coming down the stairway to gape at the falls — They are transients like the birds, summer visitors & the park is deserted for almost eight months of the year. Then what do they do — I presume make surveys of plant & animal life, writing of their habits, studying — They may look at the summer work as just temporary, interesting & important but in back of their minds is a memory of the long winters which are really preparations for the all important summer work.

August 20, 1935

As Mrs. Reid was pulling out from the dock she leaned over and told me that a short man who was on his way to Duluth, evidently Ben Mizzen, had told her that I had a beautiful mind and that someday I would have a brilliant future.

Whether he was referring to my scientific article or my way of looking at things, I would give much to know. I hope it was not the article that made him think so.

For a moment it almost brought tears to my eyes, it was so gratifying and all the world seemed worthwhile. Perhaps, I thought, I do have it, perhaps someday I will be able to do something. Perhaps it is just resting now and someday I will be able to tell the world what is in my heart.

THE DEAN

September 1935–September 1937

I CAN WRITE, I AM SURE OF THAT," Sigurd writes in late September 1935. "All I have to do is to actually cut loose from all else and begin." Just a few months later, after his dear friend and Ely Junior College dean Julius Santo died in his arms, Sigurd applied for the open position. After becoming dean, Sigurd complained about feeling more trapped than ever. Once again, he daydreamed of quitting and taking a gamble on making enough money from his writing. But he still had eleven more years to go before he would do it. "E said I wasn't a gambler," Sigurd wrote on January 25, 1937. "Well perhaps I am not." His journals indicate that Elizabeth was more willing than he was to take a chance, if it would help her husband finally find happiness.

In the meantime, though, Sigurd spent one hundred fifty dollars to renovate the single-car garage in front of his home into a writing studio. "The shack," as he came to call it, gave him space to spread out his materials, and the silence and solitude he needed to write without distraction. This chapter ends when the shack is ready, and Sigurd faces a new reality: "Now it is do or die and I am determined to find out if a steady writing program can do anything for me."

Camp on Cyprus Lake (Ottertrack Lake), 1936. Photograph by Bill Roliff, U.S. Forest Service Records, National Archives.

Answering that question depended on the answer to another question that continued to haunt him: what was his "medium," as he put it? How could he capture the emotional and spiritual depths of his outdoor experiences in a format that he could sell to magazines? And not just any magazines, but the best ones, like the *Saturday Evening Post*? He could write hunting and fishing articles for *Sports Afield* and other outdoor magazines, but those bored him and paid practically nothing. He gravitated toward essays, or shorter versions of essays he called sketches, but he couldn't sell them. If he wanted to quit the junior college and write full time, he needed to be able to write short story fiction for the better magazines.

Those were his choices, he believed. And he would struggle over them for a long time.

* * * *

September 30, 1935

Yesterday morning, paddling over in the Back Bay rice beds,[1] I was never quite so thrilled. Colors and all and the feeling of completeness that was mine, convinced me that there was only one way out. What is more I had confidence, I felt that I could do things and that the fight was all over, that the search was ended and that there was only one thing for me. Never have I been quite so satisfied that I had at last come upon the right thing. All other activity seems puerile and second hand. Only writing seems worthwhile.

Now it will take courage but I know where I am going. All of my scientific work and teaching I suppose has been for naught. Still nothing is wasted, as I have laid by a store of ideas that someday I shall use. I can write, I am sure of that. All I have to do is to actually cut loose from all else and begin.

Of course I shall carry on with my outfitting business as that will keep body and soul together, but I feel I must quit teaching or I shall not be able to work profitably. Unless perhaps I could build a cabin and have some quiet place where I could actually feel free to work, and quiet.

With my writing will come lecturing and fame that will make it possible for me to branch out in many undreamed of ways. The future will take care of itself once I make good at this thing.

I felt yesterday that I could do anything, that I had something different, something peculiar that would someday make everything worthwhile if I only did not give up my dream. The wonderful thing is that I know now where I stand, no Soil Erosion Service, no Biological Survey, no nothing but writing, writing. That alone can make me happy. All else is merely subsidiary to that.

October 5, 1935

Reading Powys' "Happiness and Culture" last night I was impressed with one thing, the stress he lays on the importance of being at one with the earth.[2] It is as though I had written that chapter myself. How often hasn't that truth burst upon me, that the main source of pleasure and happiness to me is in the daily and continual observation of little things, wind and sun, lighting, leaves, smells, movement, the very act of breathing. Here is a cult and substantiation of my belief that in nature is the cure all. Here is my religion and here what I must try to bring out in all of my writing. Burroughs did it somewhat and Thoreau but I have something new, the joy of wilderness and travel far off the beaten path, the wild fierce joy of a man who knows no roads.

October 9, 1935

The question of medium is always with me and I work on it both during my waking and sleeping hours....

Like Burroughs all I am interested in is the creation of and interpretation of beauty. If I can do it this way, then all other existence is secondary. This is more important than anything else that I can do. I am not interested in scientific research, not interested in interpreting scientific phenomena from a purely factual standpoint. I must bring in the beauty underlying it, the broad human application, the love and sympathy of a man for the earth he loves so well.

This will be different, this will perhaps be some part of the solution. It will not be fiction anymore than Burroughs or Thoreau or Emerson wrote fiction. It will be merely my interpretation of how I feel about things. Word pictures, short beautiful sketches of this that and the other thing, as different as possible from anything that has been done, no animal stuff, no travel stuff for travel's sake, but my personal reactions written into everything.

October 21, 1935

This much Powys and I have in common, an inherent love of the earth, a passion for simplicity. All in all isn't this the background of all great and lasting work, this the foundation of all they try to express, simplicity, beauty, tolerance, pantheism, Hudson, Burroughs, Emerson, Thoreau, Whitman, this they all have in common. Here is my medium, not adventure stories, not just action, not hunting and fishing for its own sake, but something deeper, a more inclusive medium that will take all I have to give and more. The essay perhaps, but much better the short story — why a man wants to work with his hands, why he loves the feel of wind and sun, why he is willing to fore-go all else — glorifying work, action, the physical — loving the earth, running water, mountains, rocks, trees — explain the philosophy of the men who have stayed on and forgotten the rest. Give of yourself here, your understanding of their viewpoint.

The essay is far too exacting, too filled with substance for all people to love. But take a beautiful short story, perhaps without any plot or love element although that may come. Put into it all you have, the love you bear toward things and you will have something.

Beautiful stories — different bringing in all a man's love for the wild — Make them so simple, so beautiful, so human that people will love them. Do not write them with the idea of making money, that will come if they are worth it. Be confident that you can, that you have something. Here I believe is a medium that will last. Not adventure for its own sake, but something deeper, something people will love to read and read again and that will bring to me the companionship I need and the sense of having created something lovely.

November 17, 1935

My years have been hard. I know now why I have been distraught, why it has been impossible for me to get excited about any field, why I could not bring myself to write the Geographic article, why outdoor stuff has palled, why the wolf paper almost nauseated me, why anything but that deep hurt feeling in my heart. One story in which I can feel the throb of my own reactions. A story which Ober, Pete, Florence, E, Bob Marshall, and the rest would read for its own sake, one that Ken would write me about, nothing cheap anymore, something that would tear at their hearts.[3] I know that more than anything else in the world right now,

I want to write that sort of thing. That to me is worthwhile. If I can do that then I shall be happy and everything will come out all right.

If I can write one such story this winter and get going then the winter will be a success. It is something to have pinned things down so far. I have chosen the hardest for me, but it is what I want and no matter how hard, I think I can do it. If this is it think how perfectly happy I shall be. All groping over with knowing that I am on my way. What made it so unbearable was the difficulty of choosing my field. At times I felt as though there was no solution.

Now I understand why "Papette" was out, why "En Roulant" was only accepted by *Sports Afield*, why "Trail's End" and the rest lagged.[4] There was no strong emotional reaction, nothing underlying of real sentiment, merely a tale of activities, pure narrative, pure adventure for its own sake. These things have their place, but for me they are meaningless. I want the pure gold, the unadulterated, the refined, the last distillate of the spirit. Nothing else will do. There is only one thing that is worthwhile and that the spiritual. As long as I feel that way, then there is nothing for me to do but try and accomplish something worthwhile. I am henceforth an explorer, a prospector. Whenever I go out, it will be to find and hunt out the pure metal.

December 9, 1935

The spell is broken and I am happier than I have been for many days. All day Saturday I worked on Silversides and whipped it fairly well into shape. It really has some possibilities and I shall try it on *Liberty* when I am through. Even E had tears in her eyes when I read the final introduction to her. That is compensation for everything.

More important than all else is the realization that once I get into the swim, that ideas come and language flows. I can write and I do have thoughts and better than all else I have a style of my own. The more I write the easier it will become, the old lesson which seemingly needs so much repeating.

As to medium, here is a partial solution. When I tell of Frank Beauchard's love for the valley of Caribou Creek, I am telling of my own love for the woods and streams. It is true that when a man writes from the heart, he is explaining his own feelings, baring his own soul to the world. My characters will see through my eyes and feel what I feel.

Wilderness Society cofounder Bob Marshall photographed by Sigurd during a canoe trip to Quetico Provincial Park in 1937. Courtesy of the Forest History Society, Durham, North Carolina.

The only difference between other rejuvenations and this is that now I am desperate, now I know and I shall keep on every opportunity I have. Only in that way can I recapture any semblance of happiness. It is really so simple, but it takes courage and persistence and dogged effort. I have it in me, I have lost nothing and have gained immeasurably. This time I will win out. Only in this way can I attain any of the happiness I have been searching for.

By Xmas I shall have Silversides completed and on the way and perhaps "Exploring." If possible I shall try another animal story.

It is enough that I have started and that I can write finis to a long period of unhappiness.

Undated, January 1936

The Dean is no better but I don't know if he is any worse.[5] I do not see how he can keep alive. The other day, he said that he had been having a communion with his God. That from the Dean, the old blasphemer, how unnatural, but toward the end when a man has suffered his thoughts unless he be a philosopher with his mind made up always turns to the infinite. It is almost time for my lecture and had better close.[6] I hope that when I write again the exhilaration that is now mine for a variety of reasons will still be with me.

January 16, 1936

Poor Dean, he seems to be in great pain. Hard to reconcile his former great energy with the poor wreck of a man lying there now. There is my old hunting pal, a hunting pal no more. When I see him lying there so helpless, all I can think of is the man he was with his old rifle in the Stoney River country, the pictures of him around our many campfires and in the duck blinds. I wonder how long it can go on. He seems to be sinking every day. Breath more and more labored, more pain in his leg and in his chest. I seem to be the only one he cares to see. Yesterday he told E that he liked to have me with him, "but Oh the long black stretches in between."

January 20, 1936

Spent some time yesterday studying narrative technique and really think for the first time I am going to get something out of it. The great trouble with me has been in working out plots and ideas and then as Uzzell said I had not the slightest idea of character delineation by action. That is what I must get out of the way. All of these years I have let this important matter go. If I had started in five years ago as I should have, I would now know something about it. Well it is never too late and I am going to begin now and perfect that part of it.

All of my time has not been wasted and I have unconsciously used many of the principles there in my work. I have a style of my own, have material and atmosphere to work with. All I have to do is iron out the final wrinkles and I think I can do something.

There will be great satisfaction to sitting down and actually begin work on a story which I know is technically correct. No matter if I don't do a single other thing this winter than work over the ideas with Uzzell that will be something. By the time I am forty I will be well on the way....

The dean is slipping fast. I can hardly sleep for I always see before me those desperate eyes, pleading for help and grasping so pitifully at every straw of hope. I always see the dean with his Springfield 30-06 on the deer trails, and in camp. Will I ever be able to go through that country again with the same joy and abandon that was mine. Every time I come to Kelly Lake, I will see him. Every time I come to the little pothole where we dragged out the big buck together, he will be with me. How can I ever camp on Low Lake without seeing him there or on Kabetogama. Each campsite will speak of him. I will still find the tent poles he cut, the firewood we did not use and which he gathered. I have his sleeping bag at home now, the old bag which through the years has become so familiar.

And the old decoys, how we knew them all, how we tinkered with them, each its own particular personality. He always worked with them and kept them in shape and now they will bob and drift without his encouragement. Up on the Stoney on the point we both loved, how can I stand there alone and think of him. Do you suppose he will be there with me, do you suppose that he will cruise over the old country.

Something has gone out of my life. An episode is ended — the Dean is gone, my old pal, my comrade of many hard trips, many sunrises and sunsets. We lived together he and I and I learned to love him. The country will be different without him. I wonder why old men sometimes do not go out into the wilds as they would like to do. Is it because they

Lake Kabetogama seen from Lute's Resort, 1937. Minnesota Historical Society Collection.

cannot bear the old associations? Would they rather stay home and hide away from memories which though pleasant bring back the torture of separation? I wonder. I know now that I have lost thirteen or fourteen of my old woods friends I somehow feel alone. Here I am for no apparent good reason left to cruise the country that was theirs and they are gone.

January 28, 1936

It is all over and my old hunting partner has gone. I was with him at the very last. Just a short time before he died, he said, "Well, it's all over." I kidded him as usual and told him that he was breathing easier, but he said "I know." I asked him then if he was going to the Happy Hunting Grounds and he nodded. Well, I admonished, "Be sure and cut some firewood and get the decoys set out and after a little bit we will all join you." He nodded again and smiled consent. That was the last the Dean ever spoke, for shortly after he was seized with pain and spasms of coughing bloody mucus. The end came very swiftly, one convulsive jerk and he fell over into my arms. I knew it was all over without even having to feel for his heart.

It was so final, his passing, here one moment and gone the next. I loved him. All last night I could only see that last agonized expression.

There is a bond, stronger than almost anything else between the men who have sat across campfires in the wilds. No matter what else they may be, the comradeship there is stronger than death. How can I ever go to the old point on Low Lake or up to the Stoney again. He will always be with me.

January 28, 1936

A chapter is closed in my life. The old days are over and I have nothing left but memories. What mattered it toward the last if we didn't go out so much. The big thing was that he was here, close by, and could go if he liked. We were like two old shoes, we knew each other so well, he and I. Never no elaborate preparation to get ready to go. We knew what was needed and could go on a moment's notice. Everywhere was home to us and we were always happy when out. I will never find another pal to take his place. Part of me is gone forever.

And now begins a new period — Farewell to you old pal, may your hunting always be good. Get the old campsite ready as you promised and someday Glenn and I and Cecil will paddle up to the campsite to stay with you forever.

February 7, 1936

Actually started writing again last night, working on the article for *Field and Stream*. Changed the title of "May We Come Along" to "Forgotten Promise," which I think is a good one. It will work up into a fine story and if I don't sell it to *Field and Stream*, I may run a chance in the *American*. Am going to send "Beauchard's Beaver" either to the *American* or to *The Country Gentleman*. Then I will have three out.

Queer the effect of writing on my peace of mind. The instant I start, I am on the heights. What it is I do not know, but I do know that I can't afford to ever stop. I must keep at something. If I don't, life isn't worth living. It is as though a sentence is hanging over my head, the commutation of which would doom me to eternal perdition.

The past week has been terrible, Santo's memory hanging over me and not working on anything in particular has been bad. Last evening in desperation I went to work and by the time to go to bed I was feeling fine....

Julius Santo, dean of Ely Junior College, 1930s. Olson Family Collection. Courtesy of David Backes.

Filed my application for the Deanship yesterday. Don't care greatly whether I get it or not but as a matter of pride I felt I had to apply.

February 14, 1936

They have made me Dean and I am taking my old pal's place. How queer it seems to know that he is here no more and that his work is now my work. The finality of his passing just begins to sink in. Forgetfulness of all the little things is also on the way and days now pass without too much the pain of memory. I can never however entirely forget and there are moments when things come up that are hard to bear. Reciting the prospector last night brought to mind the trip to the Stoney and most of all, the joyous comradeship and understanding of what was close to our hearts. "Those people can't all be wrong" and then the laughter and the realization of the childish enthusiasm and credulity of the old type of prospector and adventurer. Those things he meant to me and I will always remember.

I sometimes feel these days as though the net has wound itself more and more closely around me. Now there will be no escape and what was hard before becomes double impossible now. My leave of absence is out of the question under the new setup. However, once things get smoothly under way it might not be so bad. It is just that now, living the life out of doors approaches the impossible. All I can do now is get out as often as possible and write continually.[7]

What makes me happier than anything else is the knowledge that people are glad it came to me. So many have congratulated me and so wholeheartedly that there is no question in my mind but that they are really happy about it. It is one of the compensations of living in a small town and is recognition which usually does not come unless one dies. It is what came to Santo too late, appreciation for work well done, community interest and I suppose rather harmless living.

What I wish I could do is go into this thing joyfully and make Elizabeth happy just this once. Instead I have her worried to death and as miserable as she ever was knowing that I am still unhappy. Why cannot I resign myself to the inevitable and forget the dream that has been hounding me so long. Why don't I realize that I cannot make my living writing and that what I must do is only use it as a side line. It is hard to forget the romance and the joy of travel that might be mine had I made the grade.

March 4, 1936

As I lay in bed last night thinking all of these things over, I knew more where my field lay and medium than I ever had before. I knew it did not lie in the description of birds, animals, rocks and plants, ala Burroughs and Thoreau. It did not lie in the description for description's sake of any of these somewhat famous writers of today, it did not lie entirely in action, but that it did lie in the interpretation of that old feeling, the spiritual comradeship of men in the wilds. That is what I must bring out, using only the other to illustrate what I am trying to do. I have really not attempted anything as yet but here is the real medium, here the real thing that I have been trying to find. Nothing else for me is worth interpreting beyond that, that is everything and enough for one man to bring out in his short lifetime. Unless in my writings of the future, I can show this thing that has been eating away at my peace of mind for so long, I will not be successful.

No more animal stories for their own sake, no more tales of adventure, but rather just the feeling that men have for the life and for each other, comradeship on the out trails of the world. No sentimentality but sincere understanding and sympathy for what we hold dear....

Happier perhaps this spring than ever before. Why? Because I have been working hard, have four articles out and more in mind. My writing seems to be easier and I have actually accomplished something with it.

April 25, 1936

The year is drawing to a close and it has been an eventful one. First the passing of my old friend the Dean, may his hunting always be pleasant, and then my being given the Dean's position here. Then again all of my writing. I do not seem to remember any other year when I have been quite so busy with articles as this one, eight all told and most of them out and accepted. Have at last gotten the predatory paper out of the way which has been hanging over my head for years and also several others. Have done nothing startling as yet, but this writing does one thing for me, it gives me prestige and a sense of authority which nothing else could have done.[8] Have given a number of talks, Virginia Sportsmen's Club, University of Minnesota, St. Andrew's Club, etc etc, so have been getting before the public....

Al sends disturbing word that I am being considered for the wildlife position with the Indian Service, chief. It sounds exciting just like the Soil Erosion Service and the state biologist's job which I am sure that I could have, but again I approach it without enthusiasm. That isn't what I want. I want to write and write only. There is where I get my kick out of life and nowhere else. My eight articles this winter have meant more to me than my dean's appointment and whatever I write in the future will have as much or more meaning.

One interesting thing my writing has done for me is to show me that there is more where this material came from, namely in the subconscious regions of my mind. I have more confidence and I am developing form. I am anxious to hear what Uzzell will say this time.

April 30, 1936

My job is not to describe nature but to tell how deeply men feel about it. I am every man—in me is concentrated to a degree all of the feeling of all men. When I love the wind in my face, I love what all men love. My desires, my thrills are of them all. I shall not talk of birds, daffodils or sunsets, not of dewy mornings or the sound of wind through the pines — my job is not Rutledge's, Scoville's — Thoreau, Burroughs or Sass — I have something deeper that they can never touch or understand. They are dilettantes, they represent women's clubs, drawing rooms and gardens. I represent the wild, a deep inherent longing of masculinity for battle and hardship. I have an ideal, they have none except admiration for the prettiness of nature.

Rutledge seems anemic, & so do the rest. I am strong, virile & I appeal to the men who love the feel of nobs on rocks, packs on their backs, reality — and no longer make believe — That is the sort of thing you must never forget and which must always have as a theme song through your work.

Men are looking for a strong virile touch, masculinity—power. If I can bring this into my writing, then all will be well. Maintain this trend, never stoop to the femininity & nature class attitude of the rest. You are a man & understand all men.

May 6, 1936

Last night I felt that the time had come, that all the years had been a preparation for my writing — I recalled that only a year ago, there were doubts about wildlife work & all the rest and that now at last it was settled.

"Paint a picture of yourself" & never deviate from your ideal. What is my picture — a man of the wilds, hard & brown — a poet of the wilderness, a philosopher, a man who is not only hard as a wolf physically but who also has the finer perceptions.

Sigurd cooks over a campfire, early 1940s. Listening Point Foundation Archives.

October 1, 1936

The days go on as before, days of indecision and misery. I just saw Gay and Nels downtown all decked out in checkered shirts and laughing and I compared their lot with my own. Here was I dressed up like a sore thumb, drawing twice the money they take in but miserable to the core. Yes we can perhaps save a hundred a month but what of it. It will not make me happy and the days I know will go on through the years in about the same vein. What is the use. I cannot work up here, the problems here drive me to drink, there is no joy, no happiness of any kind. Was life meant for this or not. I should say not. On the other hand, I have financial security, nothing to worry about as far as bills are concerned, enough to pay for anything we want. That means happiness for Lib and the boys and I am purely and unutterably selfish....

It makes me sick, the way things go. I look back at the old diary and what do I read, the same old thing. I thought when the Deanship came through that I would feel differently about things, but I don't, it is the same old thing, no change whatever. I can't concentrate on writing here, that is out of the question, and in the evenings my mind is full of everything else.

Oh when will I reach the turning point?

October 10, 1936

This continual roaming around is driving me nuts. Day after day, it is the same. I try to get in some writing and only get started when someone breaks in on me. Life wasn't meant for this. What is the matter with me anyway. Is there no way out whatever or is it going to be the same old story of futility and trouble. I can see it all coming to a head again, the same old misery and lack of accomplishment. I do nothing that I want to do....

What gets me is the continual waste of time, the days on end when I do nothing. I am simply putting in my time here, nothing more. I am getting paid for it but it is not what I want to do, it is something that has to be done. That is what is really at the bottom of my unhappiness, the fact that time is slipping by without my doing anything worthwhile. It is not the fact that I am not out of doors but rather the fact that I am getting nowhere, am on a treadmill and marking time....

Why not take the world by the ears and do what you want. Ask for a leave or resign at the end of the first quarter. And actually go to it. You have the whole of the world before you. You have Canada and all the north to write about. You have some acquired ability and can really do things once you get going. Get going now and don't wait any more.

November 17, 1936

Out there, nothing is important except the sun and the snow and stars. Problems back in town seem like minor irritations and although the hunting does not assume major significance, at least it is one of those things that makes life seem more like the song it should be. We had fun, we laughed and kidded and joked and everyone had a good time. We don't laugh in town very much. There is too much tension. Why cannot we bring some of that joy and fun back with us. Why cannot things carry over more than they do.

December 12, 1936

What gets me most of all is the tremendous waste of time. Day after day it is the same, filled with little trivialities that amount to nothing. I suppose I am doing the job that I am being paid for, but it seems so inconsequential. At night there is no sense of accomplishment, no feeling of having done anything worthwhile. Contrast that with the feeling that would be mine had I written something or gone traveling or done any one of the thousand things that I should be doing normally. Shall life go on like this or should I call it quits and take a chance.

If I do quit which is probably, I must not get too discouraged if I produce nothing worthwhile for a while. I must resign myself to months of work without anything much to show for it. Surely after six months of working away steadily, will begin to come some recognition and surely in a couple of years if we can keep body and soul together will come more. Then with recognition from the outside will come offers to speak. With writing and lecturing which I know I can do, I should be able to make a couple of thousand a year. I am willing to quit and what keeps me is only the knowledge that my family may suffer. Bob and Junior and Elizabeth do not know the torment in my soul, do not realize what lies in back of my days over here. Surely I can go on here indefinitely and I suppose I could write if I forced myself to it. But when the days are gone, there is no thrill, weekends I want only to rest, and nights my mind is a blank. I need the best of the days, the time when my mind is fresh. As far as trying to write up here is concerned, it is impossible. The atmosphere is missing and the drive and the thousand and one little annoyances that are always present and the worry about how things are going to go....

The ideal thing of course is to keep on here, using this job to take care of everything and then to make my real job my writing. That is all very lovely to talk about but how does it work out. I can do no writing here at all. There is too much interference, no quiet or solitude and I need the sun and the wind for atmosphere. Could I if I had a spot at home where it was quiet or would it be the same. Is it that I haven't enough willpower to force myself to work or that I just don't care.

What gets me is day after day, wasted, wasted, wasted, nothing accomplished. Now I am getting so that I don't care very much either, letting the days and nights go easily. I don't know, I feel that the end must come soon. A good war would settle things beautifully.

January 5, 1937
Teaching wasn't so bad, but this deanship is sucking the life out of me.

January 14, 1937

E's plan of leaving Ely, disposing of all our furniture, sending the boys to Camp Miller for the summer, while she goes down to the farm to help Marie and later rents an apartment at Hayward for them to live in while going to school while I hie myself away to the sticks smacks a little bit of insanity and certainly would not work out for me. For one thing it would cost considerable to have them rent an apartment down there and furthermore, the loss of money on our furniture would be rather high, and lastly and most important, I could not consent to being without them. I admire her courage in being willing to do anything to help me. She surely is strong and brave and wants to do anything that will make it possible for me to realize my ambitions.

Then wouldn't it be much better to do this. Buy the house as we had planned without sacrificing our furniture. Then quit outright and take a gambling chance on my panning out successfully with my writing. It is a gamble to be sure, but as E says now is the time to make the break and really start, rather than waiting for several years more.

She is right when she says that I am not interested in game management or in animals or birds from a scientific standpoint. Al on the other hand is much more concerned. I do not make observations, have been forced to carry on my research. None of those things have appealed to me. I am trained along those lines, I will admit, but I am not vitally concerned one way or the other. I am interested in the aesthetic side of learning not in the scientific. My interest in wildlife and the out of doors is as a way of life, recreation rather than scientific. The truth concerns me not. My life is the other. Zoology and botany books, a means to livelihood, nothing else. My entire life is concerned with the beautiful, the interpretation of the wild and writing....

Another thing that I can do is decide definitely that I am going to quit and write, then stay on in my present capacity until I have paid for the house. That will in all probability be at least three years and I will be 41. In the meantime, write in your leisure and try and prove to yourself that you can do it. You have seen, however, how futile that has been the past years. One cannot write here or at home at night with the many things bothering my mind, all carryovers from the job.

Suppose you do make a success of it, then will come lecturing assignments, more business for the summer, prestige in other ways, but above all freedom to come and go as I wish. Of course I have more of that right now that I ever dreamed of having in the days of the past, perhaps more than I realize.

Field and Stream and Sports Afield and the rest don't offer much more than pin money. I would have to write for the big time stuff to really make any headway. The Post, Liberty, Collier's, Scribner's, Atlantic, Harper's, Esquire, the women's magazines pay well, perhaps a book later on. Lecturing assignments for a month or two might be very lucrative, if I have something to say.

More important than all else would be the sense of stimulation and aliveness that would be mine. Think of starting off in the morning for a week's jaunt into the brush, gathering material. Think how good I would feel, how hard, how brown, how at last the picture of the man I want to be....

My field is in the stuff dreams are made of. A well-rounded article in which I portray strength of feeling, emotion, in which I touch the depths of human reaction. Sorrow and joy, peace and conflict. Black and white is my canvas, words my pigments, interpretation of the wild my theme.

January 15, 1937

Stopped in to see Ernest Hanson for a little while last evening and he said something that made me think that if I could write so that he could feel through me my appreciation of the woods, then I would be doing something worthwhile....

If I can write for his type, Ray Hoefler, Kermit Wick, Bob Mueller, Bob Marshall, Ober, Reifle, Fuzzy and a hundred thousand others who feel the same way, I will have audience enough.[9] Those men feel deeply. I know how they feel for I have been with them and my own reactions are theirs.

What to write, not fiction, not essays, but rather an account of my everyday experiences when I am out deer hunting, fishing or just cruising. Tell your feelings as you go along, describe what you see, give them as Burroughs did and sometimes Thoreau a picture of the wilderness through your eyes. Not just a physical description, you have something else, what you think about as you go along, what swamps and stumps and rocks and timber and wildlife mean to you. If you can do that, then

Sigurd's friend Kermit Wick fishing on Murdoch Lake, Ontario, 1931. Wick Family Collection. Courtesy of Chuck Wick.

you will have an individual form of approach that no one else can copy because no one else can see what you see or think what you think.

Couple with that a finished form and style, describe so beautifully, so clearly that there is charm enough even there. You are a poet and your greatest happiness will come through this type of work. Everything will be all right if you discover that this is the medium for which you have been searching. Even your job here at the college will be all right, the Border Lakes will also do, my present mode of living, just so that I find my medium and can begin work on it and keep consistently producing. What I want to feel is that I have something different, something unique that the world is waiting for.

January 20, 1937

Look back over your years—the Keewatin trail, Madison, geology, Ely, still floundering but having grand experience guiding and starting with my writing, 1927 first success just ten years ago, but still uncertain, 1930–31 Champaign,[10] and research in ecology, more knowledge and prestige, with the realization growing on me that scientific work was not for me. Back at Ely, offers of jobs with U.S.F.S.—Park Service, Indian Service, Soil Erosion, my refusal to accept any an indication of my growing conviction that they were not in the books. Now it is 1937 and I am 37 years old and I know definitely that all the groping is over, that for me there is only one answer—the old old dream.

January 25, 1937

E said I wasn't a gambler. Well perhaps I am not. The stakes are high and if I do make a go of it, it will be such a success that any sacrifice will have been worthwhile. Why not take that leave for next year and trust to luck that you can make a go of it. Perhaps it will work, perhaps it won't. One can never tell till he has taken the leap.

February 24, 1937

I want something deeper, more fundamental, something solid, the primitive love of men for life in the open. J. B. Priestley in his "Arizona Desert" in the last Harper's hit it for a moment when he described the cowboy — "the men with the machines in their air-conditioned factories will always have in the backs of their minds the vision of a man with a horse, a campfire." And then again, "laughing carefree and bronzed." He hit the note several times just for a moment, but in that moment he said enough.

In my work, I want something big enough to hold me, not softly sentimental gushing, something powerful, primitive, virile, the longing of all men, no matter how sophisticated, for the smell of woodsmoke, the real thing. No nature stuff, no series of articles on the play habits of the beaver, the feeding habits of the coyote, why the spruce hen can be caught, why this and that. I want to deal in the really important things, the feelings of men for the wilderness, their love of the earth. You can't do that if you describe animals and birds ala Burroughs, Rutledge and the rest. Your sphere is bigger, deeper than theirs. You shall touch the elemental things, you shall reach down to the very depths of human emotion. Compared to Rutledge your stuff shall be heroic in mold. You have nothing to worry about as far as competition is concerned. No one has touched it as yet.

By a gradual process of elimination you shall arrive. Animal stories don't fill the void, neither do the type of article I have written with the exception of one, "Why Wilderness."[11] I do not imagine there will be many articles, rather short stories depicting a man's love of the wild and a wilderness way of living, the love of the unspoiled and space. "Muskeg" partly hit it. "Saganaga" was better. I am confident that the idea will come to me if I keep thinking about it long enough.

March 3, 1937

Last night I snowshoed over to Millers Point to get the sunset. Lovely beyond words, the sky the clear cerulean blue streaked with clouds of the faintest pink—the afterglow most beautiful and lasting of all. Most, the quiet impressed me. No sound from the busy town across the lake, no sound from the road. I stood for many minutes listening—the short bark of a dog, the quick twitter of a chickadee, then the silence. I drank it in great gulps, breathed it, wallowed in it, balm to nerves that have been frayed by constant talking and mechanical noise. I had almost forgotten there could be such silence. Life seemed purposeful and complete as I stood there, nothing seemed to matter, that an end in itself. In such a place must I live and do my writing. There would I find the peace and the stimulus for thoughts which I lack here in town. There it is beautiful, the rocky little islands to the west, cedars, gnarled pines and spruce, lichen, heather, the sort of beauty I have made a part of myself.

March 5, 1937

I want to be a leader of thought, an apostle of a new way of living. Ordinary fiction will not do that for me, neither will the ordinary type of outdoor writing of which Scoville, Rutledge, Sass and the like are a type. I want to be called upon to lecture to expound my views. I want people to ask for what I have, I want them to be impressed with the fact that I have a deeper, clearer insight than most. But what will it be. Now I am lost again as totally lost as ever. Sometimes I feel that it will come to me and that is the reason that I spring to my typewriter to catch it before it goes. But now it has gone and there doesn't seem to be a chance of catching it again.

I know that someday I will see clearly and once I do then my searching will be over, my goal clearly before me. Then there will be nothing to worry about anymore. I will just continue along my chosen and known course and every experience will be grist in my mill. I hope I do find it for unless I do life will be a futile experience.

I cannot paint word pictures of the wild, that is too common. I can perhaps paint my feeling for it, my idea of a way of life. If I am to do anything worthwhile I must reach the masses, appeal to something inherent in people as a whole, not a small select group.

March 14, 1937

Have been reading the "Psychology of Writing" and Weeks' "This Trade of Writing" and I have come to the conclusion which I have had for a long time, that once a man begins to write that nothing will stop him.[12] I know in my own case that it is all that seems worthwhile and that it is absolutely ridiculous to think that I might ever abandon the idea. Knowing that, then why not keep your job here and make a livelihood while you keep pounding away. Perhaps you will make a go of it and if you don't even then, you will have had a living and tried. The big worry in my case the past few years has been whether to go into some other profession such as wildlife work in which I could have made good. I know I shall never be a scientist....

March 14, 1937

Weeks said that sometimes it takes a man ten years to find himself. If that is true then my years of exploration have not gone to waste. My medium — I thought at one time to portray nature as seen through my eyes. I wonder now if that is as important as portraying man's love of the wilderness, the companionship of men in the wilds, the feeling of men for cold and wind, and rocks & trees and campfires — the man on the horse — the smell of wood smoke — all the trappings of wild country and the way of living that I know so well. It will be fiction no doubt of a magazine type — write the sort of story you want to read — the sort of article that you would pick out from the rest, an essay of yours will be the kind that appeals to men on the out trails of the world — the sort of thing men would want to carry with them wherever they went....

You can bring in your love & understanding in action stories, pure fiction better than by the philosophical essay —

March 23, 1937

Returning from Virginia last night,[13] pondering the old old question of what it shall be, I suddenly had a vision, one which thrilled me more than any solution I have ever had. Thinking of the type of thing I had always had in mind, emotional reactions, heart throbs and tears, a catch in your throat, sorrow over the departing wilderness and all the changes that were coming and bound to come, bemoaning the improvement of portages, the cutting of trees, the ugliness, the callousness of humanity in general. I realized that I was working into a field of bitterness and disillusionment, a terrain of tears and sadness, morbid brooding and futile regret, that these things had dominated my thinking until even when I went into the woods the old spontaneity was gone, the joy and the verve and my ultimate thrill was one of dejection.

What occurred to me was this. If I am to write and sell, I will not get far or develop much of a calling with that sort of drivel, people are tired of weeping, tired of bemoaning their fate, they are sick to death of sorrow and misery. They don't want it dinned into their ears further than it has been. What they want to read is something that will make them happy, something that will teach them the joy of living. Why not inject into your stuff the wild fierce joy of living that was yours, the ecstasy which you know so well, the romance that so easily can cover even

Canoe party on the Duncan–Moss Lake portage, 1936. Photograph by Bill Roliff, U.S. Forest Service Records, National Archives.

the commonest of scenes, the gladness that is yours when hitting the trail, love of sunshine and wind and stars and the earth itself. Occasionally pathos and sorrow will creep in, that is inevitable, but keep the general tone one of gladness and joy. . . .

Perhaps this is the turning point, perhaps this will be the solution to all of my worries about medium. Surely if I can do this, the public will want to see it. Surely it is something I want to do. Here I can picture the outdoors as seen through my eyes. Why should they be sad eyes. Why not make everything I write radiate vitality and joy. Burroughs didn't do that, neither did Emerson or Thoreau or any of the rest that I know.

March 30, 1937

The ideal for me and I need little for happiness is just this:

To have a home fairly well isolated, close to the woods and to the water where I can feel always close to that which I love, Elizabeth and the boys always within reach and time to write. As Thoreau says, what we want more than anything else is reality. That will give me reality.

I don't need the stimulus of travel. I don't need a lot of money to be happy. I don't need the car, I don't need any of the things others need. A very simple life, a chance to be out of doors as much as I would like, no scientific achievement, no honor or fame, no responsibility, no clubs, no social life. All I want to do is picture the things that are always in my mind. Why, now that you know, shouldn't you definitely plan on doing what you want. Why should you postpone it indefinitely. Cornbread and a good book before the fireplace. That is enough for me. The sympathy of good friends, the birds, the animals, the trees, the sky, and continual contact with them. That is what I want more than anything else. . . .

E asks me what I want to do. It certainly will not be the Forest Service, or the Indian Service or the Biological Survey. They only frighten me. I know now what I want to do and there is no reason why I shouldn't do it. It may take five years or more to really get anywhere, but with time will come facility, with time will come fame and ideas and at last I will be doing what I wish. I will keep my interest in the Border Lakes until I get on my feet and then will let that slide.

April 3, 1937

What worries me of course is the fact that I am faced with the money problem but surely I will take care of that. Last night it seemed so final. I had been working all of these years toward this one end, all of my training had been toward this goal, I had made my start in writing, my million words completed, a naturalist in my own right, some prestige, most of all however by a process of elimination, knowing what it was I should do with the rest of my life. These years have not been wasted. I might have quit back there in 1930, but I was not sure and if I had been, I would have done nothing for I knew very little of what it meant. During the last three or four years I have grown up and now I think I know what it is I must do. My speaking ability has improved. These years have not been wasted and now I can say truthfully with Whitman, I am 38 and full of health and can begin.

I must get me a writing place however, a room where I can be alone and not feel that I disturb. This morning, the thing to do would be to go out there at eight and work steadily until 12, then lunch, perhaps a hike of a few hours and perhaps more work until seven. The idea itself fills me with happiness. Freedom at last and still young. I do not need to look forward to retirement and I will not be whipped. I will make a success of it and even if it does take time, think how immeasurably more happy we will be.

May 14, 1937

Ken and his new job, makes me feel like a piker, he makes just double what I do at my two jobs, but is he any happier.[14] Soil Erosion, Indian Service, Forest Service, National Park Service. I wonder. E says that teaching and my influence is enough, that I am in the most wonderful work I could be in. Perhaps this is what I am fitted for more than anything else. I am happy now and am beginning to know it. Happiness is never the same for anyone. I have the boys and E and Florence and Pete and the rest. I did not know how happy I was on our little picnic of two weeks ago, the sunshine across the lake, but now as I look back upon it, I see it. Those little times, if I could only enjoy them as they come. I have always wished I was elsewhere, doing the impossible, when happiness has been so close at hand.

Perhaps things will work out all right. I want to live here and I am beginning to see it.

August 25, 1937

Do not let your duties here at school be too much of a burden. Get them out of the way the best you can, then concentrate on the writing and sooner or later you will either be able to step out and do nothing but that, or feel that the combination is all right. I have willfully sacrificed any chance of getting ahead in biological work or administrative work. They all seem second hand to the real purpose of my life which is writing.

What I will write is immaterial. There will be articles, essays, short articles for the outdoor magazines, stories perhaps, a number of things, all of which will in the end give me recognition and salve my conscience. Writing is the big end of life for me as far as recognition is concerned. There must also be the out of doors, work with my hands, sunshine and wind and water and living out of doors, getting close often and often to the real thing. Above all I must continually keep working and putting things out. I have written some passable fiction in the past, many stories, and articles, I can do the same thing again. If I hit the *Post* I am all set and if I don't hit, I am still all set. What I am determined to do this winter is to keep going and actually get on a productive basis once more. Only in that way will I regain somewhat the feeling of satisfaction and completion I need.

When I went up to Basswood the other day, I recaptured for a moment the old feeling of being able to do things as soon as I got away from this atmosphere. Up here at school whether it is an illusion or not I do not know, but I seem to be nervous and distraught. Thoughts do not seem to come to me. I am worried and ill at ease. I seem cut off from the feeling of the woods. Ideas for stories and articles seem to be in the offing. Up there in a cabin or perhaps on the hill I could do things, but here it seems impossible. That is one reason why it is imperative that I get some writing place for this winter, devoted to writing only.

I want a big pine desk, with plenty of room for paper and typewriter, plenty of room for storing—filing things away, where I can feel that I am absolutely on my own, that I will not be disturbed or disturb others, where I know that the moment I go in there I will have the place to myself and that writing must go on. Unless I have that my writing will suffer. It may cost me a few hundred dollars but that will soon be made up. I do not think that I will ever escape from what I have created here and that I might just as well go ahead with what I have and make the best of it....

The thing to do now that I feel that writing is all important is to so regulate my affairs that I can get this writing in without sacrificing everything. I can forgo night parties, work in a regular schedule of writing, at least two hours every single night, from 6:30 to 9:30, Saturdays and perhaps Sundays included, write, write write and during the day keep jotting down notes and working over ideas. You surely should not suffer from lassitude and feeling that you are not accomplishing anything. The time to write is at night. Weekends will have to be devoted to getting out of doors as much as possible and Sundays there should be no writing whatever. That day should be a day of rest for everyone.

September 13, 1937

There are many things that are entering in to the present upset state of mind. Each year it gets worse. What holds me in the $275 per mo., but the days, they become more & more miserable. Last was bad but this is unbearable. There seems no end whatever. E sees & a pleasant prospect for her — approach middle age — no security — but of what value is security when it means no happiness —

September 21, 1937

Herman Da Costa again last night on the eve of his departure for St. Louis.[15] Has great confidence in my ability, thinks that if I put in two hours a night at my writing that by spring I should be producing in good shape, that I should make this year $3600 from my writing, that I will have no trouble whatever that all I need is to go ahead and do it. He seems very confident that I will make a success of it if I only stick to it. Seems much more confident than last year and is so persistent that I practically believe him now.

The garage is being remodeled and I cannot wait until it is through. Then I will really go ahead with my writing. Before that I will have to wait. It will cost me $150.00 before I am through which seems a ridiculous waste if it were not for the fact that it will get me going at my writing with no excuse for doing otherwise.

If I begin to sell again, it will not take me long to get that $150 back again. In any case, it will be a good investment just finding out what I can do.

September 22, 1937

My writing place is almost finished and I don't know whether I am thrilled or not. For one thing, it is costing far more than I ever dreamed it would, somewhere in the neighborhood of $150.00 or so. I thought I could throw it together in a couple of days with Alex Peura's help and that the total expense would not be over $50. Well, it will help me settle for once and for all the old question.

One thing I do know and that is with the new privacy which will be mine, that there will be no excuse for not writing as I wish. I can go out there after school, lock myself in and with no possible chance for being disturbed work for several hours at a time, something that seems absolutely impossible with the old setup. This way I will not have to worry about the dining room, trying to make that into a writing sanctum. I will not have to worry about the garage for this will be my own and what happens to the rest is of no matter. This I also know, that once I get out there and get settled that I will be much more tolerant of what goes on in the big house and much less irritable. Here there is no chance for irritation, telephone calls, Bobby's tootling or anything else. Nothing will bother me out there. It is what I have wanted for a long time....

I feel terribly selfish spending all of this, but the stake is worth the gamble and I think it was the right idea. At least now I will have no alibi. Now I will have to produce and with the setup out there as it is I do not see why I shouldn't....

By tonight it should be pretty nearly ready to paint. Tomorrow, certainly we can paint the floor and get the stove and pipe in and that should be the end of fooling around.

September 24, 1937

My writing place is about finished and it looks as though it were meant for work and efficient work. It is perfectly quiet and warm, with two wonderful views of the surrounding country. It will give me the feeling that the warehouse on Fall Lake gives me, an incentive to work, a feeling that I could never get in my upstairs bedroom. Up there, with the usual domestic noises continually around me, and the closeness, smells, rustlings and the old sense of being in a house always gives me, that shut in imprisoned feeling that kills all chance of free and happy effort....

Now it will make no difference how many are in the house, what company we have or how many guests. If I can adhere to my program, I will always be glad to come in and meet people. Before, the reason for my distraught and worried attitude was the impossibility of finding quiet. I remember how I used to stroll out in the country investigating shacks, like a dog looking over woodchuck holes with the possibility of picking one for my own. Of course I never found any, but now that is settled and my jaunts into the woods can be free of that worry at least.

The woods are gorgeous, aspen just beginning to turn, some of the maples already a flaming red, the ash brilliant yellow, sumac, purple. Below us a dead white birch, its bare snowy branches silhouetted against a mass of red foliage. Autumn does something to me. I am conscious of an undercurrent of excitement and suspense. I want to be out with the color and the wind continually, seem to have an unsatisfied appetite for the beauty which I know is so transient.

September 27, 1937

The studio is finished and I have what I wanted for many years, a place to write where I will be alone and at peace for as long as I like. Here I will have no excuse for not doing what I think I want to do—write. A week ago Herman Da Costa told me when in doubt—So do it. Straight away next morning, I called Alex and together we began tearing the old garage to pieces. Within a few days it was lined and almost ready and today eight days after the first cleaning out the stove is in, lights and windows and everything ready to go. I feel a little guilty because of the expense, something better than a hundred but if I get at my writing as I should, it shouldn't take long to get that hundred out of the way and a lot more beside....

I never seemed able to settle down to my writing in the house, always afraid of disturbing someone, always conscious of the fact that my racket kept others on edge. Bob with his horn and the telephone and the heat and the lack of space for my materials was more than I could stand. All the years it has been the same, never a chance to really go ahead as I wanted to. Now it is do or die and I am determined to find out if a steady writing program can do anything for me. Surely I can pound a few stories out for the outdoor magazines and take care of the Border Lakes stuff without quite so much trouble.

Well, here at least is a good resolution, every night for at least four a week, devoted to writing, writing anything that will make something worth selling and stifling that miserable ache within me.

Grandmother's Trout

October 1937–February 1939

THE NEW WRITING SHACK gave Sigurd a burst of enthusiasm and productivity. Two months later, though, his mood soured. His work as dean of Ely Junior College drained him, not so much because it was difficult as because it bored him. Worse, he felt he was wasting so much time that he could better spend on writing. He had a good income and a certain amount of prestige but was not living what he saw as his *real* life: the life of a writer.

Throughout this chapter the struggle over medium continues. Sigurd got advice from knowledgeable friends that short story fiction was key to financial success, but he got his best reactions from other friends and Elizabeth when they read his newer batch of essays. He felt best writing them, too: they came from his heart. And so he put his hope in essays that one day would be among his most popular: "Grandmother's Trout," "Easter on the Prairie," "Farewell to Saganaga," and "Kings Point." All were rejected, and Sigurd once again felt desperate. At the end of this chapter he writes that Elizabeth asked him if he was still going to keep writing, and that he responded, "I will write until the day I die."

Trout fishing during a family vacation, circa 1941. Wisconsin Historical Society Collection, 74078.

* * * *

October 4, 1937

Last night for the first time since I began my regular writing schedule, I felt in the swim. For the first time since beginning, the words ran smoothly and easily and within an hour I had written two thousand words. It was gratifying to know that the old facility was in the offing and that I would not have to spend a winter groping for words and ideas. Another hour and I might have finished my first duck story but I was tired and preferred to wait until I was again fresh.

Da Costa was right when he said that regular habits of work would soon begin to make themselves felt and that with continuous effort I would soon surprise myself at the ease with which writing would come. I had almost begun to despair when all of a sudden it was there. I will still have many down moments but with the new setup it becomes so easy to go out there and pound off a few hundred words that I am sure everything will work out all right. The old way it was almost impossible to settle down to anything. Out there it is just as though I was a hundred miles up in the woods as far as quiet is concerned and it should contribute a great deal to my peace of mind.

October 8, 1937

This week has been rather a full one. Received a request from the *Conservationist* for an article on the deer situation and wrote it one night in an hour and got it out the next morning, showing what can be done with speed of writing when I want to.

I also have a duck story under way which I will get illustrative material for this weekend at Low Lake. As to pictures, I want to get the following: portaging, shooting if possible showing a duck coming down, picking them up, a picture of the string and the return, a picture of pushing through the rice, the tent and watching. Half a dozen good shots will be enough to carry it through.

My ease of expression is coming and when I get out there with no one to disturb I can work rapidly. I wrote most of the duck story in two hours or less and the conservation article in about the same time. About 1000 words an hour is pretty good time, that is two sheets single spaced. That much in two hours should not be impossible....

The old question of what to write, what medium to use is always with me, but I feel that if I keep on going that sooner or later it will come to me without too much further effort. The idea is to keep working away and as I work I believe that it will iron itself out. The old adage, write, write, write is the only sure way to get anywhere. I am going to work out this duck story first of all make it so finished and perfect that *Field and Stream* will have to take it. As soon as I finish with that, I am going to either go after Beauchard Beaver or a canoe trip story and finally the article for the *Post*. I do not want to go after the *Post* until I feel that I am running free, wide and handsome.[1]

November 5, 1937

In reading over *Forests & Nature* Mag[2] last evening I found that they were using about the same sort of thing that I wrote. Aldo Leopold's "Marshland Elegy" was a beautiful bit of work & I must write him about it.

I can write stuff like that but of course there is no money in it whatever. If I am to make anything it must be in fiction at which I am no good whatever.

E says I must make enough to pay for the remodeling. I can do that all right but I must begin to concentrate and no more fooling.

November 9, 1937

I have a feeling that unless I try and work in some fiction with character portrayal, that I will run out of material the same as Sass, Scoville, Rutledge and the rest. That is where they failed, they could describe but they lost out when it came to portrayal of character. That is also where I am weak, but it may be possible to do something about it.

When you stop to think about it, the time is ripe for a new writer in the outdoor field. The above-mentioned group are not producing and haven't been for some time. Perhaps this winter will see the rising of my sun.

November 10, 1937

Last night I began my winter's writing schedule with a vengeance. Duck season is over and for six months I am not going to vary. Wrote for four hours and in that time revised and recopied some 4500 words, not bad for an original beginning stint. The thing to do is go out there upon my return from school, start the fire up and then have supper, getting underway by six o'clock. I do not believe I should write two hours at a stretch, but I can write three and should average a thousand words a night either original or worked over. Five nights a week means 5000 words, the length of the ordinary story. This morning, I have a sense of accomplishment which always comes. It never fails me and should be a source of joy to me this winter. As soon as I begin I am happy. No one can take that from me.

This week we will have three days in which to work and I should get my completed articles under way. In any case it is gratifying to know that the old feeling of satisfaction is there and the days of gloom and despondency are over. One thing, out there I go to work, no more of the fiddling there used to be, that is the place writing is done and out there I do not hesitate....

The snow has come a full foot of soft and sticky whiteness. Just yesterday, the ground was dry and bare. I loved the brown withered grass, the crimson tops of the sumac and the feel of soft earth underfoot. I loved it too much for it did not give me time to work only to observe and steep myself. Planted a double row of sumac beyond the stone fence and today peeking through the snow they look as though they have always grown there. The place is getting lovely and the more we do on it, the lovelier it seems. I do not think we ever know how much happiness we have and how much daily enjoyment means until we can look backward.

"All life's failures are due to men not following their ideals."

December 9, 1937

Again the gloom has come, the sickening weight at the pit of my stomach, at spending my days up here doing a thing which means no more than a chance to eat. For a time, I thought I had it whipped, that I could work the combination of writing and dean, but the days go and my writing is neglected and with that comes gloom.

Last night & this morning I thought how wonderful if I could put in my daily stint with nothing to worry about — but then looms the ogre of $275 per month and I wonder about bills, insurance and a thousand other things.

If I could only sell one story or article to the Post, I would no longer have fear. This winter in what time I have left, I must convince myself

Duck hunting, late 1930s. Wisconsin Historical Society Collection, 74082.

that it can be done, so that if I have courage to quit, I will know where I stand. One good check & it would all be settled. A leave then for a year & I would have time to thrash it out. If I did quit, I would have $500 from the retirement, could borrow $1500 on the insurance, just enough to pay the balance on the house. Surely during the year I could make a thousand or so. Da Costa thinks I should make $3500 this winter. It is a tragedy that one should have to think of the financial end of things to the exclusion of all else.

Freedom is what I desire more than all else, freedom to do as I wish. It seems that the old solution is the only way out.

December 9, 1937

Reading Lin Yutang—I am impressed how thoroughly the Oriental classical philosophy has penetrated my own life.[3] He speaks of the Chinese garden, ordered confusion, no box hedges, no symmetry except the natural, the horror of the garden of Versailles. He speaks of the rich sensual delights of eating, the joy in food, commonplace natural things and I think of Burroughs & Thoreau. After all real culture is knowing what reality & the basis of enjoyment is. There is nothing to the false — glitter of superficial pleasures. The Oriental scholar, cynic though he may be is cynical merely of superficiality, but he understands what real happiness is.... ·

I am as much of an Oriental as Lin Yutang. Whether I know it or not, I have steeped myself in Oriental philosophy & culture. I find myself agreeing with everything he says. In my writing of the future, that can always be a safe theme, a ground upon which to build everything I create.

December 15, 1937

Ran through the fifth revision of "Outlaw" last night and had Elizabeth read it. For once she admitted that I had a good story and that it ought to sell. Quite a triumph for me in more ways than one. For one thing, I worked in a lot of action and dialogue, something that I thought was impossible before and it gave me more of a thrill than trying to work in straight description. Did not have a single paragraph of description in the whole thing that was not tied up with action and furthermore, Johnny Chabot stands out as a real character. I have done something unusual and it may be that I have solved the matter of medium that has been such a question with me all of these years. I'm going to polish it up and send it in to the Post. If they take it, then I will have made this winter more of a success than I had ever dreamed.

I have been writing now since the first of October and find that Da Costa was right. It is really getting easier and easier for me to pound my stuff off.

January 6, 1938

Again, I feel by the dead weight in my "innards" that I need an accounting. The days drag and I feel as though I could not possibly put in another. No interest whatever in my work—just putting in time....

I hope against hope that some of the winter's work will mean something, that I will see some light & encouragement soon. I think that is half the trouble. If I could actually know that the work I was doing would bring some returns, it wouldn't seem quite so hopeless & futile.

I know even though they all do come back that I will still keep on until I am convinced there is no use. If I knew that everything I wrote had a chance, then I might survive the "closed in" feeling of my days here. Knowing that in the offing were a few good checks would take out the sting.

All I can do now is keep on & grit my teeth & hope for the best.

My work as Dean of the J.C. should be full of inspiration. After all you are dealing with a beautiful medium, "you who love beauty," there is nothing finer in the world than youth, nothing more idealistic.

You are accruing as an ideal to many of them, a pattern (I hope) and there should be some compensation in that.

Why cannot you fill that gnawing pain ambition, forget about the U.S.F.S. — university job, Ralph King, Ken, Leopold, Bob M. — your fame will come through your writing, a far greater and more lasting fame than theirs. You may have to wait but it is there. In the meantime remember "Lin Yutang" & be calm.

January 12, 1938

How comforting Burroughs always is when I find myself slipping. Mss back — no success & then he tells me write with emotion, feeling, from the heart — put your soul in your work — genius is always unexpected — the world is hungry to read a new slant a new interpretation.

If I can show my world through a different slant—my own personal interpretation of things—then I will be happy, but I must strike that — Fiction is not for me — I want the other. Narrative may be necessary to bring out a truth. What I want more than anything else is to be able to write short articles giving my reactions to the world I know and love which is the physical world about me. That means of course the article or the essay—but that doesn't frighten me. I must put my soul into what I do or it means nothing to me. "Farewell to Saganaga" was my closest approach. "Sciurus nest"[4] — Muskeg — "Why Wilderness" —

What must it be — my slant on anything — deer hunting, trout fishing — camping — snowshoeing — Different — different — diff — when will I strike it? It will come, I know it if I keep working.

"Only the man who looks upon the real with passion and emotion will succeed in transmitting it to something higher and thus permanently interest Mankind in it" — Burroughs.

January 13, 1938

Reading last night Winfred Rhoades' "Adjustment to Life" brought out several things of import.[5]

1. A man must be in harmony with his environment <u>& work</u> — complete harmony.

2. Unless a man's <u>inner consciousness & desire corresponds with his outer consciousness & desire</u> there is trouble, friction, unhappiness & pain.

3. Complete harmony on the highest plane, working toward an ideal which represents the highest for the individual is the end to be desired.

4. <u>Change at once — at no matter what cost</u> to a condition where you are not forever struggling at cross purposes.

The above seemed to hit me exactly — inward strife with external activity — Right now I am conscious of the pain, a heavy weight inside — it is with me always and as far as I see will be with me the rest of my days. There is never any relief whatever. The thing to do then is make a change and make it at once. I am or will soon be 39 still comparatively young.

Read over "Muskeg" last night returned by *Collier's* & found it surprisingly well done but with a flat ending. If the ending had been different they would have taken it without question & I would have $300 at least.

I seem to be right on the verge all of the time, letters from practically all the good magazines. If I could just get over the hump, <u>I would know</u>.

Make the leap, cut all ties & go to it. Even if you do starve for a while, you can certainly make something.

E — "For 15 years we have never known what we wanted to do, never known where we should live or when we might quit." The house — Pay it up a year ahead — $480. Surely by that time things should break.

Life cannot go on like this. I just can't stand it day after day, the same old lump in the pit of my stomach.

If I can make $100.00 a month we can get along — .

I have a feeling that this year will be the end, finally & definitely.

January 18, 1938

Last night, I suddenly realized talking over the question of quitting cold with Elizabeth that we would be in a pretty pickle financially. Suppose I did not make the big mags suppose I didn't possibly make more than just a few pennies, the old supposes. I suppose it is wisest to stay on and write steadily hoping for gradual recognition and finding myself and what I can do before I make the break.

January 20, 1938

I know my dream, know what I want to do, but it will die and I will continue doing the thing that is easy, live comfortably and after a time give up entirely. Then the ghost of what once was me, the bright flame of the personality that was Sig Olson, adventurer, woodsman, explorer, author, lecturer, ideal man of the wilderness will stroll through my rooms as a ghost, looking disdainfully at the comforts I have gained. Then when I am alone and it reproaches me, I will know the meaning of the words, "He sold his birthright for a mess of pottage," for that is exactly what I have done. That is what all men do who give up their dreams.

A man who loses his dream is old, one who has it is perennially young. I see it now as I have always seen it, but now it is stark reality.

February 12, 1938

I have done practically nothing for a full month and strange as it may seem, am not too much under. Have made only one sale after the winter's feverish struggle and with most of my mss back, I have at least maintained a semblance of sanity.

My work here is not too bad, in fact I wonder if I would be happy were I to lose it. My family is a happy one. In fact I don't realize how happy we might be.

Rodin was always unhappy in fact most artistic genius is an unhappy lot, too absorbed in their work and dreams to think of making happy homes to think of solving the many intricacies of everyday living. Goethe said upon reaching old age, "I cannot remember knowing one completely happy hour." If a man is to engage in creative work, there must be a balance and a sense of perspective for surely individual happiness is more important than success of achievement.

Then again last night in the Forum — "The greatest happiness is in work." There it is again, but the work must be of a type which will allow the creative instinct some play, of a type that is not pure impersonal drudgery.

It is a funny world and a hard nut to crack. I do not think I know myself. At times I feel that I must get out and have time to myself and then again, I do not think it is so important. Is this a sign of age, complacency creeping up on me or am I resigning myself to the truth, that I have nothing great to offer, that what I might put out would be mediocre in any case. Still some of my stuff is good, good enough for people to write about, but oh it comes hard.

My best bet is to stay on here, working along, doing my best, build up the house, enjoy my family and keep pecking away at my machine. Eventually, I will sell some things and derive a little satisfaction, but not more than that.

March 2, 1938

Well the spring is on the way, with warm days, sun melting the snow, running water, and the eternal itch to be on the move.

What have I done? "Why Wilderness" to the wilderness number of *American Forests*,[6] "Song of the Bush" to *Liberty*, the Dead Line to Uzzell, Sciurus home, a new story "Grandmother's Trout" perhaps to the *Atlantic Monthly*, "Packs and Paddles" dead, not a very gorgeous performance in spite of the fact that I have been writing pretty steadily since September. However, writing is certainly easier now than it was last year and compared with my performance of last winter, it is really pretty good. Last year all I did was get off a few news stories and "Why Wilderness". I really feel that I have gotten somewhere even though I haven't sold enough to put in your eye. I have been writing steadily enough so that I could sit down with confidence and pound off most anything. Words come easily and so do ideas.

What about the future — I have not been quite so down in the mouth now that I have been working, have not known the utter desperation that used to be mine.

March 23, 1938

Have just returned from Mpls and glad to be back. Again I know that I could never live in a city of any kind out away from the wild country.

Upon my return, I find most of my mss back. It does not hurt so much now as I am somewhat resigned, but it does leave me grasping or rather gasping for air. The props are gone again and I must find something to hold to. Things look so rosy when they go out, and so hopeless when they return. "The Dead Line" and "Song of the Bush" are back but they may only mean that a certain avenue is closed.

"Grandmother's Trout" and "Fireside Pictures" are still out.[7] If they are taken, it will mean that I can never make my living at this game, but rather that I can keep putting out short skits or sketches of happenings that I have known and so paint a picture of something that has impressed me. I cannot conceive of leaving off altogether, that is impossible. But this winter's work meant a waste of time except for the practice it gave me.

April 4, 1938

As I approach 40,[8] I am conscious of one thing, a lack of the old straining at the leash, a lack of curiosity and resentment and bitterness. The fire is dying down into the old glow of age. I am becoming resigned, content and disillusioned, no longer fighting, desperate....

My writing has brought me little this year, none of the recognition I craved, still I find myself not caring too much, not too bitter. I am gaining perspective and understanding.

I still have not found the grail.

April 22, 1938

Last night reading Van Wyck Brook's "The Flowering of New England" — how well it brought back to me the old Emersonian advice....

I thought afterward of what a change it would make in my life if I gave everything up— teaching, the Border Lakes, & devoted myself entirely to what I wanted—my writing and cruising. What a tremendous shock to a system that for 40 years has been in purgatory—in prison walls of convention. I would be free for the first time—free with days & nights of my own.

All I need is a <u>sign</u>, one indication that I can produce. Once I get that, I will dare make the break, but not until then. If Uzzell should say at last — "Your stuff is good, this is worth selling," or if *Scribner's* should take "Grandmother's Trout," but without some concrete evidence it will be hard to shore up my courage sufficiently to make the great decision. I know so well now what it is that I want, if I had only known early in life.

September 21, 1938

With Herman Da Costa last night. Read "Grandmother's Trout" and thought it was good. *Good Housekeeping* — Curtis Publishing, *Ladies' Home Journal* or that group. Well it was something to have him advise that much after last night's reading of "Outlaw Beaver" which he swore was horrible.

Perhaps that is my forte, perhaps the long awaited medium. I am quite sure it is not fiction — I cannot place myself in the minds of other characters. Joe Chabot — Alex — Johnny, Waino, Ray — Florence — I don't know any of them nor do I care. I don't know any of my students. I love them but cannot see through their eyes. I am inordinately selfish and can see only my own slant. But that is exactly what Burroughs says is important. The world is interested only in what you think, what you see — Be original and different.

October 13, 1938

Yesterday I pounded off "The Mallards of Back Bay" with a facility that surprised me.[9] It will not take me long to get under way once I settle down. Last winter's work was not lost entirely. As far as medium is concerned, forget it, write furiously anything, everything, medium will come sometime, perhaps in the most unexpected manner, just as it came in "Grandmother's Trout" — Just so that you keep on writing, you will find your goal.

October 19, 1938

Burroughs was right when he said your past & your old self camps with you no matter where you are. You can never escape yourself, the real you, no matter how far you travel or what you do.

November 10, 1938

Tomorrow is Armistice Day, twenty years since the end of the war — twenty years of the best part of my life, twenty years of sorrow and grief and disappointment, twenty years of longing for something I did not know. My life has been one long succession of disappointments. What has given me happiness — what little writing success I have had — my hunting & fishing, my guiding, a certain companionship with me through the Border Lakes....

I say I have never been as low, but that is not true, I have often been that low and lower. There has never been a year when things have been different. And I suppose they will never be different as long as I stay in this tangle of conflicting emotions.

When I look back twenty years to my happy adventurous youth & realize what has gone I am sick at heart. If I broke away, would it be any different at all or would my old complex always be the same. The only way I could settle that would be to try it, perhaps that leave for a year would do it.

November 29, 1938

Now, if I had the courage to quit, but expenses seem impossible. It will have to go on this winter no matter what. I will soon be forty and will have some thirty years to go. Thirty years brings me back to the time I was ten, a boy in Prentice or Sister Bay. Think what a tremendous stretch of time.

Think what a terrible thing to die and realize that you never had the courage to take the big chance. Think what a sacrifice and also what a glorious thing if you actually make a go of it. Think of working all morning from seven to twelve and then off for a hike, none of this lethargy, none of this terrible feeling of waste. Then Thoreau will be right. Look forward to the dawn, regret the night — Burroughs — to live the bountiful life be engaged in some congenial work into which you can throw all of your energy — Emerson — to use all of the talents that are yours — follow your dream and then realize it, and many others, all the same.

December 5, 1938

The reason for fatigue, tiredness is boredom with work—detail, routine, emotional dissatisfaction. If a person can be so engrossed in his work that there is no boredom, if he can be completely absorbed so that the days "will seem too short, the nights too long" then he will never be tired. "To live the bountiful life, use to the nth degree the talents that are yours. Anyone not so engaged is filled with a growing discontent." Burroughs: — "Be engaged in some work in which you can completely lose yourself." Rest; physical, is not the answer to fatigue, nor less or easy work. Work never made anyone tired because it was work, but rather because it was uncongenial work.... Writing never wearies me.

January 12, 1939

Have no hope or enthusiasm for fiction. The little sketches are more to my liking and much easier for me to do. I can put my feeling into them and know that I am writing sincerely and what I feel. The other fiction and characters who mean nothing to me are of no interest whatever.

This week I have revised "Muskeg," which is good, and "Saganaga," which is also good, and will have eight of them out in a day which is not bad for the winter's work. Before the work shuts down, I should have ten articles and stories underway. If I could sell them all I would be sitting pretty.

January 15, 1939

Da Costa and Don[10] both said, "Lay off that sort of thing, meaning the essay, concentrate on fiction only, that is what the world is interested in and that is where the money is." I suppose they are right, that if I am to make a living, the thing to do is keep on with stories. This I do know, that as far as form is concerned it doesn't make much difference just so that I can keep on writing....

Am getting peculiar—no interest in the scouts, the commercial club, clubs of any sort or contacts of any sort, just my idea of writing. It has grown into a sort of mania with me. If I should cut loose, I know that I would drop every contact of that kind, contribute of course, but let active participation be for someone else. And why should I go through life being plagued by tasks that I despise. I have always hated club work, the 4H idea, forestry club, scouts, etc.—all good organizations and with worthy ideals, but dead to me personally. I have worked with them, hating every minute spent because there was no escape, suffering nostalgia, tortures of the mind, going through with it, speaking at banquets, get togethers.

Queer to look back upon, good experience I suppose, grist in the mill — but when I am through with this job which necessitates those things, then I will be through forever with doing anything unless I wish to do it.

In a few weeks will come the scout drive and I will have to give enthusiastic speeches to my committees, despising myself for doing it. I should go down to Chicago but I find I am not interested in conventions either, despise big gatherings. In fact there is nothing that interests me outside of my own selfish ideal. That first and foremost. I do feel, however, that were I doing what I wanted to do I would then take an active sincere part in many things that now bore me to tears.

I should try and knock out a piece of fiction before spring, just one piece to keep my hand in.

January 16, 1939

Yesterday and Saturday were unbearable, why because I did no writing, because "Grandmother's Trout" came back and "Shift of the Wind," my great hopes.[11] It does not seem possible that I can continue without my dream. The instant anything happens, then I am out on my feet.

Last night or rather before dinner, I could stand it no longer, went on a hike to Mud Lake and beyond. All along I could only think of one thing and that — No job in the whole world appeals to me in any way except the one I have worked out for myself, forestry, park service, biological survey, teaching, university jobs of any kind or caliber, governmental service, private industry, nothing that I could think of, interested me in the slightest or promised anything but food and clothing. The only thing worthwhile was my dream, to write and hike around the wilds getting material. That really would be something and as long as my mind is made up why should I not go ahead with it next year.

January 23, 1939

My being able to write on King's Point will be a triumph in more ways than one. In the first place I can demonstrate that I can do this sort of thing ad infinitum with many variations, that I can pick out almost any subject and write a lovely sketch about it and bring in enough unusual incidents and sentiment to make it worthwhile.

If you can take this subject out of a clear sky and build it up so that Florence and Elizabeth will say once more that here is something beautiful and lovely, that it is a fine bit of craftsmanship, then you can rest secure in the idea that you have something that others have not.

Do not forget through the working out of this thing that you must make it breathtakingly beautiful, that somewhere through it you must make it touchingly close, enough so that it will bring a smile of happiness or a tear, or a catch in the throat. Bring into it all of the sentiment that you have, all of the power of your description.

If you can do this, then you have nothing to worry about. There are many other subjects, all of them colored by your personality, that you can use.

> So far you have — Easter on the Prairie
>
> Grandmother's Trout
>
> Northwest Corner
>
> Shift of the Wind
>
> Saganaga
>
> Kings Point
>
> Muskeg
>
> Why Wilderness?[12]

All of them are a type — personal experience in which I show how I feel about the out of doors, not fiction, not exactly essays, each one a little sort of a story in itself and each one with a certain feeling. Perhaps here is my medium, here the thing I have been striving to find. This sort of thing I can do, where I couldn't touch fiction or outdoor stories — Here is the creation of something beautiful, a coloring of an experience with my own particular interpretation and sentiment.

Here is what Burroughs means when he said write only about what you feel deeply. If you can describe things differently than most people, then you have done something which will make the world beat a track to your door. There is no competition here for no one else will ever see things the way you do.

January 24, 1939

E told me last evening that Florence had read "Grandmother's Trout" to her sisters, that before it was through they were all weeping for the

Sigurd and Elizabeth with Pete Peterson at Peterson's Fishing Camp, early 1950s. Listening Point Foundation Archives.

sheer beauty of it—not because it was sad. Florence said Pete had signs of tears on the reading of "Easter on the Prairie" — What is it I have done — If I can write so beautifully that it affects people that way, then I have something — I have created — painted a picture as lovely in its way as though I had done a landscape — painted a mood. Here is my outlet, my opportunity, to paint the most beautiful scenes of memory —

Remember no scene is worth a thing unless it portrays some human interest, some sentiment — unless it is & embodies with itself the sort of thing that made E & F weep.

No fiction, no animal stories, only things that I would read with joy myself — write for yourself. If you would like a small leather-bound booklet of short essays to carry with you of your stuff, then it is good.

January 27, 1939

My medium: Short autobiographical essays or sketches, not over 2500 to 3000 words in length, beautifully written, each one with an emotional throb — so beautifully done that like Easter and Grandmother's Trout, the reader will feel either like laughing or crying or both.

Undated, February 1939

It will not make much difference if I don't write anything worthwhile from a financial standpoint. I must write to keep my sanity. Writing is the insulin of a disease of long standing. I must take my regular dose or go under.

February 10, 1939

A day of disappointments — "Grandmother's Trout" is back and in spite of my resolve not to let it affect me, I find that I am fighting to keep my balance. In a few days, "Easter on the Prairie" will return and then "Saganaga" and my bubble will be completely punctured....

When the time comes for giving up my dream, I begin to see red, get desperate, like a man drowning, sinking for the last time, grasping at anything, growing weaker all of the time, a few last wild spurts of energy, threshing around, growing feebler and feebler and at last resigned, sinking down into the calm ooze of mediocrity, there to disintegrate, lose my color, my vision.[13]

February 15, 1939

I want to portray the real — the feeling & hunger that was mine when I first hit Seeley — working with the earth, plowing, breaking, cultivating, doing things with horses. Chris going over the fence that night — head lighting with Jack — they all seemed real — none of the Shadow America there — that was the real thing.[14]

All of my life I have searched & found little reality — why I do not know. What is real — what is synthetic.

School is real or should be — it is a part of life — youngsters will always be going to school, college & university are as real as farms, as real as the woods —

I am continually feeling that what I am doing has no basis, no solidity—that I am on the bench watching a show but not a part of it, that I am perched as it were on a limb ready to fly; that there is no permanence—no foundation.

Perhaps for me there will never be that feeling; perhaps I am an observer, an interpreter of things which those who are anchored, settled, can never know. Perhaps my creation of bits of beauty is sufficient excuse for the feeling of detachment — perhaps without the feeling of detachment there would be no creation possible.

February 20, 1939

E's query last night, "Are you still going to keep on with your writing." My desperate answer, "I will write until the day I die" helped little but gave an inkling of the necessity of keeping on with it or dying entirely. I just cannot give up and keep my sanity.

WE USED
TO SING

March 1939–February 1940

FAMILY TENSION GREW as Sigurd's struggles became harder to hide. He was frustrated, anxious, and at times his own worst enemy. In these entries he compares himself unfavorably to his older brother, Kenneth, dean of the prestigious Medill School of Journalism at Northwestern University in Chicago. Sigurd continued to receive positive feedback for his essays but could not get them placed anywhere. Instead, literary agents and friends advised him to turn those essays into short stories, and typically panned the result.

The period covered in this chapter and the first part of the next was perhaps the most frustrating in Sigurd's "search for medium," as he put it. He got just two articles published: "The Immortals of Argo" in the July 1939 issue of *Sports Afield*, and "Mallards of Back Bay" in the October issue of the same magazine. He wrote such pieces easily, but it wasn't the kind of writing he enjoyed, and it paid very little. No matter how hard he tried, he could not find a solution. "Perhaps there is nothing that I can do," he wrote on February 7, 1940. "Perhaps it is just a wild dream."

* * * *

Elizabeth (*right*) and a fellow canoeist at Park Point on Conmee Lake, Quetico Provincial Park, 1948. Photograph by Leland J. Prater, U.S. Forest Service Records, National Archives.

161

March 9, 1939

If I could only recapture the joy of those days, the guiding — Glenn's sleeping bag — Snowbank — Twin Lakes — trout in the spring — adventure — excitement. Now there is too much gloom to suit me, not enough fun, not enough laughing or singing.

Junior said last night, "Dad, remember when we used to sing all the cowboy songs?"

It struck me hard, that accusation—for that is what it was—Why don't we sing anymore?

Always, I say, Wait until things iron out, wait until I quit and begin writing — wait — wait and the days go by — soon they will be gone and I will have to sing alone.

March 13, 1939

The following are back from Brandt and Brandt: Easter on the Prairie, Saganaga, The Pines, Shift of the Wind, Northwest Corner, Grandmother's Trout. I cannot believe that they are of no value. Don said that it is as hard to get an agent to handle your stuff as it is selling to the magazines, so must not feel that I am utterly damned, although it is hard to feel otherwise. There are three left, fiction and different than the above and expect them back also. All I regret now is that I have spent $12.00 on this one effort to break the ice, money that we could ill afford to lose.

Today and Saturday were black. When I think of giving up my dream, I don't want to go on. Nothing seems worthwhile anymore, just this. Is it that I have built up an illusion so strong, that it has displaced everything else.

I am so happy when I am producing, life is such a cheerful happy affair. It is all that keeps me going here, but without it, life doesn't seem worth living....

What I need to do is get off in the woods, work off this gloom, get a new slant on things. Right now, there is nothing that appeals. Everything is dead. The heart is gone right out of me, no spark or spunk.

At forty — my dream is over — I am through — definitely, inevitably.[1]

March 14, 1939

My disgust of yesterday is not so keen. Don said, "Don't take an agent's refusal too seriously." They won't handle non-fiction or stuff under

$100.00. They might not have read the last group at all. The same stereo-
typed letter....

Don't be too discouraged by what has happened. This is nothing.
Have faith in yourself & all will come out well.

March 21, 1939

Last night out in the shack I regained some of my old composure — answered a raft of letters which in itself was seemingly fun — also wrote
to half a dozen agencies. It may be that a critic agency will do the trick
— just a little help on a few of the things I have done — Grandmother's
Trout — Easter on the Prairie — The Pines — Shift of the Wind — Beaver
Time — Beauchard — It may just be that they can suggest a few changes
that will make them sell. I have a feeling that the Hardy outfit, possibly
A.L. Fierst might do something for me.[2] Wouldn't it be wonderful if they
broke the ice and let me in before April the 4th, broke down the barrier,
so that I could see.

I still feel that in the four essays I did this winter that I have something. If I could only know that they had a place, so that I could keep on
working at something, knowing that anything I wrote would sell, this
life would not be unbearable. I must find out this year, and I think the
critic agencies are perhaps the solution.

Uzzell was OK but my stuff didn't strike him right. I hope Jane
Hardy will have a feeling for what I have done. The fact that she is
a woman might mean something. Brandt & Brandt was a faux pas. I
should have known better than try them. They are not critic agencies,
are interested only in sales & high priced ones. As DH says,[3] if they take
you, you can count your money, "if" — they are not interested in begin-
ners whatever.

March 27, 1939

Last night we burned all of our old letters, Elizabeth & I, and today I am
sorry. They represented so many heartaches, so much happiness, that it
almost seemed a sacrilege. We were so desperately in love—could not
for an instant be separated, dreamed of being together, lived for nothing
else. Now it is all over in the past and I am a little sick at heart.

I should have saved 2 or 3 from each period, 1919 — 1920 — 21 — 22.
I would have felt better. There were certain letters telling of the farm &

teaching at Hayward, letters which gave me everything, re-enacted our first violent love, brought back the old days — Now it is all over and I am hurt & lost.

One thing it did for me was to refresh my memory, show that it was inevitable all that happened, that we could not have remained separated for long. I know now that Lib has been wonderful through it all, that the least I can do is try to be happy & keep her happy too, instead of distraught and miserable.

I will stay on here—not quit until I make my way clear, not put her to the torture of want & financial worry, at least. And above all try & be happy—cheerful—a little contented. She asks so little.

Why did I not save some of those letters — I do not know. They could bring back better than any picture the old feeling. Her letter describing her walk down through the woods and a few like it. It wasn't so much the letters as what I read into them.

One thing, it seemed to make me live again those early years, made me feel that I had something precious—something that was & is worth more than all else.

Sigurd and Elizabeth on their honeymoon, 1921. Wisconsin Historical Society Collection, 63198.

April 3, 1939

Tomorrow I shall be 40—more than the half-way mark—the best thing to do is forget the numerical value of it & just live. One doesn't think of the twenties but somehow the forties are different. Where have I come —

This past winter, I believe I have come further than ever before. In writing or rewriting N.W. Corner last night, it suddenly occurred to me how beautifully I had expressed myself. That has come this winter. I also have a feeling that before the month is over I will have made a hurdle—no more sending out of mss & watching them return. They may come back again but now they will have a chance, some consideration and I will know what is wrong....

I am more settled, perhaps — no great aspirations as far as biological work is concerned — I get my wallop out of writing and always will — I am not a scientist — research — never will be — that is over

As soon as I make my N.Y. contact then that will be over, that is any worrying about future. At 40 you have new hope. Eight years ago, I went to Champaign, not exactly a wasted year, paid for by now — but then is the time I should have broken off and started serious writing. Still I wonder if I knew enough about what I wanted.

It hasn't been too bad this drifting along, many happy days & many sad.

April 12, 1939

Back at home after a visit to the farm[4] — The farm, how permanent, how restful, how peaceful, how satisfying every hour. I do not know what it is but the instant I am there, I am happy, content, enjoy my food and want to work. Here I am all nerves, tenseness, excitement, that empty feeling inside. I wonder what it is? Is it the old childhood feeling of security that is mine or something else. Life seems to go on there in spite of everything — there is no hurry or fuss, no tremendous questions hanging fire to be decided immediately — There is time for talk, philosophy, reading, enjoyment of simple things. Then the trees and the beauty everywhere, the sunlight on the pines in the morning, the quiet rosy sunsets toward the Tobatik Hills.

If I should ever make anything with my writing so that I could live where I wished, I would most certainly want to spend some time down there every year writing and hiking, working.

April 24, 1939

When have I felt completeness — reality — When hunting — guiding — fishing — farming — working in the woods — any activity that gave me physical contact with earth, sky & water —

The instant I am too much tied in I lose my sense of reality—become a transient, a part of shadow America. My salvation & no doubt the salvation of many others is exactly that — to break away when I begin to feel unreal — get close to the earth — be a primitive once more — Too many thousands of years have gone by to so forcibly change a man that living artificially he no longer missed the earth & water.

My writing-cruising combination would be perfect — Days like today should never be spent indoors — They are far too lovely —

April 25, 1939

These days have been hard in many ways. For the first, the coming of warm weather is always disconcerting. I do not want to work inside, only be outside working with my muscles. Have taken some of that out by working on the new raspberry patch and there is still much to do. But that is not the main reason. "Kings Point" is back and "Beaver Time" and "The Dead Line," not a one my best work but disconcerting just the same.[5]

There is the same old report, no plot, no action, things move too slowly, not the sort of thing a fiction loving public will go for. I am beginning to realize that that sort of thing is not for me, that fiction might well be left for someone else, that I had better stick to the sort of thing that "Grandmother's Trout" and "The Pines" and "Northwest Corner" represent. Those things are real experiences of mine, they are colored by my own personal slant on life.

They are my way of reporting the out of doors. If as Burroughs says, you can make your reader see what you see, think and feel what you feel, then you have approached literature. That is my forte, not the other and if I can cash in there, somehow, that will be enough....

I am of the opinion that no man dealing with blood and thunder stuff will ever want to take care of my stuff, that it takes a woman's greater sensitiveness to understand what it is I am trying to do. Burroughs found the same thing, that women were his greatest audience, that men as a rule were too thick-skinned to understand or appreciate what he did. So it will be Jane Hardy or Ann Elmo.[6] One of the two and I hope it will be Jane Hardy.

April 25, 1939

What is getting me down is I think my lack of recognition. We need at least I do something more than this local situation to make me content. My writing would take care of it for me and if I stayed on would compensate for my small position. But the writing must materialize, or something will break. If I could sell half a dozen articles or stories a year, then it would not make much difference if I stayed on or not.

April 27, 1939

These days go on and on and each one leaves me more and more sick with life. I know the trouble, that I am not writing, but it seems impossible to write not knowing if the stuff I write is worth the paper it is written upon. I just cannot try another essay with joy and abandon, feeling that it is not worth the effort, nor can I even write a fishing story or a hunting yarn with any hope.

May 11, 1939

Jane Hardy writes that my writing "is perfectly lovely," that I write charmingly, that these two lovely pieces are sketches, not short stories, that I shall never sell unless I inject action, suspense, all the other requirements for a short story. Well, it is something to have her call my stuff "lovely," to know that at least I write beautifully and I wonder if I can ever make the hurdle of suspense and drama.[7]

In the first place none of this stuff was intended to be short story material. They were all intended as sketches, nothing more. The big question is, is there any place for sketches of that type in the publishing field today. The Atlantic, Harper's, Scribner's and the rest will have none of them and they are the only media I know who want them....

I have proved to myself that there is no market for "Grandmother's Trout," "The Pines," "Shift of the Wind," "Easter on the Prairie," "Muskeg," "Northwest Corner," no market for personal anecdotes, personal reflective observations, philosophic essays. There might be just a chance but a bare one, certainly not the type of thing that might bring me any money, much as I love to do them. As Da Costa said, forget them, they are not what the readers want. They want action and suspense. They have been an interesting experiment and perhaps have placed me on the way to my final medium and if they have done that it is enough.

I feel if I could have a little more time to think things out, I could do something. Give me a month and I know I could revamp the whole works, make a dramatic sequence that would put their eyes out, <u>make each little incident a vital, gripping one</u>, hold them breathless, not with blood and thunder stuff, but with the old emotional appeal. All my things have been running narratives only, no single emotional effect, no complications, no heart-tearing climax. I begin to see what it is they want. As Jane Hardy said, "It will be hard, but I think you can do it." If I finally do it then my way will be clear, then there will be no further questioning. And write only about the things you know and feel deeply on. Do not write about people who cannot see things as you do. Create a thing of beauty. The creation of beauty is far more important than anything else. Make each one of your stories so breathtaking and at the same time so alive and full of drama that they cannot help but sell.

May 17, 1939

It is drawing toward the end and today I feel as though I would crack. For better than a month, I have been going too fast, home to work away at some project in the yard, then at my letters, working always until late, then the Scout Drive and the Prairie Portage matter, everything piling up until I could see no end. Last night planting shrubbery I flew off at E about some little matter. She does not know how close I am to snapping, thinks I cannot stand criticism. What I need is rest and calm.

Then too, I suppose the fact that I have done no writing whatever for about two months is a contributing factor. While I write a peace descends over me and all life is wonderful. When I stop and let other things take precedence, then there is apt to be trouble. In other words, I cannot busy myself to the exclusion of all else or life loses all purpose.

No word from Ann Elmo as yet and I wonder. I know what it will be however. Pretty soon, some of them will come winging back and then the 1939 experiment will be all over. Jane Hardy came back and told me that all I was doing was beautiful sketches not shorts. She is right and I must ask her if there is no room for sketch material. Somehow, someway, I must begin to put out the sort of stuff that will sell. If I only had time to work on that alone, I know I could do something.

June 6, 1939

Ann Elmo comes back with the old story. She has received my three pieces but of course I realize that they have limited appeal and that the only possible market is with outdoor magazines, that they are exceedingly well handled but that as short stories they would go much further. Thinks that I should by all means try the Post, Collier's etc with short stories.[8]

The only ray of sunshine is this — she does admit and so does Jane Hardy, that they are well written, rather lovely in fact, she does advise the Post and Collier's which she would not do if they did not show promise, also that she is keeping them in the hope that they will pan out somewhere.

My conclusions are that I will have to work up a plot with the necessary complications and climax, using what skill I have worked up in bringing them out. In other words, my only hope is the short story, not the article, not the essay or sketch. Unless I work along the short story lines my chances of making any money are nil, absolutely nil. That much I have discovered this past year. My dream of making good with the above stuff is out. It is a pleasure writing it and it has a limited appeal, but there is no money in it whatever. Unless I can write a thriller with a wallop, I might as well fold up and quit. Outdoor stuff I can do, but there is no future in that. Short stories is the answer.

July 1, 1939

<u>Time, the thing that any sort of a regular job robs you of.</u> Time is so precious especially when you feel that you must be stealing it for something other than what you are doing at the present. At times in the morning, I feel that time is endless, that it would be only too wonderful if I could call it my own. On the job here as it would be on any job run on schedule, the greatest loss and worry is <u>the loss of time</u>, the loss of hours when I feel I should be doing something else. I sometimes feel that this is the chief reason for my discontent, that if my time was my own to do with as I wished that there would be no trouble with my happiness or sense of accomplishment.

How wonderful not to feel that you must keep appointments with meals, with schedules, with deadlines, that the days are full twenty-four hours in length, that nights made no difference just so long as you got a reasonable quota of sleep, that the hours put in on a writing stint would not be counted as hours. That would be compensation enough for any sacrifice material.

Reading the *Harper's* last night "One Man's Meat" I was impressed with the idea there of freedom, "<u>So few men have real freedom anymore, freedom to come and go</u> and do as they like, freedom to sail the broad seas, to come and go, to act with the tides and the sunsets and moon-rises." He struck a kindred note there with what I have been feeling all of these years, that with me the keynote to happiness is personal independence and about the only way it can be achieved is to give up everything and take a chance on my writing.

September 13, 1939

Up against the old problem, but this time it is more in the nature of an ultimatum than ever before. Now they want me to take over the super-intendency of the Sunday School. That is the last straw, then they want me to reorganize the League, another straw, then leading the singing in church gatherings, the assemblies at school, taking part in a hundred things that go against me. It seems that the very things I am good at are the things I despise myself for doing.

Vestal's little chapter on why writers write hits me square, freedom to move, act and think, to do the things that I want to do, working at something I love, escaping the responsibilities of a small town, independence is perhaps the secret of my longing.[9]

The days up at school are more and more stifling, but how can I resign now.

September 14, 1939

<u>Yesterday we came to a definite decision, that the thing to do is make the break. E at last feels that</u> the coast is clear that there is one thing for me to do and that is write. Tells me she knows I can do as well as Don Hough and a number of others, that she does not want me to stagnate here on this job that my horizons must be larger and will be if I make the break.

September 21, 1939

I have sent off a couple of letters to Wallie sounding him out on the proposition of giving me a yearly salary with the Border Lakes. If it is O.K. with him, I will approach Pete and if O.K. with him, it might settle things for good.

One short story for the slicks at $500 every two or three months would take care of me. That should not be impossible.

What gets me is the ease with which the money comes in on this job. How simple it would be to keep on going this way, pay up the house and live comfortably and all of that. But the fact remains that in twenty years, all of this will be behind me and I will not have done what I wanted to do. I <u>feel that no matter what the sacrifice, it is worthwhile, just so that I can feel that I have taken the leap</u>....

<u>If I could achieve some peace of mind</u> on this job, I might be tempted to keep it, <u>but that seems impossible</u>. There is no peace, no balance at all. I am continually ridden by the realization that I am wasting my time. And I know that will go on for the rest of my life, no matter where I might happen to be, if I am not writing.

Peace of mind — how I want to recapture the peace that was mine down on the farm, while guiding up in the Canadian wilds, while trout fishing, while working with the geological survey. Peace and contentment. If I can inject that atmosphere into my writings, show my readers that there is such a peace to be gotten out of just normal healthful living, then that is enough. I must demonstrate however to myself that there is such a thing and get away from this strident note that dogs every hour of my day.

September 22, 1939

Last night was typical, so is every gathering. I go with the rest, laugh and joke and supposedly have a good time, but underneath it all I feel that I should not be wasting my time, that I should be away somewhere writing. Writing, writing—it never leaves me. The duck hunting coming up will be the same. I will finally manage to get the gang to Basswood and while there will try and get enthusiastic, will try and lose myself as Wilson, and Ray, and Alex and Junior do, but it will be the same. It has been the same for years. I can never forget, can never get over the idea that I am marking time, am part of shadow America....

Last night in the *Atlantic*, "Town and Country," I knew what it was, the feeling that what I was doing was not worthwhile, that the people living natural country lives being close to the earth, doing natural things, were those who really lived. A countryman lives as he works, he does not have to look forward to a vacation, but enjoys his life day by day. That is why vacationists seem somewhat puerile, somewhat unstable to him. That was why the feeling as a boy on the farm, I resented the

Kahshahpiwi Lake at Hunter's Island, Ontario, north of Basswood Lake, 1944. Photograph by Francis Lee Jaques. Courtesy of University of Minnesota Archives.

visits of city folks, resented their coming out in a supercilious way to look over what we common country folk were doing.

From that early feeling no doubt came my love of farming and natural things, a love that has during later years expressed itself in my wilderness roving. A seeking after the natural, the fundamental, with no chance of finding peace until I return to that.

October 17, 1939

I must write and I must work out my own salvation. News that Ken is still on the rise makes me feel that I am stagnating here, that if I make a break with this setup, that there is a chance of really going to town and making good.

October 25, 1939

This I do know, that when I make the break, it will be forever, that all of my energy will go into the new venture, that I must succeed somehow and when I do, it will be different.[10]

To sit down in the morning or after a workout and pound away for several hours, to be able to get out when I wished, the feeling of frustration will then be gone. To get rid of this deadly weight, the sickness inside of me, the suicidal frame of mind with which I greet every day. Anything is worth the sacrifice, anything to get away. We can cut down, we can make it pan out. Drop Molly $13.00 per month.[11] Cut the phone, $1.75 per month. Cut a lot of my own wood, cut out the use of the car except for emergencies, cut out trips, cut out movies, cut down my own clothes, small running expenses, even cut some of the insurance. It can be done and any sacrifice is worth it.

When it does happen, I must not expect too much. I must resign myself to the idea that it may be a year before I really do anything worthwhile, several months at least before I send anything in. Remember that it will take months before you get your old facility back, that it takes time to develop smoothness and form and ideas. Don't get too discouraged if only rejection slips come in instead of checks. It is the first year that counts.

October 26, 1939

The road seems to be opening up and all I need now is the courage to walk out and do what I want. With $150 from the Border Lakes, another

$100.00 from my outdoor stuff, why I could make a good living. It isn't the desperate chance I had thought it might be, nothing really desperate about it at all.

It does my heart good to talk to fellows like Handy,[12] men who without solicitation approach me with their belief in me, tell me that I have big things in store.

What gets me is the many years of pounding away at nothing at all, the years of frustration and worry and sickness. It is time to make the break, time to call things quits and go to town. I know I can do it, I have the ability, have the brains the background, everything. But I must make the move or nothing at all will happen.

The time may come and not in the too distant future when I can either buy out Wallie or Pete or both, perhaps get the whole business, or cut away from the Border Lakes entirely when my writing gets to the point where it will really take care of things.

October 27, 1939

<u>E seems to think that the time is ripe to make the break</u> and Pete's note of yesterday "Perhaps next year, we will all be able to go," meaning of course that if I make the break there will be no more schedules to keep....

To think that *Field and Stream* or *Outdoor Life* might pay a hundred or better for a story, might mean the difference between success and failure of this writing business, that would mean that I could make between $250 and $300 just from my Border Lakes business and the writing. With three or four good outdoor magazines would mean only three or four for each of them during the course of a year, enough to keep the wolf from the door if nothing else panned out.

There will be other things too, of that I am sure — just a thought this morning, write the supremely beautiful, the sort of thing that makes you catch your breath for the sheer loveliness of it, the sort of thing that "Grandmother's Trout" did to Florence and Pete and the rest, the sort of thing I caught in "Easter on the Prairie," that is what counts, that is what you must elaborate, work on that to the exclusion of all else and sooner or later you will crash. That will not be work, that will be the creation of beauty.

Sigurd at the Border Lakes company store, early 1940s. Photograph by Wallace Kirkland, Wisconsin Historical Society Collection, 74077.

October 30, 1939

What you want to do of course is paint with words, color your experiences in the belief that the way you see things is important enough to thrill the world. That pheasant hunting trip of two weeks ago might do it, the morning, the birds, the rustle of wind in the corn, mallards, dogs and cattle. Whatever you write must bring out that certain something—the deep feeling, a certain thrill, a surge of genuine emotion for doing a certain thing. No story or article is worth its salt to me unless it embodies this high emotional factor. I am not only an entertainer. I am more than that, I am an artist, a dealer in emotional effects. "Grandmother's Trout" is a type of what I mean, the sort of thing that brought tears to the eyes of Florence and hard-boiled Pete. To actually read a magazine story that will do that to you is a remarkable experience. Somehow, someway I should be able to work that sort of thing into a form that is worthwhile.

November 8, 1939

Nothing is more damning to a man's soul than to put in day after day of what he considers sheer idleness, even though he might spend the day on busy work, chasing here and there, doing any one of the thousands of little things that most people would think as work. That to me however is violating one of the first essentials of happiness, that is putting in your day doing something useful and to you constructive....

Contrast that with the feeling of being on my own, of working away every morning on some writing or other. Think of the difference there would be in my leisure if there was any, of the way I would feel after having done a decent piece of work.

It won't all be short stories. After I finish a bit for one of the magazines, I can work away on some of the types of things I did last year, then work away at a book or two and then perhaps on the stories Lib wants me to write.

Anyone seeing me here would think I was insane to think of shifting from the security I have now to something entirely different and insecure, but if they could see my state of mind, if they could see that no matter how secure this seems, no matter how easy that it is driving me swiftly insane, they would feel that I was justified.

November 15, 1939

Today I am strangely happy and fit again — why simply because yesterday I spent the afternoon out of doors over in the Camp Four Creek country calling mallards and more because last night I wrote for several hours. It never fails. I should know that there is no use trying to hold it off. I must write for peace of mind. Once I start then I am all right. Tonight I am going to do it again. It seems to provide its own fuel as I work along.

November 24, 1939

The best part of my little jaunt into fiction is that it opens up an almost limitless field for me. As long as I stayed with the idea of articles and essays, I was in the doldrums, no way out, not a chance of making any money. With working on "The Girl in Red Flannels" I find that it is not too difficult, that there is infinitely more where that came from. The balance of this winter, I am going to work along those lines and I have a feeling that something is going to come of it. I have more confidence now, more of the feeling that I know what it is all about than I had before.

December 13, 1939

The only part of writing that I really like is the first draft where you are really getting your ideas down. After that the endless polishing and revision is just plain back-breaking work. Occasionally when a new idea slips through it is fun again, but mostly just work.

January 19, 1940

Reading "Grapes of Wrath" — one thought stayed with me — the picture of the toughness & brownness of men who work out of doors — the soft pot-bellied men and their soft women — the softness of everyone who does not work out of doors — who is not toughened by the elements — whose hands are soft, whose spirits are softer — The reason that appealed to me was that it struck home — it is what I am fighting all of the time — Why do I crave the sun — it covers with a tan the pallor of my days inside — to toughen the muscles from soft long days at a desk.

It seems any sort of a release will do the trick — If I could get some sort of a sign this winter — any sort of encouragement whatever — that is enough, for if I can do it once I can do it again. That is why it is so important to finish "Grandmother's Trout," show that I can change those essays around & make fiction out of them. I see now where I made a horrible mistake, see now where there wasn't a chance of getting anywhere with them in the form they were — As fiction it might be entirely different but I'll have to keep the suspense at a high pitch — will have to keep my reader guessing until the end & not permit a lull or dead spot during the fishing — it will take clever work — the big thing — the excitement & adventure of a little boy going off alone for the first time — actually seeing things anew — losing his way — The climax when he finally sees the light in the kitchen window — finds Grandmother waiting and the feast — 80 etc — Action & suspense all the way through — not a dull or slow moment — this is not an essay — This is fiction —

January 25, 1940[13]

At times like this when nothing seems to come easily, I might just as well forget it and not despair. There will come times when it will again flow easily. Today is not one of them and I am letting it get me down. I can't even get a clear story idea and thoughts are clumsy and stiff. Any writing I might do would be of no value. I have been working too hard and steadily, have finished four stories since I began about the 1st of December. Here it is the last of January, which averages about one every ten days completed which is not too bad.

January 29, 1940

Now again on the verge of a break — resigning from my old pit here — taking a crack at my writing — hoping it will be enough. In the meantime hoping I am not jeopardizing the future for them all, Bob & Jr. — Nearing school and getting started[14] — no one worried about me — no one helped me very much. —

"You haven't any guts — afraid to make the break" — trying to shame me into taking a chance.

What gets her down is the constant feeling of impermanence — unhappiness — discontent that is mine. If I could get away from that, I believe E would be perfectly happy & willing to undergo any hardship. Well if it is all as easy as that why hesitate any longer.

February 5, 1940

It came—both mss back from Don and Elmo and with most scathing criticisms. Somehow I had the feeling that this time I had crashed the gates, was not quite prepared for what awaited me, but now it feels like the end of everything. What concerns me is that I see no chance of dropping out of the picture here this year, no possible chance of breaking loose from the treadmill ever. When I think of staying, I get panicky, realize that all that has kept me going is that I thought I might leave. It is like being in prison and waiting for the day and then having it come and find your reprieve postponed for a year. Hope is gone, gladness, everything. At this point, I would like to drown it all and go off on a bender for a month. Here I am forty, twenty years of trying and then failure.

Now if I quit forever, then what shall I do, give up the idea of writing entirely, never write another line — cross off the list all aspirations — all hopes for happiness — all dreams of the past years, the formulas of Burroughs and Thoreau — of Hubbard and Lin Yutang. All that was for nothing and <u>now I see myself a shell of the thing</u> the world had hoped for — <u>man of the wilds, writer of outdoor subjects, outdoor stories</u> — <u>lecturer sought after by clubs and organizations, the interpreter of wilderness.</u>

Don intimates that fiction is not for me—certainly not funny stuff, the serious side bringing in my love of the wilds, the woods, the lore at my finger tips, that is me, nothing else, or is it the picture that he has built up in his mind for me.

Maybe I am insane trying to do this sort of thing—"Grandmother's Trout," "the Pines," "Northwest Corner," but such a limited theme. I can write outdoor stuff, but that isn't enough, I must do the other and I believe I can if I have the time to put on it.

February 7, 1940

Don's reply took the wind out of my sails more than any rebuff I've ever had — My short stories have to be accounts of people in action — their reactions above all else — no description — no reflection — nothing that will detract in the slightest from the end in view — the climax with Gloria etc. My stuff is too light — it doesn't ring true — isn't worth a damn — "a million miles from fiction" that hurt.

Even Ann Elmo says she likes the original "Grandmother's Trout" better than the revision — this sounds forced, padded —

Well the question is again — What is my medium — Perhaps it is not fiction at all — perhaps it is something else entirely — You are not interested in blood & thunder stuff — in the ramifications of love & intrigue — you want something more, something that is akin to poetry — your interpretation of the country and the way you feel about the woods and streams — perhaps you are off on the wrong track entirely with fiction.

Undated, February 1940

Sam Campbell says that someday I will find the medium and the way to express the fine things that are constantly seeking expression in me, that I mustn't let the world make me commonplace, that I must keep on seeking and trying and sooner or later it will come.[15]

What I have tried to do the past two months is to descend to common ordinary fiction. I thought once that I wouldn't want Sam to see that I was writing stuff like that, that it would detract from the effect I wished to give, "Gloria's Red Flannels" would strike a harsh note, so would Beaverwood Inc. and after they were all through, I would have no deep satisfaction, nothing that really meant a thing.

I must keep up the search for the proper way of bringing it out. If I can do it in speaking, then I can do it in writing too. One thing that will never lead to lecturing is being able to write ordinary fiction — Don would never get a bid on the strength of his stuff, but an interesting character with a philosophy of his own would — and that is where I am different than Don. He can write fiction, he can weave a clever tale, but I have depths of feeling and understanding of natural things that he can never hope to touch. I am a poet, a philosopher, and as such must paint the world as I see it, not as a fictioneer. In other words, I am not a writer of fiction — to be one I think would cheapen me to a certain extent — it would certainly make a different man out of me than Sam Campbell envisages. What does he feel, what would Ober feel, what would my audiences feel, they want to get my feeling about the woods. As Bob says, I have reached the ability of making others go with me, feel what I feel and have done it with words.[16] Well that is something. Perhaps I had better concentrate on my hunting and fishing yarns, not a recitation of events but in that telling of events bring in the way I feel about things.

In everything you write, remember that you are telling what you feel, that what you feel the world is hungry for, that you are a poet, a sage, a prophet, not a teller of funny stories. You are the spiritual incarnation of Thoreau, Burroughs, Muir, and thousands and millions of sportsmen anxiously await your stuff every month. Short beautiful pieces covering my reactions on many things — eventually books — eventually peace of mind and soul — that would be being true to yourself and striving for the highest — that I think is what I must do. "Grandmother's Trout" was a start, "The Pines," "Northwest Corner," "Saganaga" — and the others — perhaps there must be a different approach, I do not know, but I must keep on working and eventually it will come, if I know where I am going.

Perhaps it will be such things as "Saganaga," trout fishing, "Grandmother's Trout," "Easter on the Prairie," "The Pines"—short flashes of beauty which I will give the world, highlights, things so beautiful that to read them brings tears. I did that with "Grandmother's Trout" and "Easter"—if I can do it once, I can again. Things so breathtakingly beautiful, that no one in the world can ever imitate them. That is perfection — that is what I want to do.

As Florence says, "you are different, you have more beautiful thoughts and experiences than most people."

February 7, 1940

Perhaps there is nothing that I can do. Perhaps it is just a wild dream. This I do know, that I can speak and hold an audience. I shall not speak on adventures but rather on spiritual experiences, the meaning of getting out. It gets back to the old premise that runs through all of my diaries, my reaction to the woods, my feelings about things, my slant on life, the world as seen through my experience and background. That is what the world wants to see. It doesn't want to be entertained, it wants something deeper than that.

Perhaps I have it in my outdoor stuff — in other words when you write an outdoor story in the future, it will not be how I shot a thousand ducks but rather what such an experience does to me, what ice fishing does to me, what a walk down the Lucky Boy does to me. I am egotistical enough to feel that my slant is different, my slant worth something.

Perhaps that is your best approach, write a different outdoor story entirely than the rank and file could do, write your book, write any stuff that will appeal to the outdoorsman. Develop something of your own. Your "Last Mallard" may have been a start. "Shift of the Wind" another and "Gold in Them Hills" a third.[17] They are different. Well, work along that vein and perhaps you will get somewhere. In other words do the thing you know and make them so startlingly beautiful, that there is no chance of their going wrong. You have enough outdoor mags around to work with if you can continually produce.

Lay off fiction — these are real experiences and there are many many others, weaving into them a thread of philosophy that all the others lack. Perhaps this is the answer. At least I can do that easily and well. There is my chance to say what I want, to create the atmosphere of the swamp and woods which fiction never allows.

February 7, 1940

E says that the boys are worried about me, wishes I could be happier than I am, that it isn't fair to them, that there should be more laughter and good feeling around. She is right, but I do not seem to be able to help myself. Each day seems impossible to live through. I wake in the morning wishing I could die and I know it is ridiculous in the extreme. I have reached such an impasse that I know no matter what the odds, I cannot go on another year. It is impossible. As long as I was teaching and could get interested in my lab work it was not so bad, but cut off even from that and immersed in problems that do not interest in the slightest is what is driving me mad. Little problems seem to get me down, problems that should be ridden over with no trouble at all. The annual,[18] teaching of zoo and botany, gym work, activities, assemblies, I force myself to take care of them and the Boy Scouts and the Izaak Walton League — they have pyramided until I see no way out whatever. Next year if I have the courage, there will be an end to all of that, and never again will I become entangled, not in this life.[19]

February 22, 1940

I told Elizabeth last night that I could not go on another year, that I did not see how I could last through the next three months, and she answered that she had already resigned herself to that, that she was confident that I would go to town with my writing, that I wrote well and that all I needed was time to roam around, get outdoors, that ideas would then come to me and that I would speedily make some good sales.

That was the first encouragement I have really gotten from her and for once it really warmed me. I did not know how necessary that faith and encouragement was to my peace of mind and resolve. Queer how the thing has finally come to a head. I have reached the point where I can not possibly go on, where any alternative is better than this, where it is absolutely necessary that I make a change. It is no longer a case of whether it is the wise thing to do. Now there is no choice for I know that nothing can ever change the present situation, that I shall always be unhappy and increasingly so, that time will not help, nor that I will ever develop any enthusiasm.

This morning — a pit in the center of my stomach, more like vomiting than going to breakfast, forcing down the food, trying to smile and be cheerful, gritting my teeth and going off to work. It can not last without something breaking.

Imagine on a morning like this, going off on a snowshoe jaunt or skiing, sitting down peacefully to my typewriter and working happily for several hours, working and thinking about only one thing. I hope soon that I shall be able to sing and play, again able to enjoy the world about me.

Elizabeth fishing with the boys, 1930s. Wisconsin Historical Society Collection, 74089.

February 23, 1940

The reason for my inner turmoil at this time is twofold. First, because I have not been doing any writing since the first of the month which always has its repercussions in state of mind, and second, because of the desperate plight of the Finns.[20] How I would like to be over there with them fighting. Nothing seems worthwhile beside that. All other activity, writing, painting of pictures, scribbling, worrying about my job, the house or vacations or the Border Lakes, all of it seems puerile compared to the odds they are fighting against. It makes one think that after all, after all the froth has been stripped away, that only one thing is worthwhile, the ability of a people to live in peace and happiness.

Any little troubles I have are insignificant alongside of that, writing of funny little stories, or even serious little stories telling of a man's love of the earth and the wilderness, seem foolish when men are dying and suffering, giving their all, when women and children are being bombed. The only important thing at all is the maintenance of the kind of civilization that we think is worthwhile.

Big Brother's
Big Idea

February–December 1940

A S 1940 GOT UNDERWAY, Sigurd continued to struggle over the kind of writing that would work best for him. "I know now that the finding of my medium is the most important thing in life to me," he wrote on May 15, "more important than my job, comforts, travel, money, I almost said friends and family." His big break finally came shortly before Labor Day. His brother Kenneth came to Ely for a visit and urged Sigurd to consider trying to become a syndicated newspaper columnist. That would allow him to write the short sketches he was most comfortable with, mixing natural history with philosophy and human emotion. On September 2, relieved and enthused, Sigurd wrote, "After fifteen years of searching for my medium, I feel at last that it is close."

Much of the content of this chapter relates Sigurd's prodigious work of preparing a large set of sample columns to choose from and send to prospective syndicates. By Christmas he had a stockpile of more than a hundred. Having put so much work into it, he was excited but also worried about whether it would all be for nothing. And those fears only grew when his big brother was slow in responding to the sample Sigurd sent for feedback. Still, at the end of the year Sigurd felt he had found his niche.

Camping at Basswood Lake, 1947. Photograph by Ray Gordon, Minnesota Historical Society Collection.

* * * *

February 24, 1940

Last night coming back from my walk, thinking over the eternal problem of medium, I thought of the advice of the sages, "Write only what you cannot help but write, what comes easily, what pours from your inner self with an unceasing flood. Pay no attention to technique, or form. That will take care of itself and is of no concern when you are writing from the heart. Keep true only to what you sincerely have to say. The world will beat a pathway to your door if you have something worthwhile saying."...

Well what do I write easily—just the sort of thing I am writing this morning, the sort of thing I write every morning when I am at school. Those little pages run from me as easily as breathing—but are they things the world is hungry for. That is the question, are they only the searchings of my own mind for the solution to my personal question.

In other words, the field of philosophy is much more important than short stories. To give my slant on life, to give my impressions, give the way things appear to me alone, my own particular, individual slant, how I feel and what I think about when I am out, short 1000 word essays perhaps woven through and through with thoughts that come to me as I walk or hunt or fish. Have them alive enough and good enough so that when I sit down, the magazines and the newspapers will take every word I write. Perhaps syndicate will answer my question, perhaps a series in some outdoor magazine, like *Field and Stream* or *Sports Afield*, perhaps well illustrated short articles in the women's magazines, perhaps the *Atlantic* and others. Write on a variety of subjects, on everything that you do or see.

It also came to me that it did not make much difference if I kept on with my job, if I could only find my medium, if I could only feel that I was getting toward the goal that I have been searching for, so far aimlessly. To know that would make all else worthwhile. Then I would know. It is more important that I find that, than anything else in the world right now. The thing to do is to try your hand at the type of thing you have in mind. "Easter on the Prairie," parts at least had some of it, "Grandmother's Trout," some, "The Pines" some, and "Northwest Corner," but that isn't the answer as yet. "Fireside Pictures" had also a touch of it.[1] In other words, I have started and in my groping I have begun to come close, but still do not have the answer.

To someday make a booklet, <u>a small book, leather bound, that men on a wilderness canoe trip would want to take with them to read around the campfire at night, that duck hunters would want to read when they came back from the hills to the cabin at the end of a November day, that trout fishermen would want to read and carry with them to pore over at noon on some favorite stream. That my boy is an ideal</u>. If you can work up into that sort of thing, then you have gone far beyond the realm of the short story, then you have gone way and beyond what pure fiction might ever hold for you.

I think there is a need for this sort of thing. I personally would want such a small book, I would like to have it as a gift for Christmas or my birthday, something that I would think of as precious, a real man's philosophy of the wilds and the out of doors. Then after that would come lecture engagements and a spreading of my philosophy. Then would come the recognition that I had hoped for, but more important than all of that would be the fact that I had done something worthwhile, that I had endeared my philosophy to the clan I know, the sportsmen of America. That is the recognition I want.

I do not want to write the pretty type of thing Scoville or Sass would write, none of the "see the pretty bird" type of thing, none of the pretty spring flowers stuff, but rather, bring out a stronger, more masculine philosophy of the out of doors that will strike a kindred feeling in the hearts of all men and do away with the prissy, Audubon Society, garden clubs of America sort of thing. Not that I do not cherish the work they are doing, but I want something else, something so worthwhile that there can be no mistake, that the demand will grow and so that my eternal question may be answered at last.

I must before the spring completely snows me under begin work and do something worthwhile. A series of short articles, so different and so appealing that men will want to read them. The thing to do is make them different from anything that has ever been written. Call one of them "Quetico Days," another "Mallards of the Storm" and another "Trout Streams of the Earth" or just "Trout Streams" — Portages — Rapids, etc. The ideas will come to me, the important thing is to get started on something, something that will strike the note. Another on Wilderness.

Make it about 1000 or 1500 words and something that will strike a kindred note, not an account of any particular hunting or fishing or camping. The outdoor magazines are full of that sort of thing, but rather a philosophy that runs through even an ordinary yarn and so beautifully and simply written that there is no possible chance of its failure.

February 26, 1940

Yesterday while hiking over the Mitchell Lake route — I had a vision — a vision of a booklet for hunters & fishermen — a book they would want to carry with them — leather bound, beautiful — a composite of sketches — 1000-1500 words of experiences of mine — call it "Flashes of the Trail" — "Fireside Pictures" — "Masterpieces" — ...

Write for yourself — something you would want to read — sincerity — genuineness — Only that is worthwhile. Write what comes easily, naturally for you. Write for Fuzzy — Bill Rom[2] — Doc Knowles[3] — Fred — Ober — Bob Mueller — Kermit Wick.

In other words — if you are vivid enough — if your reaction is good enough, that is all you need. The question is — are your reactions good enough & vivid enough —

Bill Rom, Sigurd's former student at Ely Junior College and founder of Canoe Country Outfitters, 1940s. Rom Family Collection. Courtesy of Rebecca Rom.

Write so that a man can pick up the book — turn a page anywhere and find himself for ten minutes transported to the Northwoods — the Manitou River — a blind in Wind Bay — a fisherman on Basswood — a summer camp in the Quetico — a ride with a Canadian ranger on the border — "Flashes" —

Nothing like it has ever been done — It is worth trying & it might work up into something pretty good —

April 2, 1940

Success Formula — "Doing what you can do best as well as you are able." Dorothea Brande

The above formula might well be amended to read, "Doing what you can do best and like to do best and would rather do best than anything else, as well as you are able to do it."

The question with me is whether or not I have been barking up the wrong tree. Is writing nature stuff and interpreting it what I can do best. Is that what I should be working toward. Surely it is shown by now that what I can do best is not writing fiction, not making the regular magazines. I simply cannot do that best. The definition of best is a difficult one. She does not mean that, she means the thing you want to do and would give your life to do.

What can I do best to date — I can teach well — my students like me — I cannot carry on research however and cannot do that best.

I can run an outfitting station and I can guide and I can make people enthusiastic about the woods on field trips and on guiding trips. I am a good guide, can do that well, in fact very well.

I am also a good speaker and can do that well and when I get a chance I always do the best I am able to do.

Looking at me—Sig Olson—as an outsider or a friend or even a stranger might, what is the answer to the question, "What can he do best?" Is it counseling students, talking to students, getting their sympathy and love, is it running around the woods and then writing about them — is it conducting a zoology class or a botany class or a field trip — yes I am good at it, but isn't there anything else I can do better. On field trips it was always the same, I never could get the feeling that I wasn't just playing around doing nothing worthwhile.

"Doing what you can do best, as well as you are able."

I am a pretty good writer and am just coming into my own — is that what I can now do best. I can certainly string words together. I like bumming around the woods and coming back to write about them.

Would I be happy, passing up my contacts with students, wouldn't I miss the companionship and the joy they give me. Wouldn't I be happier teaching or would the old lecture and the days indoors drive me mad as they used to. Could I forget my wanting to write?

"The Rugged Four," 1926: Sigurd (*second from left*) with Dr. James Burrill, Dr. Sidney J. Knowles, and Ray Allen. Wisconsin Historical Society Collection, 74080.

April 9, 1940

These days are in the doldrums. Last night taking my walk, I tried to unravel the old problem, wondering what medium would be the best, but the solution seems as far away as ever. The essay, the short story, the outdoor story, they all seem the wrong answer. I might as well decide as I decided some time ago that the answer is to write everything, that sooner or later something will pop that is good, that among much dross there will be some gold, that writing something every day is the answer.

The reason for my slump now is that I have not written for some time....

To describe a beautiful scene, Lac La Croix in the moonlight or the sunset, the winding channels of Crooked Lake in the morning with the light upon the pines, a swamp or a marsh in the evening with the ducks coming in, that is nothing, not worthwhile to put one's time upon, unless—and here is the secret of success—unless one can embody in one's writing the portrayal of some emotion distinctly one's own.

April 29, 1940

The important things in life are the emotions, the eternal ability to appreciate things, imagination, the inner things, not scientific achievement, not the outward things of show, the material. The occasional glimpses we have of sheer beauty, of ecstasy, are peeps we have under the veil. They are peeps into eternity. I have known them at times, on Sarah Lake in the moonlight, on Robinson Peak, overlooking Mud Lake Bog, and other times on the Lucky Boy Trail. Those things are real, and here is reality itself. I have often wondered what it was I wanted out of life and now I see what it is, the chance to interpret those moments of insight, those flashes into the real things of life, those high spots of living. No amount of material comfort or success will ever mean anything to me. Only this, that I satisfy repeatedly the urge to see and feel.

Today, I have been happy, for no particular reason perhaps, except that I am beginning to see my way out of the morass. Once I make the break, I will begin to live and once I begin to live, my writing will work out all right. My days up at school are wasted, a dead loss. It is only when I am out here and on my own that I feel I am really living. If I resign and pay for the house and have that worry out of the way and the car and some additional insurance, we will make enough off the Border Lakes and my writing to get along and I know that soon will come enough success so that I will make ends meet. That cannot help but come with the time to work and live as I will.

Think of writing every day, of being on Basswood for a week or two in the fall, of writing steadily and hunting and fishing and working the way I wish. Think of living out of doors all I want, of using my body until I am tired, of not being cluttered with details which mean nothing to me, no speeches, no reports, no antagonisms, only my writing. The future looks happy and secure and adventurous. No I don't want to write hunting and fishing stuff, that is merely the mark of the amateur, I don't want to build a great resort and make a lot of money or discover a gold mine or do any of the things that other men want to do. All I want to do is write and work out of doors at the things I feel will give me inspiration. My years here have not been lost for now my work really begins. I am just in the prime and have at least twenty to thirty good years ahead of me, the best quarter of a century. I could not have written sooner, because I did not know what it was I wanted to do for sure. I know now and that is everything.

I am still young and full of life and enthusiasm and my insight is deeper and better than ever. In ten years if I keep on, I will really have my feet on the ground and know that I have done the right thing. I would rather work here than anywhere I know and if I can make the arrangements to get along, then it is simple. Tonight I am fairly happy and serene.

April 30, 1940

If the world of emotion and feeling and sentiment is the real life, the inner life, the love life, all that is worthwhile, then dealing with those things, trying to picture them, give the world your interpretation of them is a worthwhile objective. And that is exactly what I shall be doing through my writing. That to me is real and worthwhile, more so than anything else that I might do.

It will not be hunting and fishing stuff, except as a medium, or stories except as a medium. Through it all will be an attempt to give the world some of my experience of life as seen through my eyes. Florence told me once that I was different, that I had more beautiful thoughts than the rest. Well, it is those thoughts that are worthwhile and which will someday amount to something, that will someday be the basis of stories.

The narrows at Sarah Lake, Quetico Provincial Park, 1948. Photograph by Leland J. Prater, U.S. Forest Service Records, National Archives.

I have contacts now, Ann Elmo, Don Hough, Fierst, Uzzell, enough so that I can make the grade once I begin to produce and I am confident that with enough time to put in that there will be no question of making something worthwhile. Even though I haven't done anything this winter in the way of sales I have more confidence than before, feel that if I had the time, I could really go to town.

"You have that inner flame" — the fifth time it's happened. It means that there is something unusual that others recognize and that someday will be worth something.

Right in this connection, in writing of the hunting or fishing, it is how a man feels about things, not the ducks or the fish he took. In writing about farming, it is not the crops that count, the heads of cattle, but how a man feels about these things he has produced. It is not the gold that counts but the hunting and finding of it. It is not the material gain of anything a man might do, but the spiritual gain that is really worthwhile and real.

"What does it profit a man if he gain the whole world and loses his soul." There it is again in a nutshell. Paradise is within us, each man has the making of happiness within himself. To try and find it anywhere else is hopeless.

Burroughs said it — "Wherever a man goes, his old self camps or walks with him." We never escape ourselves.

May 1, 1940

As I take over a zoology class, I realize that it is all over, that I can never do much in the way of teaching because I know nothing about my subject and am not particularly interested. Look at the exhibit material, the collections, the paucity of stuff after twenty years in the department. That is due to lack of enthusiasm and the pigeon-holing of my interest in other channels.

Tonight I make two speeches to the Rotary and the Legion Auxiliary, both of which make today a case of nerves. These days are entirely too much cases of nerves. I am nervous all of the time, come to work as I have for ten years or so, upset and miserable. If this is life, then I am missing much joy....

Surely, I will make something off my writing. If I sold one story for $200.00 that is $20.00 per month. I can do that much on outdoor stuff alone. Field and Stream will pay close to $100.00, so will Outdoors and Sports Afield. They should if I sell them one story each give me the $200.00 or $250 for $25.00 per month. That is the minimum, surely I can crash some of the others. If I hit the Post with one, it will mean $500.00 or $50.00 per month which will settle all troubles. This is sure, unless I see my way clear there will never be any writing. Think of having nothing to do but write, what satisfaction there will be and how different my days will be. I will learn to sing again, will sleep out of doors, hike and paddle and cruise around, do a million things that now I am divorced from entirely. Life will begin all over again and I shall be a new person and have a new outlook. Only one great if, how about the war, will everything go crash, will there be no sale for stories or books, will the market for everything drop out of sight. Of course, if that happens there will be no market for anything and the whole economic system will go haywire and we will also be in the same boat.

May 2, 1940

Last night two speeches and successful ones judging by the response of my audience, proving to me again that I can talk and sway listeners. Made me realize that my real talent is along those lines, that I cannot tell stories or amuse any more than I can write fiction or amuse in that way. That my long suit is serious articles of the essay type similar to what I can do best when I speak.

If I can write as I speak, then I have something. The words come easily and fluidly, all I have to do is start and they come. Writing should be as easy as that and always at the end have a clear thought, a conclusion. That is what counts. In planning an article, you should go at it as painstakingly as planning a speech. One or two or at most three main ideas, each one dovetailing into the other and finally a clear, crystal clear idea, leaving your hearers with one thought, one impression. Yesterday, I thought a long time until I found what I wanted to bring out. Finally when the idea was clear, then there was nothing to it and that is why it was successful.

E says she <u>does not think I can write fiction of any</u> kind and I almost think she is right. It is <u>the essay, the serious article that will count</u>, which will lay the foundation for any speaking I might do. <u>I will never be in demand as a writer of short stories</u>. The world is full of short story and fiction writers and they have no appeal....

But the world <u>would welcome anyone who had a new and stimulating philosophy of life, a brilliant essayist</u>, one <u>who had a fresh view of living and life and the world at large</u>. That is what will be mine if I can make things go, that is the only way out. Fiction means a living, but the essay, the serious article, <u>possibly the syndicate</u>, will be the real answer.[4]

May 2, 1940

Character sketches do not appeal, because I do not understand or care to understand others. I am so egotistical that I care only for my own reactions. <u>I am a harp on whose sensitive strings the winds of the world blow and my task is to set to music the strains I alone can hear</u>. I must give ear forever to celestial music — each day when I go abroad, I must look for it, try and catch the strange something. This will <u>of necessity be essays or short sketches of things I do and see</u>, <u>the thoughts that are mine</u> in the <u>doing & seeing</u> —

May 7, 1940

"Don't let yourself be so tortured, don't allow all of these things to hurt you. You have a beautiful mind and I hope that someday you will let it go and do the things you know you can do."

And so it goes, they all believe in me, feel that I can do something worthwhile if I have the chance. These weeks are nightmares, more details than I can possibly handle, one thing right after another until I wonder if I can bear up. To think of writing now would be absolute folly. There is no time for anything except just getting the routine work out of the way....

The days go on and I have no chance of doing any writing. I am too busy to really think very much about it, but this I know, that if I ever am to accomplish very much, I must divorce myself from all of this activity, all of this running around and concentrate on what I really need to do. There is no chance, no matter if I cut out the Border Lakes Co. The year or ten months of it would be as full of stuff as ever. Only by cutting all of these ties can I find time or leisure enough to go ahead. It is days and nights. Sunday afternoon, sitting visiting, how I hated it and how that rebellion made me realize that I wouldn't feel that way if I had plenty of time to myself to spend out of doors. That if I had my time to myself that there would be no question.

May 14, 1940

I do not have to interpret nature, that has been done, what I <u>want to interpret is how I feel about nature</u>, my reflections on life in general, using my knowledge of the out of doors as atmosphere and background. There is where I think best, there is where I am at home and contented. My frequent sojourns into the wilds are necessary for my equilibrium and to give me perspective....

It is <u>not description</u> or <u>painting of word pictures</u>. They are merely <u>incidental</u>. It is <u>not action</u>, <u>the catching of fish</u>, the <u>running of rapids</u>, the <u>shooting of game</u>, or <u>the torture of portages</u> and <u>work on the trails</u>. Rather <u>it is what these things mean to you personally</u> or to others that counts. Right in this category, I am mindful of what Burroughs finally discovered, that it is not scenery unless it has human emotion tied up with it, not any action unless it has meaning. He described too many birds and scenes to suit me.

Unloading canoes at Basswood Lake, 1940. Photograph by Leland J. Prater, U.S. Forest Service Records, National Archives.

May 15, 1940

Just glancing over Stewart Edward White's new book, "Flying Geese" or something like that and I knew again that I could never write a book like that, would never want to.[5] I know nothing of primitive urges, the quest of a man for new frontiers, the battle with the soil, primitive men and primitive women, all I know is the poetic, the higher feelings, the interpretation of beauty, philosophy, things that Sally and John were strangers to except in rare instances. Reading such a book makes me feel strangely ineffective, as though I could never do the thing that I was supposed to do, but then when I think it over, I know that he could never do what I want to do, either. He is the typical outdoor writer of yarns of the big timber, exploration, frontiers, Alaska. Mine is more than that, mine the feelings of Thoreau, Burroughs, Muir, Emerson, Walt Whitman. Mine are deeper, subtler feelings and at night I go to sleep wondering what shape they will take. In the mornings I wake wondering if this day will give me the solution. I <u>know now that the finding of my medium is the most important thing in life to me</u>, more important than my job, comforts, travel, money, I almost said friends and family. I sometimes wonder if it will take all of my life, if I shall ever discover what it really is.

Last night, I felt that if I only had time to think things out, if I could only be quiet and reflective, if I could only think clearly and see the problem through. Life is so hurried and harassed with a thousand things that I never have time. Coming down the lakes the other day, I knew that here was a time of hours when nothing could disturb me, looking down the long blue misty reaches of Knife and Moose and Newfound, the diamond studded water, the many islands the cliffs, fleecy clouds and all I could think of was how beautiful it all was, and what a grand thing it was to be there seeing it. No room for philosophy or introspection, merely time for living it and breathing it.

That is usually the way with me, when I am out, I can see nothing, think of nothing, feel nothing but what is around me. It is when I return that my ideas come. On long walks, I think little out, things soak into me and then on my return they come to life and sometimes I capture them. What should I write, will be my own feelings about everything, not only the out of doors but life in general, using my beloved outdoors as a backdrop, with never an attempt to commercialize it at all.

The thought occurred to me that if I could only look at the lakes and canoe travel as pure recreation, not as material, not as grist in my mill, not as a means to an end, but simply something as necessary as air to my well being, that I could enjoy it more. If I could feel that a picnic supper on a rock overlooking the lake was the most important thing in life, give way to all of its beauty, give myself over to its enjoyment without restraint, then it would be so much more worthwhile. It is when I try and study it, make it cash in on my ability to portray, that I begin to lose. In other words, one cannot find what one is looking for unless one forgets the search. What is worthwhile comes when least expected and when unsought for.

To get the most out of the woods, out of trout fishing, out of any outdoor experience, I must be absolutely unconscious of any effect. In the back of the mind must be no sought-for objective, no plan, no idea except enjoyment. Is this not also true for anything, looking at pictures, work, music, friendships, anything we might name. To get the most out of any experience, we must be unconscious of any desired result no matter how subtle or remote. The result must come, and it will come.

May 27, 1940

Last night Elizabeth and Bob trying to figure me out. Both of them trying to help me reach my objective. Bob is so sweet and E so desperately anxious and I knowing as the rest of them know that sooner or later I must make the break and try to fulfill my destiny.

I know now that part of that destiny is speaking to audiences. I can do that and I like to do that. I do have a talent there without question. I can plead a cause if I believe in it, if it has to do with wilderness or the land or streams or the sun and wind. That I can do better than most. Emotional reactions are my meat and drink and transmitting them to others....

James Hilton — last night telling of a moment of transcendent beauty which came to him on a mountain top, as it came to me on Robinson Peak and on the hills overlooking Mud Lake.[6] For a moment, he was supremely happy and it wasn't the happiness of success or wealth or anything else, he was just happy and contented. I know that so well, because it shows that happiness is fleeting, comes quickly and goes and does not depend on material possessions at all, certainly not directly. Happiness comes from a certain realization that things are right, that for the moment everything is right. Happiness is made up of little things, everyday things, not the big long looked-for things.

Sigurd (*left*) on Robinson Peak, Quetico Provincial Park, 1948. Wisconsin Historical Society Collection, 117099.

James Hilton thought he would be happy if he achieved success in his writing, but he admits at forty that he has never been any happier or successful than he was that day up looking over the Jungfrau and the peaks of the Swiss Alps. This all goes to show that we are happy at times, desperately happy and do not know it or cannot pin it down, that we should strive to increase those moments, capture them, make the most of them, not look forward continually to the big things. In other words every day there should be some moment when this might come to you, the smell of food, the glance of sunlight on a leaf, the wet pavement, the sound of chimes, the smile of a girl, a look of recognition, sympathy, the joy of a bulb coming through the ground, bird songs, the glint of sunlight on a swallow's breast, a thousand things which we pass up each day. Those are the things that are worthwhile, they are the essence of happiness, things that we pass up, because we are absorbed in other things. If each day we could be aware of one or two such things, take them for what they are worth and pin them down as unforgettable moments, would it not make in the end our whole lives happier and more successful?

If that is the secret carried on over a long period, it should be possible to change a man's entire outlook on life. We look over the horizons, forget to look at home. Happiness is about us, within us, everywhere we look, if we have eyes to see and ears to hear. Happiness or the source thereof, of course, is always within. Without the ability to analyze or appreciate, or to make one's mind still and receptive, there is no happiness or possibility of it.

June 5, 1940

The year is about over, that is the shouting and I am both sad and glad. Today is the big picnic out to Halfway, tomorrow commencement and then on Friday goodbyes.

I sometimes wonder seriously if it will be the last windup for me. If this war hadn't come along, I think it would be, but now one can't tell what to plan on.

September 2, 1940

After fifteen years of searching for my medium, I feel at last that it is close. For the past ten years, I have been probing my mind, searching, lying awake nights trying to find out what it would be, trying fiction, outdoor articles, rather sentimental stuff from the past, trying desperately to sell and getting nowhere and more and more discouraged and hopeless. It took Ken's visit of this weekend to crack the problem and now it all seems so simple. For years, I had the dream of hiking around and then coming home to pound off my thoughts, my reactions to things, hoping that I would be able to give my interpretation of things out of doors a new and original slant. That is what I wanted to do but in stories it was impossible — in the ordinary article, no more chance. I found out that I didn't have the fiction slant, that there was no money in articles, not enough to keep going, that hunting and fishing stuff palled, that there was no incentive to keep going. Periods of gloom and desperation came, when I felt that it was all over, that there wasn't a chance of getting anywhere.

Now Ken comes with an idea I have toyed with for some time but not seriously. Why not try for an outdoor column incorporating in it some of the philosophy and feeling that is yours alone, making it a different sort of column, not just a where-to-go, how-to-do-it sort of thing, but the type of article that the average sportsman might want to sit down for five minutes and enjoy, reactions on the out of doors, trees, rocks, vandalism, conservation, water, fish, almost anything that you might want to mention, making it from 500 to 1000 words, every one a gem of its own. What would you like to sit down and read, what about Fuzzy, Doc Knowles, Doc Bacon, Kynaston, Mueller, Sheldon Coleman, Gere Stoddard, Bob Watts, Ober, Fred, Ken Reid,[7] Walters and many others, including all the fellows who come up here.

This appeals to me more than any other. My audience will be larger, I will develop a bigger following, possibly work up more lecture opportunities than if I ever tried to work into the slick magazine group. There are 2000 newspapers in the field. If I could get the group in the middle west who know the north, you would have something. The stuff you would put out would be alive and fresh, nothing stuffy, stereotyped. You would be working all of the time, could work as you pleased, be living exactly the sort of a life you have always wanted to live, could write up your reactions as you see them — "The Pays Plat River" as a thought and the peace that was there as we drove by.

Every trip you make would give you material, every trip you ever made would be sources for additional work. Your whole lifetime would

be there waiting to be tapped — "The trips to Sister Bay for perch,"
Northwest Corner — The path through the woods and the coons, Jump
River — First Canoe Trip — The first Buck — Heine's Snowshoes —
Guiding, trout fishing — duck hunting, all in season — reminiscence
— make these little articles something so vivid, so touching, bringing in
with each one a little of your own philosophy and reaction.

This then looks like the answer to all of my questions, and the first
job is to get a dozen or so ready, perhaps 500 to 1000 words, shoot them
down to Ken, and get his reaction. Thoreau did not have this opportunity, neither did Burroughs, nor Muir, nor Emerson, but I have. Each day,
they came in and wrote their notes of the
day's happenings, jotted down in diary
form what they thought. They went into
their biographical volumes we know
today, but if there had been columns in
those days, what a chance might have
been theirs.

A thousand words—two single-
spaced pages—almost too much for the
real thing, too much to keep going. Make
it one single-spaced page or 500 words,
that is about all a man can do in a day or
for a daily column and keep up interest.
A man can rattle off a page in no time and
keep his interest supreme and without a
chance to flag. Make it longer and it gets
too much in the short story class — one

Sigurd's brother Kenneth Olson,
circa 1940. Courtesy of the West
Virginia and Regional History
Center, WVU Libraries.

page is a vivid flash, one single reminiscence, one high spot, one thought,
never more than one, never so long that it will drag in the slightest.

What will it be for a starter — write at white heat, while you are
fresh, while stuff is vivid, alive, pulsating, these are your thoughts, yours
alone, your own special ideas, each one enough of interest so that others
will want to hear them and enjoy them. Strike the proper keynote once
and you are set for life, no one can quite hit your slant or try and take
it away from you. This may be the answer and this winter you must
try and find out if it is. This appeals tremendously because I feel that
this is what I am suited for. I am not a character analyst, no plotter, no

fictioneer, my long suit is vivid flashes, high spots, reflection, introspection of a sort. I cannot concentrate my attention long enough to do
lengthy articles or stories. I seem suited only to this, the short flash, the
peek through the mist of the commonplace, the vision of the new, horizons, visions of immortality. Perhaps this is what I thought was my own
particular genius, and because one is in contact with the world daily,
perhaps this is enough.

September 2, 1940

In line with my recent decision, I plan on writing an article every day
from now on. By stealing half an hour or an hour sometime during the
day, it will be possible, and by the end of the month I will have something to choose from in addition to working away and getting used to
the idea.

Just what it will be I do not know as yet but evidently something
along the lines Ken and I discussed, some philosophical slant on what
you have been doing, something that will appeal to the common man,
the fisherman, the canoe man, the hunter, the man who loves to get out
and cruise around, if only in his dreams, the average man in every town
in the country, that is the market you must shoot at.

If I can do that sort of thing, then it will not seem so bad up here as
I will feel I have an objective, something definite to shoot at that will
occupy my spare time and give me the feeling that I am getting somewhere. One article a day instead of working around on stories and revising the things I tried to do last year will be entirely different. Now I
know where I am going, now I know that I have something definite to
shoot at.

The whole idea appeals to me and it seems to be right in line with
what I have been working toward all of these years. In the back of my
mind, I had hoped it would be possible to do this sort of thing, but had
not the slightest idea of how to go about it. Ken's suggestion of an outdoor column seems to be the logical answer to everything.

It will give me the chance to work in my own personal and individual reactions to things, will give me a chance to use my spare time, the
knowledge of everything I have ever done. In an hour before breakfast,
I might pound off something worthwhile, while I am fresh and uncluttered with ideas from school or the Border Lakes. During the year, if this

thing pans out, I will feel that I am doing something that is the expression of all the creative yearnings I have ever felt.

Well, now that that is settled and I have pinned down these ideas to paper, then the thing to do is to get under way with something definite. Don't worry too much about what it is going to be. Write about anything that may come. That will be the story later on so it might as well start right now.

September 6, 1940

For four days I have pounded off little sketches on a variety of subjects, from hunting and fishing to planting of trees and Finnish Baths, in each one bringing my thoughts about things. One might call the column "Sketch Book."

Finnish Bath — Stone Wall — The Planting — On Getting Close to Things — First Day of Duck Season — Last Day of Trout Season — On Flying from Basswood — Good Housekeeping in the Woods — a total of eight so far all of around 500 words, some 4000 words all told.

These sketches have been good practice so far, have given me a few ideas on how things will run, what they will be about, what I like to do. They are easy to do, in fact I pound them off so easily it is no work, which brings me to the old adage, write what you like to write, what you would write if only for fun, what you must write — be sincere, write only of what you know. This all ties into my old dream and if this is the kind of writing I will do ultimately, then I am satisfied. I think I could pound off one of these sketches every day for many many days or many years. It is surprising how easily they come and what a wealth of material there is. Everything I have ever done is at my beck and call. There is nothing that is not material and as Elsie Robinson says, the joy of a columnist's life is being able to share everyday experiences with others.[8]

I see that it is not going to be hunting and fishing stuff entirely, rather sketches of things I like to do, things I have thought about and done. Everything I have done in the past is of significance and I can write about most anything. Five hundred words is enough—long enough to hold interest, short enough to bear a single thought or two or three. No plot is necessary, no conscious planning or writing. These things are impromptu, unplanned and as natural as talking. They will give me a chance to express my philosophy and how I feel about things.

I have always been a philosopher, always one who thought about things and saw more meaning than the average. My years of jotting things down in the morning will now stand me in good stead.

This will appeal not only to the hunter and fisherman but to women and children, all those who have a feeling for the out of doors and natural things. It should have a name however that appeals, and that is my next problem.

> Why not call it "Sketch Book"
>
> "Philosopher's Corner"
>
> "Wilderness Note Book"
>
> "Outdoorsman's Note Book"
>
> Northwoods —
>
> "Northern Lights" by Sig Olson
>
> "Wilderness Jottings"
>
> "Wilderness Notes"
>
> Call of the Wild [added by hand]

September 7, 1940

Elizabeth thinks that my short sketches should not embody the word I, that I should make it in the third person, as impersonal as possible, that all the other columnists do it this way, that she tires of reading anyone who is continually talking of himself, of his own reactions. Perhaps she is right, but on the other hand this is not what I wish to do. If I ever hope to do anything along the lines of my dreaming, then it must be my personal reactions to things. Of course there is no question of how the idea will get across. It is your reactions and ideas no matter what the person.

The things I have done are different so far, not mere enumerations of events or things seen. I could describe a trip in the woods, talk about the chickadees, the nuthatches, the tracks of game, make it merely a running narrative account of the things I had seen which in itself would be unimportant unless I could inject in that some of philosophy and interpretation that was mine alone. The world is full of photographic recorders and the papers full of such columns. There is nothing so far in the way of complete sketches. Each one a masterpiece in itself, a complete little gem, a story which can stand alone — what I am working toward is a series of sketches embodying my personal reactions toward everything I see and do.

September 17, 1940

Last night for the first time I felt that I had hit my pace, had for a moment struck my medium, the medium that for years I have been looking for. Pounded off three short items all within the space limit — all rather of the essay type, all of them my reactions to things I had done — out of the air came the reaction to the cowpuncher silhouette at Cody, something that has stayed with me for years, developed finally into a sketch on the real people of the west, the smell of sage, dust and heat, horseflesh, the hunger of a man for reality. Then another on getting close to things, an elaboration of the idea that came to me paddling down Back Bay on Sunday — the wish to be alone and be a part of the picture. The third I do not remember, but they were all of a vein, struck much the same note.

This is what I have wanted to do. It will not be matter-of-fact stuff, no where-to-go, no how-to-do, how to kill ducks or fish, no factual material at all. Let the others take care of that. This will be of a philosophical turn, a reflective turn, my personal reactions to the world I live in, each event, each happening an adventure of the spirit. This is where the effect of Burroughs, Thoreau and the rest will come in. The reason I delved there was because I wanted to know the feeling of these men for the things they did.

By the time you have worked over half a hundred of these things, watched them develop into a regular pattern, then you will have done something. By then, they should begin to take form, show the proper direction and what is best for me to do. Already the pattern is beginning to form and I do not think it will be much different when I write the hundredth.

September 17, 1940

It seems like most of the things I write are short essays, and the question is will short essays be acceptable to the average man, Wilson, Art, Johnny and the rest. Will they read essays. Not if they are too somber or too scholarly, not unless they have a gem of something in each one.

You struck the note properly when you mentioned the toughness of the real paddle, when you explained how it grew in a cold swamp, how the seasons it fought gradually gave it the much prized resilience, that toughness only comes when life has been hard, that it takes living and combat and adversity to develop toughness in paddles as well as men. That is what is known as a gem, that is what will make men appreciate a paddle more than they have before. That is the whole excuse for such an article. It is not the description of the paddle. That is of no value, but the insight you might get into the virtues of paddles in general that makes it appeal.

September 20, 1940

E suggested last night that I call my column "Woodland Philosophy," a name that isn't half bad. It is more inclusive than Wilderness Philosophy or Jottings or Notes, will give me an opportunity to write about most anything out of doors. If I go down into the farming more settled regions, then I will have grist for my mill down there. If it was Wilderness, I must keep myself to the big woods entirely. Of course there is no reason why I cannot bring in all of the wilderness I wish, but the title is confusing.

E thought last night that I have something and I think she is right. My piece on choosing a paddle seemed to click with her and she thought that if I could continue in that vein that I might do something worthwhile. It seems to me as I said last night that this sort of thing is what I have been working toward all of the time. Here is a chance for me to use all of the knowledge all of the reactions that are mine and mine alone.

There is nothing to prevent me either from pounding off an occasional short story or an article for one of the magazines in addition to my columnist work. This column will be bread and butter and a chance to express my philosophy and reach an audience. I feel that I have something different than anything that has ever been done....

This is what I have been trending toward these last ten years. Since 1930, I have been feeling around, searching for my medium without any success. Now I seem at last to have found it. This seems the only logical outcome and it might be that it will be the solution to all of my troubles. At least this winter, I am going to work on this and nothing but this and try and make a few contacts.

If I can do this then the rest is easy. This is the sort of thing I like to do, the sort of thing that I do easily and well. I am not for long continued thought. Mine are short inspirational flashes, no character analysis, no prolonged meditations, but short birds-eye-view insights into what gives me pleasure in the out of doors.

As Ken says there is no fiction in either of us. I have sold a little but very little, enough so that I am convinced that I can never do it easily. In fact it makes me rather sick to think of it, but this column business seems a natural for me. As I might look back through my notes for the past ten years and the record of my search for a medium, what do I find, simply this — I want more than anything else to be able to go out into the woods and write my own interpretations of things as I see them. Burroughs was right when he said there is no competition in this field of writing because no two people see things exactly alike. I have tried again and again to hit this note in various types of stories and have failed. This seems like the solution.

October 7, 1940

The whole past has been working toward this one ideal — all the jottings — all the ideas — all the work I've done —

And the marvelous thing about it — is that this is writing that I like to do — I like to catch these things, elaborate on them — keep catching them all the time — get up at night & dash them down if they come —

If this could work out, it wouldn't make much difference what else happened — I would just keep on working running my column, and doing anything else I had time for — I would also stop fretting my heart out because I could not do the longer sustained essays — fiction for the Post or books — although the books — might come — consolidation of these little articles — one for each day, grouped according to seasons perhaps — Gift books of various types — ...

First of all is getting your column sold & that is what you must do now — Polish up your present ones until they read as smoothly as silk until you really have them in a form that will appeal to everyone — Try your darnedest to sell them — This is the answer to everything.

Ken — Stuffy Walters — Paul Meyers — America Out of Doors — perhaps an extra there — Take it over for a pittance — at so much per — once a week.[9]

You have a number of chances.

October 14, 1940

Yesterday cruising around Basswood in search of ducks the thought came to me that if I wished to continue writing indefinitely that the thing to do would be to work up a popularization of scientific things, such as geology, botany, zoology and natural history, my particular slant on each one. Take subjects such as pollen grains, terminal buds, adaptations, ecology and the balance of life, interrelationships, dependence, predators, parasites and the way a parasitical life has meant the breakdown of bodily perfection. Embryology, zoning, environment and how animals seek their own, temperatures, paleontology, climaxes, natural selection, sex, food, predation, color, specialization, dinosaur tracks, mosaics in plant growth, peat, etc.

The above might work but I would have to be careful not to make it just another science popularizing proposition. How can you work in the emotional angle in discussing temperatures or climaxes or predation or paleontology. Wouldn't it seem queer trying to work in any feeling about this no matter how sincere this interpretation. Much better to let these ideas seep in as reflections, indirectly. If you don't then this will be just another science column with no more appeal than any other.

Yesterday coming down past Bill Wenstrom's Point, saw Bill out there on the beach picking up wood, cleaning things up, and a vision came to me of how happy he was, how clean and beautiful a picture it was and how Bill had made a place for himself the past year. Now he owns boats, several cabins and a beautiful point. In a way I was envious and wondered why I hadn't done the same thing ten years ago instead of going to Champaign to study. I wondered if that wasn't the answer to things I wished for and wanted, if Bill wasn't happier than I could ever hope to be. I am supposed to be a woodsman and then I live in town, get out only on weekdays or weekend. Bill lives in the woods, lives the sort of a life I write about.[10]

On the point in Windy Bay — I thought of my new setup, Dean of the Junior College, <u>Nationally known columnist</u>, Border Lakes Outfitting Co. guide and outdoorsman. Being Dean of a College does not mean that I can't do these things, rather it is a feather in my cap and seems to work with the other. Being Dean of a College would give my writings added weight.

Another thing, be happy about your writing, be light-hearted and gay, don't write heavily or sadly. Pound off these things without too much forethought, give them the verve that would make people read them. Don't be heavy, give your stuff the lightness of touch that will make people look forward to it every day.

"Big Bill" Wenstrom at the East Bearskin Lake Ranger Station, circa 1920. Wenstrom Family Collection. Courtesy of Barbara Wenstrom Shank.

October 16, 1940

More and more, I find myself working away more happily. This morning I felt as though at last things were working out and it comes from the realization that I have no other dreams or ambitions than what is offered here — no fish & game jobs — no conservation jobs — no university department head of wildlife or wildlife surveys — or deanships — Here is a good place to live and work and if you work out your writing angle here, there is no reason for discontent. I will not eat out my heart anymore because this may be my medium—this what I have been searching for all of my life. Medium—my notes are full of it, searching everywhere, with no success — at last it seems I have the answer — short descriptions with philosophical aspects, personal slants on what I have seen and done. <u>Write easily, sincerely, only what gives you pleasure</u>, what <u>you would like to read yourself</u> — <u>write only what you know</u> — <u>only what you would write in any case for the pure joy of writing</u> — The one on being lost is good, so also "The Raven" — I like them & feel they are good — flashes of memory — highlights — the vividness — insight of a mind fresh & uncluttered — The world will welcome with open arms anyone who sees with an original slant, who shows that through his eyes things look different — Original observation — genius and sincerity —

October 18, 1940

Sent my first batch of mss to Ken yesterday and now for his reaction. Lib seems to like them and so does Mother and I do myself. At least they are different and it seems that I can pound them off easily. They are somewhat wordy and there is repetition, but that can be corrected. The big question now is whether or not the average reader will enjoy them. As I look over the columns that are being written practically all of them on political stuff and general observations on life in general, I fail to see where they are so terribly good. There is nothing of half this type of thing and it may be that fellows like Doc Knowles, Fuzzy, Al, Mort Cooper, La Budde, Wilson and the rest of my canoe trip following might get a tremendous bang out of them....

This much I have learned. Do not try and compose for perfection the first time. Write fast and as it comes and when the time comes for your revision, don't do it too seriously lest you break the thread of your thought and the smoothness of your style. It might be that this sort of thing will appeal tremendously to Ken. If it does, I hope that he will go to town with it and give it a break sometime in the near future. Some of his syndicate pals might consent out of their friendship for him to give them a try. If they should go over and I am sure they will once they start, then to receive a contract for a steady series will keep me busy and happy the rest of the winter. To know that I am definitely on the way, that my writing has assumed direction will be all I will want. What has bothered me in the past is that I haven't been able to see any real objective except the Post and the pulps and the out of door bunch. That is why I hesitate even thinking of resigning. But if this goes through the rest will be pure velvet and I will write only for the magazines when and what I want to.

October 28, 1940

I don't see why Ken doesn't answer my letter and at least give me a slant on what he thinks....

The fact that he hasn't written indicates to me that he doesn't think they are much good, thirteen days today since I sent them to him. That means only one thing that he can't bear to write me about them.

I can't expect too much, but I still think they are good and that the idea is worth working on. I can only hope and pray that he will find time soon to let me know.

In this day of wars and death, why bother with thoughts of quitting, trying to do the ethereal sort of thing you have dreamed about. Life is serious, far too serious.

October 31, 1940

Right now I have reached one of those impasses when I am physically sick. It happens every year and now it is worse than ever — Don't seem to be able to hang on — would blow up in a minute at the slightest provocation — — Something every day would do the trick — keep me fairly happy & contented — Right now it is suicide —

Read last night — the man who takes the chance — the big chance grows in stature — the one who fails is lost & dwarfs —

I am suicidally sick & the only way I can pull myself out of the morass is to keep on writing — I have some 30 odd done, one for each 2 days since I started — which isn't bad — but I don't care to go on until I get Ken's slant —

He will say — no punch — no general appeal — poor elocution — poor construction — too much repetition — & will say thumbs down on it — Then what — short stories, articles — again — keep plugging away — no I can't do it — this time it is the end and I am 40[11] —

If on the other hand things should pan out — you will perhaps be the happiest mortal on earth — In the meantime keep things dark — don't let on — keep a stiff upper lip — don't let down at all —

Tonight I will attack 11 new ones, finish them off & send them to Ken. That will give him 32 — a full month's supply —

October 31, 1940

The big question now is what Ken thinks of the column idea and then how to revise it should he think it is not worthwhile working on. I know he is busy, is putting off the evil day of letting me know what he thinks until he can do it gracefully and easily without hurting my feelings too much. I have another dozen or so done and should work them up and shoot them in to him for further stimulation. Perhaps I should do them tonight, get them off in the morning so that he will have some additional material to judge me from. With some thirty odd pieces, 32 to be exact, he will have a full month's supply of work or almost five weeks if they do not run them Sundays. Surely he will be able to judge whether or not they might ring the bell. They are really better these last pieces than most of the first, "Indian Summer," "Call of the Loon," "First Snowfall," "Good Housekeeping in the Woods," "On Standing in a Blind," etc, all of them of some general interest.

E asks me what we should do with our reserve and I always tell her it depends on what Ken says. If he is enthusiastic then it may be the end of all this or I may keep on for a while. But it will make all the difference in the world to me in what we decide to do with what we have.

November 5, 1940

Today, I mailed to Ken the last twelve of the Field Notes that I have prepared and I believe they are better by far than the old and original ones. At least they are finished which is more than can be said for the first batch. This makes thirty-four that have gone in, thirty-four original ideas all of about five hundred words and all as alike as two peas. The fact that he hasn't acknowledged what I have sent in, does not make much difference. I like to believe that he is trying to get them all in line for something, before shooting them down to me. Perhaps he is seeing some of his syndicate friends, perhaps he is working them over so that they will be somewhat in the shape he thinks they should be before sending them back.

November 6, 1940

Your objective before Thanksgiving is to get 50 items sent to Ken, which means a total of some 25,000 words. With that as a base, he certainly should be able to tell me where I am off and what to do to improve what I have done.

I puzzle over his long silence. Can it be that he is so disappointed in what I have done that he doesn't dare write me, that he hates to let me down, that he hasn't had time. There is this much about it, if he was wild about them, he would have come back pronto, be all enthusiastic. He might know what it means to me to get some reaction after all of the work. Perhaps he is sick, perhaps so tied up with the election that he can't even find a moment.

Perhaps he thinks in view of the seriousness of world affairs that this is no time to be writing piddling philosophy, this no time to be prattling about daffodils and sunsets and moonlight through the trees. If that is so, then I can't agree with him because I feel more than ever that now people need to feel some of the primitive philosophy I am trying to express, more than ever do they need escape and release from the spirit of war and suffering.

Burroughs last night — how close we see the truth, how much the same his ideals and mine — "Unless in a description of any natural thing, it be infused with a spiritual light, colored by one's own emotional reaction, invested with some meaning then it is not literature, has no place in the hearts of men." Scientific description is cold and without sentiment, my description is warm with feeling. No scene of beauty is worth describing for itself alone, no action or even unless one can color it with the light of personality, unless one can inject something of the soul. And so, nothing that I ever write can be otherwise.

November 13, 1940

Word from Ken — says my stuff is very good — Thinks I have something — Have seven more done which makes 41 all told — If I can do nine more before Thanksgiving, then I will have fifty pieces finished which should give whoever is going to pass on them a pretty good idea of what I can do — — Fifty at 500 words is 25,000 words — Surely it will mean something — surely at least it will indicate a trend —

Undated, ca. November 24, 1940

Ken's comments

Nov 6, 1940

"Read the first dozen or so the other night and they sounded very good to me. I'll go over them all carefully and then will take them to Dilley or Anderson unless I get any ideas for polishing them further. I really think you have something."

Nov. 16th

"I really think Sig has something in the 'Column' he is working on. I have a syndicate man out to see me tomorrow and I'm going to have him take the articles and see what he can do about selling them."

Nov 23rd.

"I turned over Sig's articles to a Mr. Anderson, head of the publishers syndicate this past week and I'll probably be hearing from him soon. He warned us not to get our hopes too high for a column of this kind is very difficult to sell. But we'll be hoping for Sig's sake. I thought some of the articles were excellent. If Anderson doesn't take them I'll try them on other syndicate friends of mine."

Mickey[12] —

"I did so enjoy reading Sig's columns — They are so different from the ordinary run of newspaper columns, it seems to me they should have real appeal and not just to men alone. I am very eager to hear what Harold Anderson of Publishers Syndicate will say about them."

In other words, my criticism is all just general as yet and Ken doesn't know what to say. I have a feeling in my bones that they will go the way of "Grandmother's Trout," "Northwest Corner" and "Shift of the Wind," "The Pines" etc. Not enough punch to make them appeal to a general reading public. Nice writing but that is all — no wallop — nothing sensational enough to make them worthwhile to the mob. And the big question arises what will I do when the blow falls — will I go into the doldrums or let it be merely an incentive to more and better work. I can't be slapped down much more than I have been. There must be a way out soon and I thought this was the answer. I have written sixty now and have a dozen more in the making — short personal observations seems to be the answer and it still seems to be the answer if someone else can see it.

November 28, 1940

My one ambition in life is to write a good outdoor column bringing in my interpretation of life as I see it. Already I have written 60 odd items totaling about 30,000 words which should be a good sample of what I can do. By Christmas time, I should have 40 more, at least I shall make that my goal which will be about 50,000 words and a good start for any column that is being considered. If they are as good as the stuff I have already put out, then I think I will really have something. No newspaper syndicate can afford to turn down 50,000 words of any material especially if it has something of general interest.

As I think of the League[13] and wildlife conservation in general, I see that my sole interest is no longer purely conservation, that it has gone beyond that into the realms of the spiritual, that I have gotten over this amateurish material and interest down to something really individual and distinctive. The meeting tonight, I think I shall pass up as it will be just another repetition of what I have been through before. I hate these meetings and endure them because I feel I should. Then why go to them. Why not declare your independence and let others get the glory and go through the grief....

I do wish Ken would give me an inkling of what he thinks so that I can guide myself in the future and not feel that I am doing too much groping in the dark. It is hard to know what he is thinking of or whether or not these things are just reposing under a heap of rubbish on his desk. I can't imagine that being the case. There must be some other reason.

If this thing goes, then I will be satisfied with life and want nothing else. Then I will realize that I am at last doing what I was cut out to do, that my purpose in life is the interpretation that I have written about all these years. Perhaps now after a decade, since 1930 when this introspection started, I have finally reached the point where I shall reap the harvest and really produce what is in me.

Sigurd stocks bass fingerlings for the U.S. Forest Service at Crooked Lake, 1940. Photographs by Leland J. Prater, U.S. Forest Service Records, National Archives.

December 3, 1940

The more I think of the column idea, the better it seems. It may be that what I have done so far is merely an approach that the winter will have to be devoted to polishing, perfecting, getting a better medium of approach & finishing. Develop a light heartedness — a freshness — an unusual & unique slant. Make every one so <u>alive</u> & <u>fresh</u> — & vivid — and <u>beautiful</u> — so smoothly written — that anyone would turn to it every day —

Last night I thought that if I could feel that I was functioning at top speed — that my brain & energy were at premium, then & only then would I be happy — Then would come demand & recognition — Ding Darling — Henry Ward — Al — All the friends I know would then admit that I was contributing something. I want the feeling that I am doing something of which I am proud — something that my genius dictates — An excellent column would be the answer — but it must be so good that there would be no question of its excellence. Of course it will not be written for Henry Ward but rather for the mob of illiterates — those who don't read or think too much —

December 5, 1940

Your ambition now should be to produce the finest outdoor column of interpretation in the world — Be the outstanding columnist in your field — be so good that newspapers will beg for your stuff — It doesn't make much difference where you live on the earth — your reactions are the same — North — South — East or West — what you say is of general interest to everyone —

December 5, 1940

I have ten more ready to mail, and they are getting progressively better, at least so I feel. The name Field Notes seems to be the best of the lot, Harp of the Winds being too poetic to allow of much freedom. A few of my pieces might fit into it but not many and it would rule out all matter-of-fact observations such as any slants on wilderness.

Still no word from Ken, it must be that he is waiting before committing himself or wants to surprise me with a real bit of news before he even admits having gone through them....

My writing seems to be improving, getting smoother and my form

is taking shape — an introductory episode — the body of the idea — con-
cluding reactions — all invariably within 500 words. With the ten I have
now, I have written 71, four more would make it 75.

December 9, 1940

I was thinking tonight that if this works then my troubles will be over.
I can keep going as I please or quit as I please and no one will ever again
have anything to say about what I shall do. This will be justification
enough. If I can write one of these things each day, then I will not think
about fiction or anything else. It will absorb all of my time and energy
and make me feel that at last I am doing what I am supposed to be doing.
I have no hankering to get into government work of any kind, conservation work, or any of the highfalutin school jobs that might be mine if
I went after them. This is as far as I want to go. This is my limit and I do
not believe that I can do anything higher than this.

To realize that will mean a great deal in contentment. I will then
know where my talents lie, will know that this is what I am cut out for
and all my preparation has been for. This will be the answer, of that I am
sure.

If Chicago does not feel that it can handle my stuff, there are many
other syndicates to try and Ken can help me with them all. To know at
last where the answer lies that is a satisfaction that can only come once.
Articles and books on the interpretation of nature, that is enough for
me. I care for no place in the field of novelists or short stories or plays.
That is a closed book, but if that works out then I will have no aspirations. My one job in life should be to run a good column and perhaps to
carry on with my talking, which will come without question.

December 11, 1940

Still Ken does not write — I feel that he is waiting — hopes to give me a
surprise for Xmas, that this will be the turning point — surely he is not
letting it go after all I have written him. There can be no other answer —
If nothing happens — I shall keep on — By spring — I will have perhaps
200 of them — 100,000 words and will have spent the winter perfecting
them — They should be in good shape then.

I see now where they are improving how in each one there is a new
slant — a different feeling — something to bite into —

If I can keep going — work out a couple of dozen or so that during Xmas I can polish them off — that will be enough — For a time, the idea frightened me of material but that ogre is laid low now — I think I can keep going indefinitely and bring a new slant on anything —

"Every new genius is an impossibility until he appears; we cannot forecast his type. He is a revelation, and through his eyes we shall see undreamed of effects." — Burroughs.

"When a man speaks of real insight & conviction of his own, men are always glad to hear him."

And so I hope it is with me or will be — More than anything, I need recognition and the feeling that what I am doing is wanted —

December 16, 1940

What I must try and bring out in order to sell this column is that it is different from the ordinary outdoor column, that it is world wide in its implications, that even though I might talk about things I do up here, they should be of interest to anyone living anywhere. Would Thoreau have been accused of being regional just because he wrote from Concord, would Emerson or Burroughs have been called regional. No, what they wrote about were things of universal interest using merely the medium of their own experience to bring it into light. These things of mine are not regional, they are of the whole U.S. and for that matter of the world and the sooner we can convince the syndicate people that this is the real reason for them, they will get an entirely different picture of them.

There is no where-to-go, how-to-do-it angle here at all. Never once do I give camping, gardening or fishing or hunting hints. If I give them it is merely incidental. Neither do I describe a squirrel or a hawk or a raven for the sake of the description. They happen to be mediums at the time for an idea I am trying to put over.

The only ones that are regional at all may be some of the things on wilderness or paddling or camping or skiing, but even they are not regional. They apply and can apply to camping or paddling or skiing anywhere, and with each one there is a thought or an idea that covers the whole country.

Our approach on the last batch was wrong. We must impress whoever considers them next that these little essays are interpretations of things of universal interest that though they stem from the north, the precepts and principles underlying them are the same as though they had stemmed from Africa. This is a universal philosophy of living, a philosophy of simplicity and contact with the earth. This is different—I could write these things anywhere, on any subject and they would be the same. Running through them all is the idea of living close to the earth, of simplicity, of sun and water and what the out of doors means to me as an individual and through that perhaps be of some interest to others.

I must write Ken immediately and try and put this across to him. Get him to feel that these things of universal interest can be run at any time in any kind of a paper and under any conditions. Such things as sitting in a blind may be local, still when you think that what I try and bring out is the sense of security and aloneness that comes there, it immediately becomes of general interest. The instant a man speaks of things that may concern others and gives them a fresh peek at the world beyond, the world of the spirit and the emotions, then what he has to say is important.

December 20, 1940

Since September 2nd I have written over a hundred "Field Notes" close to 50,000 words & I have a real feeling of accomplishment. The items are getting more and more polished, better than ever. I am going to keep on working and I know that by the time the rush starts in March or April, I will have another 100 — I have 3 on the way now — 97 to go — that will be 100,000 words — By that time my form should be getting pretty good —

December 25, 1940

At last I seem to have hit my pace to have started writing the sort of thing that I have always wanted to write, short descriptive essays of the out of doors, essays that are more paintings in words with all of the mood, all of the imagination and emotion and the spiritual that I have always felt.

Florence and Lib read "The Climax" and "Cherne's Pond" and Robinson Peak and "Balm of Gilead" and they both felt the same way, that I had done something beautiful that would live and be accepted by all.

Perhaps not as newspaper stuff but rather as books of essays for young people, reference and gift books that will make the north country live for those who have learned to love it, the Smiths, the Knowles,

Kermit Wicks, Goodarts, and many others who like the sort of thing I have been trying to depict. It may not come at once, it may be that I will have to search around but surely before the year is up if I keep on working and polishing what I have done, there will be an outlet and once that happens then I am all set.

I have here enough material already for several books of essays, one on hunting and fishing, one on the type of Cherne's Pond, one on wilderness, one on gardening, etc, canoeing. There are the makings here of a number of books and with the books will come other things requests for contributions to magazines, lectures, all the things that I have dreamed of. This Christmas time in spite of the war, I have a feeling that at last I am on the trail, that now after ten years of search, I have at last arrived at my goal.

AMERICA
OUT OF DOORS

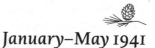

January–May 1941

T HE FIRST PART OF 1941 was an emotional roller coaster for Sigurd. Having written 150 columns, he alternated between anxiety and confidence as he sought advice and tried a few syndicate possibilities. His first break came in February, when Basil Walters, new executive editor of the *Minneapolis Star-Journal*, said he loved the twenty samples Sigurd had sent. "Man, you can write," he said. "This stuff simply yells for outlet in my opinion." Wanting to help, Walters ran a series of them for a couple of months as Sunday features.[1]

The break he wanted most came in mid-March. Paul Meyers, manager of the North American Sportsman's Bureau in Chicago, wanted to see some of Sigurd's samples. Meyers then passed these on to a number of newspaper outdoor editors. The feedback wasn't unanimous, but overall it was positive enough that Meyers wanted to give Sigurd a chance.

They cemented the deal in May. Sigurd would become the sole writer of the syndicate's "America Out of Doors" column, which ran in dozens of papers throughout the Great Lakes region and some states to the south. Sigurd was afraid the mixed reviews would lead Meyers

Promotional photograph for Sigurd's "America Out of Doors" column, circa 1941. Olson Family Collection. Courtesy of David Backes.

to demand that Sigurd drop his interpretive style for a more traditional one. But Meyers was ready to try something different. His only demand was to make the first six months probationary, providing no income to Sigurd.[2]

* * * *

January 6, 1941

The holidays are over and I have finished as per my schedule the 100 essays for the column. Now I have done about 50,000 words and that is more than I had actually planned, but as I write finis to this first batch, I have a sinking feeling in my heart for I wonder if all this work was wasted effort, if there is going to be any chance to market them, if I am through writing and must try to make a go of short stories, articles or outdoor stuff as in the past. Or the big If, am I through forever. That is what really frightens me, but there must be some way out. Ken will surely write me soon and give me some encouragement.

In any case I must not lose sight of the book which might some day come of this—a book of essays illustrated perhaps by Jaques[3] or some other good black and white etcher or perhaps by photographs of the subjects I have in mind.

January 16, 1941

For almost five months I have been working consistently on one project, the news column of essays suggested in September through my talk with Ken. I have written and completed 100 of these and have about twenty five more in stages of revision, a group that I could complete in a week if I had to. One thing I wanted to prove to myself when I began was that I would not run out of material. The fact that I have done 125 or an average of 1 each day since I began seems to indicate that I will not run out immediately. There is some repetition in thought which I suppose is natural starting in, but not too much. They are original and unique enough to stand alone.

The longer I work on this, the surer I am that this is my medium and that eventually this will be the answer to my long search. The short picture of an idea, a flash so to speak of something I have seen and thought about and felt, that is what I am trying to do. Five hundred to six hun-

Francis Lee Jaques sketching at Lake Superior, early 1940s. Courtesy of University of Minnesota Archives.

dred words seems to be the answer. Essays these days, that is the normal ones, are too long for people to read. These short flashes, kernels of meat so to speak, should fill a need without the necessity of great elaboration or repetition. I usually plow through an essay of two or three thousand words for a kernel of truth and am willing to get the gross material for the small net, but here I have eliminated the roughage and gone directly to the point. In that way, it might satisfy a need.

I hear nothing from Ken and at times I am ready to wire for his reactions. Why should I let it disturb me. After all it is just four months since all of this started and I should perhaps work a year at least before I feel I really have something. The thing to do is to keep on working without a break. Everything you write will not be good, but some of it is bound to be. If one in five is passable, that is a pretty good average. The point is that if you keep on pouring out these things which seems to be the answer to your problem, eventually you will build up enough material for a series of books. I often wondered how Burroughs wrote as many books as he did. If I keep on writing what is in my heart eventually I'll have enough for a series. Suppose out of this first group of 150 essays there is enough for book number one. If I keep on writing away another year, there will be enough for a second, possibly one every two years or so. In ten years there will be five, each one a miscellaneous collection of short essays of what I have seen and thought about. These books will be the story of my life and what I have thought about during my years in the woods. They will tell as much about me as a biography, they will be my contribution to literature. In a sense they will be poems, but much more readable than poems. They will be prose poems, each one with as sure a germ of thought as any poem could be and much more understandable to the mass. If they create a demand, so that the public is waiting for them to come out, then I will be secure.

There is no use in my wasting time on short stories or long essays, or outdoor articles or narrative of happenings. All I ever wrote them for in the first place was for an opportunity to work in what little picturing and philosophy I could. Each one was an attempt to work in a little of what I had in my heart almost as riders to the running narrative. Usually the story was weak and surely my heart was not in it — so that phase is definitely over. From now on, it will be these short descriptive flashes or essays, come what may. It is all I care to write and eventually they will make a place for themselves. If one must follow the advice of writing what is in your heart, writing sincerely and what bubbles out of its own accord, write what you must write and write for yourself, the sort of thing you would like to read, then you are doing the right thing.

January 17, 1941

Just wired Ken this morning telling him that I would call him tonight regarding the column. That will make him think about it today and have ready some sort of an answer to my questions. When I call tonight I will ask him first of all what he is doing with them, where they are, whether or not he sent them on to Des Moines—what I should do. I am also going to ask him why he hasn't written, what his personal reactions to them are. Then if he has done nothing, I will ask him to send them all back immediately.

It is hard for me to be rational when I think of how he has ignored my requests for help and advice. At least he could have been brotherly and told me where I was wrong. But none of that, not a word.

Well, tonight I will find out, will see what it means. I know already—he has not had time, or taken time. They are laying in his office covered with a lot of catalogs, old correspondence.

January 23, 1941

Last night Elizabeth read "Caribou Moss," "The Esker" and Witches Broom, said they were the best I had ever done—that all of the last bunch were better than anything of the past. It made me very happy for I felt that I had gotten somewhere, that I had hit my stride. When I finish this bunch I will have done 120 or 60,000 words — Do not think I could do one a day but I can do one a week or two a week, if I can make $25.00 per week or $100 per month that will be all I want. That is an additional thousand a year and with what I make with the Border Lakes will take care of us very nicely. I will stay with my school job however until the house is all paid for, the car and all of the improvements, but what a relief it will be, and what a joy to know that at last I am working on the right track. Already I feel differently about the whole business of writing than I did before, feel more secure, self-confident and sure of myself.

Last night on my skis I paused over a great spruce swamp, stood there for a few minutes watching the fading of the last streak of orange in the west, watched the swamp getting darker and gloomier than ever. Down there it was quiet and black, there it was primitive and safe. That was sanctuary, the last refuge in the wild.

Elected finance chairman for the Scouts for 1941 — took it without a quiver, same old stuff — will make it go somehow, not so desperate a venture this year in view of my new peace of mind.

January 27, 1941

The Des Moines syndicate has turned the idea down and now I begin to wonder if there is any use going on. Of course as Ken says there is New York, but newspapers are the same I suppose.

Last night driving home — Why not the old book idea, make a book of short outdoor essays of enough interest so that everyone will want a copy. Long essays people will not read — neither will they want short stories, but a book that is a collection of outdoor philosophy, so that a person can turn to it anywhere and get something worthwhile, perhaps five minutes before going to sleep or ten minutes, something to chew on and read over and over again. Something they will want to carry with them wherever they go, canoe trips, fishing trips, pack trips, a book, they will never want to be without, such a book would be better by far than a play or a novel for they take only one reading and you are through. Each essay the meat, the sum and substance of how a man or woman feels about the out of doors, the sort of thing you like to read — then you will have something.

February 3, 1941

Sent 20 items in to Tubby Walters today.[4] I suppose it will come back the same as ever, but then I will have to go around and try and sell them myself to the local editors. There might be the sole solution.

In a week or so I should hear from both Holland[5] and Walters and possibly from Ken so that by the middle of this month I should know somewhat more definitely where I am at. Ken—how he exasperates me with his silence. Will wire him soon.

Starting in September, I wrote steadily for five months, now am on the sixth, have work mapped out for a couple of years and some 60,000 words all done which is not bad for a starter. Tonight I am going to spend the night reading, not a letter, not a Field Note, no skiing, nothing but reading — Ernest Hemingway "For Whom the Bell Tolls." It will be fun being on my own for that once.

February 5, 1941

Have made a sort of survey of some of my early stuff with the last I have written, keeping in mind what Ken told me about the matter of being "preachy." I can see what he meant and think I have the solution. As I look back over the early stuff, especially the culls from the articles, it all is very plain. They are preachy and the philosophizing is entirely too evident. If that comes in it must be subtly so that no one will suspect.

The last things I have done are much better than the first, The Esker, Witches Broom, Beaver Dam etc are excellent, much better than Pinnacles, Saganaga, the Squirrel and others. E seems to like those with information in them and so does Pete.

I also see certain roughnesses in some. That will mean rewriting for smoothness, also for clarification and simplification of the thought. What I should really do now is sit down and rewrite everything I have written to date, polish them until there is no chance for any roughness at all and so the thought stands out as clearly and well defined as possible. In other words, these things should each one of them be perfect, so that I can say when I am through with them, that nothing can be done to improve them.

The bunch I send around the syndicates must be letter perfect and so beautiful they shine of their own accord. I could take several weeks to do that, but I haven't the time now. When I hear from Holland and Walters, I will know a little better what to do.

February 6, 1941

These days of waiting are hard, nothing done, nothing accomplished, seem to be standing still and when I am in the doldrums, I am down completely.

With Holland and Walters to hear from and they have a good selection, it should not be too impossible. Think, however, that I will do nothing until I do hear from them. Then I shall go after the syndicates that Ken talked about.

Speaking of syndicates — the thing to do is pick out perhaps 25 of the finest things you have done, look them over carefully for errors or smoothing or clarity, and do the whole bunch over so that when they go out, you will really have something so perfect that you can be proud of them. Also, you had better for the syndicate bunch pick things that are so general and non regional in scope that they will not have that criticism.

Among this group will come such things as:

The Climax Stand

Chernes Pond

Dog Days

Caribou Moss

Something about Moonlight

Moonlight Escapade

Rose Quartz

Scrub Oak

The Stone Wall

The Little River

Balm of Gilead

The Dream Net

Arbutus

The Crossbills

Easter on the Prairie

February 11, 1941

Ray Holland says "I sometimes feel as though you did not have the power of expression to put over your own feeling for the woods." Also that some of my stuff is overdone and that I have a tendency to get off the deep end. By that he means that sometimes I go further than I should, that I don't know where to stop, that I go to the point of embarrassment, where a man might feel a little sheepish at the undue exposure of himself. In other words a man can be too naked with his feelings.

Liable to go off the deep end — in other words, liable to get beyond my depth, and flounder — not being able to speak clearly and lucidly. Simplicity again, dear old simplicity.

There are plenty of others who admit that my stuff is good, well written and all that sort of thing, but this crack of Holland's hurts —

lukewarm as it were — "Some of them are doggone good and in some of the stuff you get the feeling of the out of doors." In some of your material, however, I have had a feeling as though you had gone a little too far, beyond your depth. Your powers of feeling and experience are better than your ability to express yourself.

Well—that hurt, but I should take it to heart and in the future watch myself, simplify, be subtle in your philosophizing, never come out and say what you think, infer it.

I hope and pray that Walters will give me the break I need.

February 13, 1941

Heard from Basil Walters today and the first real recognition I have gotten. "Man you can write — that stuff simply yells for an outlet — I want to see you go ahead with it" does something for me.

Of course there is no money in it at $5.00 a throw, but it will as he says open the way and that is what I need. Suppose I get half a dozen papers here in Minnesota at $5.00 a throw, that is $30.00 per week or $120 per month and then gradually increase it to ten or a dozen, ten would mean $50.00 per week. Once I get the *Star Journal* to run a few, I will have something to work on and the way might be opened up. A weekly thing is the answer not a daily and it might be possible to sell it on that basis once it gets under way. *Minneapolis Tribune*, *St. Paul Dispatch*, *Duluth Herald*, and say the Hibbing and Virginia papers, there are five for a starter. Suppose the *Star Journal* eventually brought it to $10.00, then they alone would bring my $40.00 per month or $500 per year. Well, in any case this is a starter and if they come out for a while and create a demand, the book proposition will be easy to sell the Minnesota Press people on.

I wonder if I should tell Walters about myself and my writing, *Field and Stream*, *Sports Afield*, etc and the recognition I have already achieved. I wonder if *Sports Afield* would take one a month and pay me their standing rate of $10.00 to $15.00. They might take two or three and make it work out that way.

No matter what happens, I feel that this time, I have a chance, that this is the best type of outlet for me, that this will give me the opening I need, that given several months or a year of this stuff that the way will clear and I will see where I am going.

To date, everything has been lukewarm, polite and nice refusals to hurt me, but this being Minnesota is the real thing. This is down to the ground and worthwhile.

Funny about hunches or dreams — night before last a dream that the *Star* would offer me $100 per month if I would work for them alone.

February 18, 1941

Have been in the doldrums for the past week, no writing, nothing, just sitting tight. Suppose it is the let down after finding that my stuff was not syndicate material, that Walters of the *Mpls Star Journal* must try them out at $5.00 a throw and the slowness that entails.

If that does go, then there will be the chance of a book. If there is a real demand, then it might spread into other channels, perhaps another newspaper or two. This much is true, after the *Star Journal* has run a bunch of them, and I have some clippings, it will be possible to run through some of the syndicates with the printed stuff which will be better than sending them unprinted stuff....

In the *Atlantic*, "No man is truly happy unless he is living the sort of a life that suits him," climate, surroundings, comforts mean nothing unless the life itself suits.

Well in my case — just what would suit — freedom to come and go, freedom to run the woods and be in the sun, freedom to write when and about what I please. No city life for me, no university life, no classes, no committees, none of that. I suppose it simmers down to the old premise — write or be damned.

Do I like teaching? I have liked it, loved it in fact, lab days in winter dissecting, labs studying rocks, field trips, explaining this and that — geology, botany, zoology. Yes, there is much pleasure there, a great deal. I am a strange cosmos of conflicting desires. What gets me now is that I am not teaching, this administrative stuff is stifling.

February 27, 1941

Today, after almost a month of writing nothing, a few revisions perhaps, I took three of the first and worked them over. I was amazed at the ease with which they improved, how even after a month, it was possible to see them more clearly. "Rose Quartz" with the idiotic poetry tie-up was fixed up so that now it at least is not gushy and then there are always a few words that can be made smoother. I took "Stone Wall" and really made a masterpiece out of it. Never did like the last line "and now they make my wall" that was lame, terribly lame and there were other places as well that could stand polishing. Well, the upshot of this is simply that I can take most of my old stuff and work it over. Before I ever attempt to publish either in a book or magazine stuff, this should all be whipped into perfect shape. What I should do is start at the beginning and work right through. Some of them don't need any changing but there are many that do.

March 5, 1941

The winter is about over and no results as yet, but I hope soon that I will know if what I have done is worth the time I have put in on it. It will be terrible to think that nothing will come out of all this effort. I have polished my form and I have developed a type and a medium....

Do not lose heart, but keep working away. You have been working now since September, six full months and going on the seventh. During this time, you already see a tremendous improvement. Take "The Breaking," take any of the first crop, how immature they sound, and unfinished. Contrast them with the last, "The Coloring of Leaves," or "Scrub Oak" or "The Beaver Dam" or the revised "Stone Wall" or "The Breaking" and you can see how far you have come. I am developing form and type after a winter of work. "This is material that a person would want to come back to and read and re-read time and again, a book that people would love, would want to carry with them, make part of themselves." That is what I first had in mind, that is worth far more to me than any financial recompense, worth more than anything else in life. That will come, of that I am sure and think that at last I am on the right track. Make these things so beautiful, so much like poetry and so much better that those who love the out of doors and have a feeling for it will ask me to keep on working — a shelf of books, all small, all beautifully illustrated — the work of my life, nothing but that, better than poetry, better than sonnets, better than anything that has ever been written before.

March 10, 1941

Have just returned from the farm with the same old reaction — that the farm is home, that I am camping up here in Ely, that this is not my home in spite of the fact that I have lived up here 20 years. Queer that I cannot get that out of my system.

If I should ever make a go of my writing, I am going to spend some of every summer down there working away at something or other.

Hiking over to the river again — open now, goldeneyes and the rush of the water — I was hurt inside trying to recapture the old days, now gone forever. The pines and the borders of the fields, home to me.

Back here last night — back to the camp in the woods, home looked unreal, unstable — temporary. Will it always be that way. Here I have spent most of my life, here my children have been born, here I have lived and worked and still it is not home. Wisconsin is home to me, the pines and the soil, there I should have stayed. There I would have found reality and happiness.

I am a queer makeup — I get queerer all of the time. Will I ever feel at home again, anywhere, will I ever strike my roots into the soil and stay there or will I always be a wanderer with home nowhere. I want more than anything else to feel that I belong.

March 12, 1941

Paul Meyers & his syndicate "America Out of Doors" — suppose he has 25 papers & they pay him $250 a week as a source of income that is $50 per week — Could it be that he would use my stuff, possibly.

"America Out of Doors" could be sold at a price & I buy in to the syndicate — on my own —

Pictures — 1. Standing with a packsack against pines.

2. Snowshoes —

3. Close up of head

4. Various poses with pines in background —

5. Stream

Get large port and camera —

Look over guiding pictures of last two trips — canoe trips family — La Budde — Smiths — family — duck hunting —

Shoot down half a dozen good shots if possible.

After a hunt with Bob (*left*) and Sig Jr. (*center*), early 1940s. Wisconsin Historical Society Collection, 74092.

March 15, 1941

Last night the snow was hard and glassy on the south slopes and when coming down a hill the skis would slide as though on glass, but it was beautiful with the reflection and coming down the north slopes where the snow was still powdery, no effort at all, a push on the sticks and you had the sensation of flying.

A flash of white wings behind a bank of snow as though the crest of it had suddenly taken to the air and was winging toward the tree tops — a snowy owl that had drifted down out of the north, the first for many years, flapped its way slowly to the top of a spruce, sat there a ball of white until I was past.

A night of full moon, the moon coming up hazy and warm before the west was entirely free of color. Orange in the east and the stillness that comes with the full moon, rose in the west and in the north the greenish yellow flash of northern lights. I stopped on a great hill overlooking town where I could not only see the white and red lights of the streets, but also the four horizons. It was warm and beautiful and the light effects were unreal, so beautiful were they. From the mine came the clanking of heavy metal, ore coming up for the mills.

Down the last final slope toward home, my skis fairly flying over the crust, a few wild turns, still on my feet, a shot between the gateposts of the last fence and it was over, perhaps the last skiing of the year. For three gorgeous months it has been perfect and I have learned more and enjoyed it more than for many a year. Now the skis will be put away for another year. I think of next December and wonder what the world will be then, if there will be any time or inclination for any skiing or any kind of fun such as we have known here in the north.

March 15, 1941

Wrote Paul Meyers yesterday and it will be interesting to get his reaction. Don't expect much but you never can tell. The idea just might intrigue him, especially if he is out of material and is having a devil's own time getting stuff. After all, he is a syndicate and has some distribution, perhaps some good papers. If he is willing to take a chance, I would be crazy not to try him out. With a toehold, you can never tell what will happen. I am too, don't forget, one of his eight writers and that means something.

March 17, 1941

St. Patrick's Day & wearing of the green but what a strange unhappy-unsettled anniversary, the world at war and uncertainty in the offing — dire predictions for the future — war — disaster — I wonder if it will be the last happy St. Patrick's Day we will ever know.

Wonder what I will be learning from Paul Meyers — Sports Afield — Readers Digest — three weeks now since the material went in. Shouldn't think about R.D. too much as they always wait a month —

March 21, 1941

Sent in 18 articles to Paul Meyers today and really feel that it might develop into something as they are pretty good and he has the feeling for the stuff that is necessary to make it go. The big question is — can I possibly get out enough of it to keep it going every day, 365 of them a year, 30 of them or 26 of them every month, one a day, that is almost too much to do. I think I will have to insist on using it merely as a Sunday feature. I could get out one a week but that would be all. I don't think I could possibly do one a day. That would exhaust me in no time at all.

March 22, 1941

A final snowshoe hike with the crust hard enough in the open to make good going. Seemed good after all the months of skiing, out to Mitchell Lake and then down the river.

Flashes:

Stopped in for a cup of coffee with the caretaker — the cabin was immaculate and while I was there, he kept moving around, arranging a paper here, picking something up there, the cabin shone with cleanliness and order, but what I remember was the woodpile and the chickadees out there and the feeling of peace and content that was there. I thought if I could only sit there and work for a while looking out at that woodpile with its chickadees, what more contentment could a man wish for.

Snowshoeing down the shore of the lake toward the river mouth, part of the old feeling came back to me of joy in being out. I'd almost forgotten what it was like, but I really felt it when I stopped at the beaver dam and sat down on the dry grass under the pine. Looking out over the creek and the beaver meadow, and watching the storm and the snow sweeping out of the east, it looked so good to me that I laughed, yes I laughed just to see it, it seemed so free and good and exciting.

The gurgling of water running full under the snow and ice, in spots wide open eating at the crust, trying to break free. Another month and it will be in flood.

What gorgeous vistas over the hills toward the lake, pine and rocks and spruce in the valleys — as wild and fine a picture as could be mine anywhere and here it was at my back door within an hour of where I sit and write.

It was a happy hike this morning — happy because the *Star Journal* is coming out with the first — "The Bohemians" and because Paul is going to work on them and because no matter what happens, this is the answer.[6]

I knew as I went along, that only one thing mattered for me, not the adventures of me with men or the physical adventures of men with things of the earth — excitement, valor, disaster and triumph are of no significance compared to a man's feelings toward the universe — that is what I have been trying to do, paint pictures of just that, my personal interpretation of things of the earth and how they affect the spirit.

A photograph taken near Ely to publicize "America Out of Doors," circa 1941. Listening Point Foundation Archives.

March 30, 1941

The *Star Journal* came out with the second of their series this morning "Arbutus" and with the usual fine layout of artist's work.[7] The piece sounded well and should attract some attention. At least the *Journal* has almost a quarter of a million circulation and that is as much as the magazines. I begin to see what Paul Meyers meant when he said the newspapers don't want magazine competition. If these things go for a while, it should not be hard to interest the Minnesota Press in a book or a larger syndicate. Paul should get a wallop out of these and it might convince him of their salability. I must mail him one tomorrow with the others so that he can see how they work up....

I wonder if my 42nd birthday will be a turning point, if this April 4th will be the answer. At least I seem closer to the goal than ever before.

April 1, 1941

A vision just came to me of what it would mean if the column actually goes through and I could give up the outfitting game, the teaching, all else and devote myself to this and this alone. That would mean an entirely different world for me, one in which I could concentrate on one thing. Then I should be perfectly happy and content.

What I am afraid of now is that the world will blow up just as I am getting it organized to suit me. A life of preparation and getting ready and then everything lost just as victory is in my grasp.

April 3, 1941

Another birthday in the offing and if anything more tortured and distraught than at any other time in my life. I have felt suicidal before but never quite like this — I hope & pray this will be the end — that my 42nd year will see the finish to the dull pain I always carry with me —

If Paul <u>Meyers</u> comes through & decides to take a chance on the syndicate idea — if he is willing to run them for nothing to get them started that will be OK. If they get going — it will mean full time for me — 50 newspapers at $2.50 a week will mean $125 a week or $500 a month — $10 a mo — is $500 — If 20 take it it will mean $200 — If 10 take it $100 — Even 10 would start me —

I would have to cut down on my length & hit general things — one a week seems all I could do however not 6 a week — that frightens me to death — unless I cut it to 200 words or so & left out 300 or 400 —

If the *Star Journal* keeps on building reader interest — in a year they will have something & there should be demand — perhaps the stuff for a book —

April 4, 1941

This is April the 4th and as usual I am calm and thoughtful and perhaps reflectful of the past and future. This morning I knew that perhaps the most important attribute of man was to be calm and reflective, in full control of his environment, understanding and poised. I thought of the men I knew and did not envy anyone his place—mining engineers, doctors, lawyers, teachers, resort men—it is all the same.

I am a peculiar hodgepodge of desires and I wonder if the day will ever come when it will be different with me. For twenty years I have done something that never did particularly appeal. Nevertheless I have been fairly happy and have gotten considerable out of life. What will the next twenty bring, will it be the same or will I at last get recognition. I have a feeling now, that if this column idea goes through that there will be the answer, not the magazines, not other mediums. Finally will come the book or a series of them. I know that to be happy, I must work to capacity all the time and if the column goes through, I will be doing that, thinking, working, writing. I must be working at top pitch to the full extent of all the interpretive abilities I have to be content.

Today is the 4th and I wonder if such a coincidence could be possible that I would hear from Paul today. About ten days since he last wrote — about four days since he got the big bunch of articles. It would almost be too much to know that actually they might work out.

April 4, 1941

Heard from Paul Meyers today and he is debating whether or not to discontinue the old column and work in mine. If that is true then I have a build-up and a group of papers already to run it as it stands.

Buell Patterson's idea to inject some of the old where-to-go, how-to-do-it element into some of my stuff and thereby get the ideal column is an idea worth working on.[8] Just how to approach it, I don't know. Climax Stand is perhaps as good a bet as any to work on although I cannot see myself trying to do that sort of thing without breaking down the original atmosphere I created.

In each one of these things there is something factual, all right — isn't that enough — shorten them perhaps. Make them breezier but that is all, a running patter perhaps on the out of doors — one each day of my life — six or seven days a week — 300 words —

The stuff I have been writing this past winter is too stodgy — what I have to work in is a running swift patter such as the nature of a speckle's spots, the horns of a deer — quick thoughts, things you can do quickly— and easily—one on pine knots, or using an axe or cutting grass or hauling gravel, outdoors stuff, not necessarily sportsman's stuff.

You want to write about what you see and what you have thought about — well this is the answer. To sit down every morning and at white heat dash off 300-400 words of comment on what you have seen and done — that might be the answer, perhaps not too much of the sort of thing you have done, but rather a running patter much as the columnists in other lines have done, but make yours intimate and personal and somewhat philosophical.

April 25, 1941

Paul Meyers is coming up next Wednesday or Thursday and it should be something definite after that. I am afraid that he will want me to break down my style.

I must write Basil Walters at once and get his reaction before I give anything definite to Paul. I should get his advice on what to do, whether to wait for other bids or to keep my style, whether or not this could be daily stuff.

He could get an answer back to me by the middle of next week without trouble and then I would know my ground when Paul counters with a proposition.

At least my stuff is out in the public eye and getting favorable reactions — that is better than disappointment and wondering if it would ever see the light of day.

April 29, 1941

In a few days Paul Meyers will be here and I am afraid he will want me to change my style and write a swift running commentary on the out of doors, but the longer I think of this idea of a daily column of that kind of stuff, the more I cool.

This morning I wrote "The Whistling Swan" and I wrote it as I have written the rest, a short essay type of sketch, very simple, and I hope beautiful, rhapsodic in a sense, certainly nothing like what he has in mind. Which makes me think that the only thing I want to do with this writing a column idea is to do it my own way or not at all. Write only as you have been writing and about things that appeal to you, write so that anyone anywhere might read it with pleasure and profit and forget the stuff Paul has in mind.

Wagner said that I could not change it without ruining it and doubted if it would run each day. Bob said they are timeless and will run forever and not to hurry about making a choice. I hope he is right.

If I change, I will sell my soul and make myself unhappy. I know nothing about gadgets and how to do things, where to go, and the details of fishing equipment, that means nothing to me and I would be the last to write for the public as an authority of kinks. That would be plain work.

May 14, 1941

The winter is gone and I have written some 140 items for the old column, a brilliant idea and for once in my life one that seems destined to amount to something. For seven weeks, articles have been running in the *Minneapolis Star Journal* and with success and acclaim. It looks as though they might run for some time and gradually build up a good audience.

Now comes Paul Meyers with a more or less definite offer to write for his syndicate. He wants ten articles before June 1st, ten originals and these ten will be more or less of a test of my ability to do something along the lines he has in mind. Short 500 word things, entirely seasonal and inspirational, but also factual and informative — not entirely hunting and fishing but general outdoors stuff — This is a job and a test job and I must get it to him if possible this weekend, forgetting for the time being all my correspondence, all things that might interfere with me. If I could go home today and sit down to work, I think I might do something.

Write about canoe trips, about the first spring trout fishing trip, about catching walleyes — on taking a picnic, on working in the garden and getting the perennial bed ready, of getting the lawn in shape — of going on a pack trip — of bird houses and birds, the swallows and the wrens — the brown thrasher — the whistling swan — about Boots[9] —

cherry blossoms — the large-toothed aspen — each one with a nucleus of truth and fact, but never for a moment forgetting your slant and your old idea of somewhat philosophical enjoyment.

I believe that this stint will more or less prove to Paul that I can do it. Here it is Wednesday. If I can start in tonight and write Thursday, Friday, and over the weekend, then I might be able to do it. At three times a week, he wants about three weeks or a month's supply. Can I or can't I, that is the question.

I can but it will take freedom of mind and removal from small irritations — I must sit down with my mind at fever pitch write these things as I wrote last winter — watch them take shape and turn into something beautiful — Of course there are the things I have not sent down to him which might be worked over — whatever it is — they must be finished and gotten to him and these ten are so important because they are going to be the selling media for Paul's new idea.

More than ever before, I have to concentrate and do my best.

CASUALTY
OF WAR

May 1941–March 1944

F ROM MAY 1941 THROUGH THAT SUMMER, Sigurd wrote another hundred columns, making a total of 250 since he had started a year earlier, and for which he had not received any pay. Kenneth Olson worried that Meyers might be taking advantage of his brother. Sigurd vacillated between confidence and anxiety.

But the column took off. Sigurd started to get paid after the probationary period ended on December 16, and he felt his long search for medium was over. His fears about the column and about Meyers were unfounded. Except for one, that is. He wrote it down on April 1: "What I am afraid of now is that the world will blow up just as I am getting it organized to suit me. A life of preparation and getting ready and then everything lost just as victory is in my grasp."

He was right. Nine days before his probationary period ended, the Japanese bombed the U.S. naval base at Pearl Harbor. For the Olson family it was a deeply personal tragedy: Sigurd and Elizabeth's nephew Curtis Uhrenholdt, who had lived with the Olsons for two years while attending Ely Junior College, was among the thousand-plus men who died when the USS *Arizona* exploded and sank. Sigurd tried to enlist in 1942, but the Marines said he was too old at the age of forty-three.

Falls on the Basswood River, 1940s. Photograph by Leland J. Prater, U.S. Forest Service Records, National Archives.

The war effort added a lot to Sigurd's workload; he had to take on the work of two others at the junior college in addition to his own work as dean. More important, the war claimed the life of his syndicated column. The massive conversion of industry to war footing led to a sharp drop in advertising that forced newspapers to begin cutting features. Syndicated columns were an easy target. In addition, at the end of 1942 the war production board ordered publishers to cut their use of paper by 10 percent, with steeper cuts on the horizon. Sigurd soldiered on for a little over another year at a fraction of the pay, but in March 1944, when only four newspapers still subscribed, he ended the column. A year later he would look back and write that "America Out of Doors" was "the closest I ever came to really arriving."[1]

* * * *

May 21, 1941

Yesterday I sent off fifteen new articles to Paul Meyers and a letter on the proposed contract. All to the good so far but what I forget is this:

I am close to my goal—the goal of sitting down and writing about things I have done and thought about. For years I have thought of nothing but that, have mentioned it time and again, hoped and prayed for a medium and a chance to market something of that type. Now it is close and I am on the threshold of achievement.

Yes, it seems good and I suppose I have achieved a certain success already, getting this far. A year ago it seemed impossible, three months ago the same. Then I used to lie away nights wondering what it would be — "Grandmother's Trout" — "Easter on the Prairie" — "The Pines" — "Spray of Heather" — "Beaverwood Inc" etc, all desperate attempts to find a way out. Now I seem to have it.

And what's more, I feel that this is the answer. I do not care to write short stories or novels only essays and articles of the type I have been doing this winter. That is outlet enough, will make me more money and fame and give me more satisfaction than anything else. That will be the answer. Forget then all magazine stuff, forget everything but that.

Well, suppose it all works out, you resign your job and go to your writing — then a dream will have come true and you should be as supremely happy as it is possible to be. As far as work is concerned, you will be doing something for which you are fitted superbly by nature and temperament. You will have chosen and won out and will have no yearnings for anything else—in short you will have reached a goal.

Remember the mornings when you said, "If I could only sit down and write now, how much I could do." Well, it is close now and it is ten years since the first dream, ten long years of effort and striving. It was 1930 when I began my notes and now it is 1941. Up to 1930 I had dabbled but done nothing serious but during the past ten years, I have been formed and crystallized into something definite.

May 22, 1941

I must somehow convince myself of the import of what I have done & if it works out be content with life — For 20 years I have wondered — pondered, getting nowhere, experimenting, talking, writing continually with little success — Now it has come & I am on the threshold — at last —

If there is contentment in the world & there is happiness in work—then this should be it, to write the sort of thing I want & make a living at it. Forget my Deanship or hold it one year. If I hold it one year — I will be able to put $3000 on our home & bills — & will be clear forever.

Then at 43 I can live as I please & be happy — Happiness will consist in knowing that at last I am on the way.

May 26, 1941

It is or will be just a week since I wrote Paul Meyers about the new deal in the contract and I am a little worried about the outcome. Still he should not cool off now, just as it is working into a position where it will amount to something.

He got the letter on Wednesday, read it then, may have been out of town, but supposing he was not, he would not have a chance to really get at it until the weekend and that would not give me a chance to get anything done or finished until now.

Suppose I don't hear for a couple of weeks. Don't let that worry you—just keep a stiff upper lip. In the meantime, get off that biographical material and the pictures for him to use, so that will be in there with him before June 1st.

There is no use writing any more until I hear from him definitely. I do feel that he has stuff now that really should work in good shape. Surely this last batch is more along the line he would want.

June 25, 1941

I do not think I want to run every day. If I could hold Paul down to three or four a week, or say 15 or 16 per month, that will be enough. That is one every two days and should not be impossible to keep up.

I can at least write in a hurry. My facility is improving and I can pound off anything at short notice that I can develop in my mind.

I dare not look ahead through the years however — that frightens me but I will just have to quit thinking and write as though there was nothing to worry about. What do other columnists think about and do. You have to keep on going and with my full time on the job, I shouldn't have too much difficulty.

I have developed speed and smoothness. If Paul can sell this to a hundred papers so that my income becomes enough to live on, then it will be enough and I won't have to worry.

June 26, 1941

I am doing what Robert Frost has done make the commonplace glow with the white heat of my insight, the woodpile, the northern lights, the wood road, the ice, the coming of the birds, catching a fish, catching trout or what have you. Instead of poetry, I have prose but if I can make my prose so beautiful that they cannot evade its glory then I have arrived. Someday soon the papers will recognize that I have something unusual and then the struggle will be over. And if I keep on writing this year and next without getting more than recognition perhaps that is enough for eventually when I keep on doing these things I will arrive.

July 31, 1941

The days go by with increasing lethargy and disgust and I just tumbled to the fact that I am not writing, have not written for a long time and the only thing that will keep me happy is just that. I learned my lesson long ago and should not have to discover it each time there is a slump in my production but that is nevertheless the case.

After my canoe trip with the Roberts which was a beauty from all angles concerned, I thought I could come back and be perfectly happy for the rest of the summer. While out there I actually wished I was home again but after a short time here, the monotony got me and I wanted to return. I know the old feeling from my guiding days. It is the same now.

The only way for me to conquer this feeling is to begin writing and keep on continually writing. I should start now on some September stuff and get that out of the way and not let it drag until the end.

The more I think of my stuff the more I realize that I must hew to the line that I cannot write factual stuff and keep going, that if I am to be different that I must be consistently different. So many have remarked about the *Star Journal* articles and wished I would keep them just that way the human interest slant more than any other.

I wonder what has happened to Paul, what will happen to our idea this fall, if anything will come of it. I will not know that is sure and cannot make a break until I do. But if the thing pans out and I have an auxiliary income of $200 per month, then I will be all set and we can do anything we wish. I suppose the thing to do is get all set for this fall in the old channels and forget about breaking off. Do not break away until this other has worked out. Then there will be time enough.

August 25, 1941

Ken Reid likes "The Worth of a Tree" as of course he would.[2] He is going to put in a good word for me when he can, says most of the outdoor stuff is pure pap and that papers need what I can give them. Hope he is right.

Now on this other stuff, if Paul goes to town, November 16th should be the beginning and by December 1st I should get my first check. If they are running in 20 papers @ $20.00 per month, my take will be $135.00. If they have 30, my take is $200, if 40, my take is $265.00 per month. That is on the basis of $20.00 per month or $5.00 per week. If it is only $15.00 per month $3.50 per week, then my take is $100.00 — 30 - $150 — 40 - $200.00.

The old column grossed about $500 a month or $165.00 for me. In other words I should stand to make something off this deal that is sure. It becomes a Sig Olson column Nov. 16th and on Dec 1st I get my 1st cut of 32½% or about $75 to $80 enough for Xmas money. Then on Jan 1st I get my 1st full check of possibly $150 or $200 and I will be all set.[3]

August 28, 1941

By the end of this month I will have about $430 coming from school, about $600 coming from the Border Lakes and possibly a dividend of $800 which will give me at least $1800 to spend. The thing to do at once is pay off the house so we won't have that bleeding $45.00 per month bill to pay each time a check comes in. Also pay off the car. There is about $1300 left on the house which with the car will take everything we have, but with no outside payments, we will be sitting pretty well.

The salary will take care of us nicely and any improvements we may wish to make.

Then there is the matter of the syndicate. If that begins producing by Christmas time, there should be an income of from $100 to $200 per month on that, which with what I am making here will give us plenty for all purposes.

This year is the deciding year without question. Financially we are more secure than ever before and there is the chance that the break will come before Spring.

The thing to do now is not to worry yourself sick, but instead develop a certain calmness and surety from knowing that this end of your life is beginning to work out all right. Keep plugging along, working and producing and being happy and contented.

You don't want any other combination than this, don't want any other job, no other ambitions. If you can write a good column, then that is enough. You don't want to do a novel, no short stories, all you want to do is write a distinctive column that will pay enough and take your energy and creativeness. Once that is established, the other will come.

All I need now is the assurance that it will go, that the market will develop, that you have something that will go over. That assurance will come this fall or will blow up entirely. I do not believe there is a chance of its petering out, not after a year of working. It has to go through and from what I have heard they will be accepted.

Then when that is established, continue with your Deanship with its $3000 per year as a backlog, keep on with the Border Lakes and its backlog, and with the syndicate and you will have enough to keep you going and then some without worry.

September 8, 1941

Have just finished Kieran's "Nature Notes"[4] — Mine are so infinitely better that there is no comparison. His very simple, almost childish — mine mature and finished — If the column goes through it will be simple to put out a book of the best for sportsmen and nature lovers generally — must see my contract on that.

Paul should be writing soon — 2 full weeks since I sent in my last batch of mss — Aug. 28 or 29th to be exact — now 9/8 — really only 10 or 12 days — seems like a year — His reaction on this bunch should be the final proof of my ability to do this thing —

I hope he is not sick or under the weather — that he is working hard and that there is some success to report.

Sept. 9th — by Sept 16th — 4 mo will be up — by Oct 16th 5 and by Nov 16th — 6 mo will be up and Dec. 1st I will begin to take in something —

What gets me now is the uncertainty of not knowing what is going to happen — once I know that — then it will all be different entirely —

And knowing that I can break off with equanimity —

Not knowing, I can't make a move. I only hope & pray by Xmas — I will know for sure —

September 11, 1941

This fall is starting in like the last — waiting — waiting — waiting for word. It is now 18 days since Paul got my stuff. Almost 3 weeks. Of course he may be sick or busy lining up stuff. After all I didn't write him for a month — By the 28th of Sept it will be just a month — Perhaps I had better ship in another bunch of articles to him so he will know I am working —

The whole point is this. If this does not pan out—then the bottom is out of everything. Nothing else counts at all and I will be completely sunk no hope whatever. I cannot approach other writing with hope any more — This was the one way out.

This thing must pan out. It cannot be lost. It has gone too far. A whole year has gone into it. Sept to Sept.

During this time, I have written about 250 articles — 160 last spring — 40 in one batch — 25 — 15 — about right. The Star Journal has published — I have signed a contract and have had advance publicity — Now I am on the hot box — don't know if I will live or die.

September 16, 1941

Been working on some 25 new ones for Nov release — many of them good — all of them with a decided timing worked in somewhere. Isn't this what I had hoped for—to record my flashes as I am doing now.

Marshfield — Green Bay — Cincinnati — Pittsburgh that I know of & there must be many more.

What I need now is the assurance that what I write is OK will be accepted and run that each work is worth something & will be judged by the world —

This time as with the last I will get them out in time & send them off with the same hope & uncertainty. 8 done now, possibly 15 without too much work — the ones on deer tracking should go in also but will take more time.

September 18, 1941

Last night, I finished twenty one new items for Meyers. Most of them were fairly good, some better than the others. One thing I have noticed now is that I can run them off very smoothly, that the writing is not difficult at all, that if I have an idea that the rest comes without much effort.

After finishing this bunch, I felt as though I couldn't write another thing. My mind was as barren as a desert and anything I might have written would have been no good. Sat down and tried to do something on ducks but found it was impossible. I'll have to wait now until I catch up before any ideas will come that are worthwhile, just like a well filling up again after it has been drained completely dry.

After each effort, I sit down and wonder how in the name of all creation it will be possible to do anything more and I wonder if there is anything to write about. However, I know that when my mind gets surcharged again that they will all come a-running. The half dozen or so that I have milling around in the back of my mind will soon take shape and so will plenty of other things.

Now Paul will have about fifty good fall items which should hold him well through November and possibly in December. What gets me is that none of this stuff will be paid for until November 16th, but that isn't all true as the contract reads any new Sig Olson columns will be mine.

As I read over my stuff and realize that actually I am doing what I have always wanted to do, that my mind is working like lightning on a thousand things, then I begin to see that after all this dream of mine is actually coming true.

The contract says all book rights are mine. Well, I do not see why it should be impossible to work up a fine book of short descriptive essays, much on the order of what I had in mind, short beautiful interpretive things that a man might want to take with him into the woods, or keep by his bedside or give away as a gift, selling perhaps at a dollar or perhaps two. And what is more, there can be a regular series of them, perhaps a book every year or two. That is enough for one man. That is enough to keep me occupied and happy without any further ambitions. That will be the end I seek, nothing more.

It will be marvelous to know that at last I am doing exactly what I have always wanted to do, that I have found my creative outlet at last, that there will be no more looking around and wondering.

September 22, 1941

My letter from Paul was encouraging, says a check is forthcoming for my personal releases the past 2 mos — and then after Dec 16th — the end of 6 mos — that my checks will be substantially larger — our plans to release America Out of Doors — 100% your column — If they are grossing 600 per mo — my take is 200 which will not be too bad — Once I start that everything will be set. —

Undated, ca. October 6, 1941

Last Friday, my mind was barren, needed new scenes and experiences to recharge it. I am like a run down battery after a session of writing, need new current to bring me to top amperage. When out, I am like a sponge, soaking up impressions around me as a sponge soaks up moisture. I don't need to take notes, the things that are worthwhile stay with me. I need to jot them down immediately upon my return however, so they are not lost in the maze of other interests before they are caught. Now I have some fifty new titles ready for use in Jan and Feb. Ten more titles and I'll have enough for two solid months and with what Paul already has, enough for three months.

October 8, 1941

An idea after reading review of Needham's book "About Ourselves."[5] Feel a book would give me a host of ideas — about which I could weave my own interpretation. I would have to have time to read & explore the thoughts of others. A book would do as much as a thousand trips afield. That has been done during the past 30 years or so. —

Last night thinking of Nashwauk & the feeling I knew back in 1920 and '21 — What a marvelous sensation — hiking down the road to McCarty Lake — Kennedy Lake — Shoal Lake — Buck Lake — The uplift I knew — the clean air the color — the adventure — the camps — the hunting — That was the harvest of those years — the real harvest — those days & nights were the real thing[6] —

I had the feeling then of wanting to write — Remember Keewatin that day when I decided.[7] Then I was all impressionistic — uncultured — unmapped. I was a boy with a poet's soul enjoying a primitive life to the utmost. Things went perhaps as they should. If I had wanted to enough I would have gone to Alaska & tried it or to Le Pas, Manitoba or gone prospecting — but there wasn't enough of adventure in my soul. I was still too much of a poet to want to leave the familiar —

October 14, 1941

Pete said last night that he could not see why the titles I had chosen should not be interesting — the titles themselves, he said were intriguing.

Paul worries me continually — Is this thing going to crash or not. Will the war curtail features entirely or will this one go on.

Will this be enough of an unusual article type to keep going —

The thing to do now is send Paul Meyers — the titles you are working on some 65 odd to show him you are not letting go. Also remind him of Si Peterman — sports writer — & the Philadelphia Enquirer — just to show you are working along —

This week is Oct 16 — Nov 16 is one month off — in other words it should not be long now —

October 16, 1941

I set out on Monday to jot down the ideas accumulated over the weekend, some twenty six of them all told and then proceeded systematically to work them up. Today four days later, I have twenty pretty well whipped into shape. Now for a session of typing and final revision and I will be through. I think the way to work these is to type each one of these for a first draft and then go over them again for final revisions. I could do it with one attempt, but they will be more finished if I go through them a second time.

A campsite in the Quetico–Superior wilderness, 1940s. Listening Point Foundation Archives.

This has shown me that I can sit down and with twenty odd titles work up twenty articles. I think that with leisure it would be no stint at all to do my twenty eight or so per month.

Now for better than a year, I have been doing this and have written several hundred similar things, possibly 150,000 words all told, enough to show me that I can carry on. For a time I thought one a week would be enough, but I see now that that is only a drop in the bucket that I can and am capable of doing much more than that.

Now if I had the consolation of knowing that Paul was actually going ahead with the stuff, that there was no question about the stuff being used. What is hard is playing with the idea that perhaps it is all for nothing, that my work is valueless, that there will be no outlet after all. Once that is cleared up then it will be a different matter entirely. For then I will know that things are actual and working out.

Today is the 16th of October, one month more of probation and then that period will be over and either they will have to come across or tell me when they will.

My letter of the other day will show Paul that I am working steadily that he is under an obligation of some sort to make it right with me. All I can do is live in hope and pray that he will come through. I don't know why I should be so skeptical, but I am continually so. Perhaps Ken was right when he intimated that he didn't want to see Paul take me for a ride.

I can't believe that after all the work that has been done on it that he will fizzle out. Soon I shall hear again of that I am sure.

If he comes through, it will mean that pretty soon I will have an income of about 150 to 200 per month in addition to what I have here. That will be enough to keep me going beautifully. I have some 45 articles well under way now, have some 60 odd in fairly good shape for the next bunch. I must work in now some of the winter shots, keeping that in mind to sandwich in with the rest.

October 18, 1941
Spent a beautiful weekend up at Basswood and saw again what my life might be if I didn't have to come home to the many problems of the college. Up there I really seem to live, I get so much out of doing just the ordinary things. See so many things that give me ideas, get so much genuine pleasure out of everything.

Seeing that FISH NET gave me a picture — the fact that it belonged to the Indians gave me a slant on their freedom and the primitive dependence they have on wildlife. The net laying there so serenely, so patiently waiting, so different from the speed and fuss of ordinary fishing. That was the real thing. I pulled it and saw two suckers, enough for a meal, but what impressed me was that here was something real, back to earth, primitive and simple, the quiet calmness of that little bay, the smooth water, the corks floating there, waiting, waiting for the catch.

Sitting in the sun today, I fell asleep, asleep watching the decoys, grew tired of watching the blue water and the shifting flocks.

November 11, 1941
Last Trip to Basswood

Queer going up for the last time, all the potholes and sloughs frozen solid, the landing in Hoist Bay firm with two inches, even around all the shores, masses of solidifying slush ice and broken cakes. Yes it was time

A motor launch prepares to leave the Border Lakes Outfitting Company docks at Fall Lake, 1940. Photograph by Leland J. Prater, U.S. Forest Service Records, National Archives.

to be getting out so we stacked the canoes away, checked out all the extra grub, hung the blankets over a rafter and closed the door.

Made one final sashay after bluebills — a great raft sitting at the mouth of Back Bay, took to the air with a roar as we approached but would not come back, killed three close ones but that was all. As I stood there looking over the lake with the ice forming, the rosy west, it looked too good to me, I knew and I felt then the old joy in doing what we had all fall. In fact I had not for years felt so completely happy and content and convinced that that was the answer. I came closer to finding the old joy on these last trips than I had since I used to go with Santo to Low and the Stoney. I think part of the realization is knowing that I never care to change from this setup, no advancement, no government jobs, no change of residence, that this life is enough and that I should stop fretting. I think part of that has come from the writing I have done, part from knowing that I want nothing more out of life than this. In other words my philosophy is hardening.

I have my doubts about Paul and will not urge him but if it should fizzle out, then I can only do one other thing, make these essay sketches into book form. That perhaps will be the real answer though it would be interesting if the other panned out. At least it has given me much peace of mind.

In view of all this settling down, the thought comes, why not fix the house up as you wish, why not get all of the things you need to keep you happy rather than wait and wait until you are too old to enjoy it, why not change the fireplace, why not build the porch, why not put up the dormer to Bob's room, why not spend a couple of thousand doing what you wish, rather than wait. And I think, well, why not, what is the difference if I stay here the rest of my life.

My dreams and my philosophy have jelled and no longer shall I reach for the moon and keep myself unhappy. I know what makes me happy now. I wonder about the Border Lakes, if I could let that go, if I could get along without that source of income.

February 18, 1942

Perhaps through your writing, you may be able to give to others something of what you have. Perhaps that is the answer of real service to others. That must be the driving force. If you can give people the feeling that used to be yours in the old days, the supreme joy and sense of glory and elation when on a trout stream, when hiking through the woods, when exploring, when skiing, and hunting. If you can give them that in books they might enjoy, then you have done your share. That is your job to do and the world will be better for your having lived. For what I felt there, it is possible for all to feel, if I show them how.

March 1, 1942

E says my last batch of stuff is far too good to send to Paul and I really think she meant it.

Read Van Loon this morning — told the story of the old Chinese artist who on his deathbed when asked if his work and sacrifice was worthwhile, pointed to a painting he had made of a single leaf of grass. The grass was more than a painting for it lived and breathed and moved, it was all blades of grass that had ever been born.

That painting made the artist akin to the gods, he had touched the hem of eternity and therefore was divine. It is given to few to do that.[8]

Sigurd on a summer hike, circa 1942. Listening Point Foundation Archives.

The thing that impressed me was the similarity. If I can paint a word picture of something eternal, if I can catch the divine spirit in something I do, that is justification enough, no matter whether I starve or die of exposure.

All his life this man had devoted himself to his dream. Starvation and hardship had dogged his steps and he had nothing to show for what he had done, nothing in the way of spiritual things, but he had done what he wished to do and that was enough, he had created and never for a moment lost his goal. At last he had painted that blade of grass and that was enough.

March 19, 1942

Crows back, a whole flock of them sitting in the birches, a half dozen grouse flying sedately, soaring across the open field, the morning sun and the mist and the feeling of unbounded energy. Hard to believe it is nearing April and my 43rd birthday and the country at war.

But so it is and it is hard to tell what another year will bring. As I look back over my other birthdays, I see the answer clearly. Never any peace until you can devote all of your time to the business at hand. For thirteen years or fifteen years to be exact since 1927 this has been your passion, years of learning and improving. That is all that counts now and all that will ever count.

Reading over "The Marks of Genius" I see so many things that I have learned the truth of during this period, staying with your goal, not being distracted, not allowing anything to sway or change your ideas, loneliness, differentness, all of those things come in and also the great satisfactions.

What I must do is get rid of the Border Lakes, get rid of everything that might interfere, devote my whole life to doing what I know now is my life work, "The Interpreting of the Out of Doors," making myself as Walters says, "The finest outdoor writer in America."[9]

April 22, 1942

The whole trouble with me is that I am not writing anymore. I recognize the signs. As soon as I quit, the bottom drops out. I must write in order to keep my sanity. Nothing else counts, all the joy and the verve is gone and I am in the depths.

I am waiting for Paul, have heard nothing since the 10th of April—12 days now. Evidently nothing has happened, either there or with NBC.

All I can do is hope and pray, but if nothing does happen, I feel that I must keep on with my writing, no matter what happens. I must write if not for the newspapers, then stuff for the magazines.

It is possible to work up combinations of material for the magazines along certain lines. I must keep on working continually, and then there is the book possibility.

I cannot let the drive disappear. There must be movement and accomplishment.

Undated, November 1942–February 1943

I feel a real passion in giving of myself. I want people to know how I feel because I believe that in so doing they can get more out of life and be happier. I feel that I have a message, something to contribute, something real and vital that many are missing. If I can make them feel about the woods and hills and waters as I do, about every little thing that gives me pleasure, then I have done enough.

There is something of the crusader in me, the evangelist. I cannot rest unless it comes out and I will never be happy unless I give myself wholly to the task at hand. And it will not be stories but rather articles much as I have done and through them try and bring out my ideas. Somehow in reading them, I feel that people will begin to find what I have found, see what I have seen, know what I know.

January 20, 1943

The more I work on the idea of the book the better I feel about it. Now that the first preliminary work is done it does not seem such an impossible task. At first when it was all one grand jumble I did not know where to begin, but now order is coming and it is possible to know just what to do.

HOURS AFIELD does not seem too bad a title — grouped in Spring, Summer, Autumn, Winter might make an attractive layout.

What impressed me as I worked through the grouping last night was that we picked the pieces that had a spiritual appeal, not the factual ones at all, spirit, emotion, feeling they were the ones we remembered. The beautiful things stayed with us and the poor ones were forgotten.

February 24, 1943

Last night reading Thoreau — "I want to enjoy only those simple, common everyday things, make capital of them, for they are what make life significant."

That is what I have tried to do. I have forgotten the great adventures, dramatized and made heroic and meaningful the thousand and one things that lie about. If I have any fame, then it will be based on that, for only through them will people be reached. . . . I do not have to go to Alaska or Tibet or Australia or anywhere else. The whole world is here at my door. Ely is the hub of the universe. I can learn as much here as anywhere in the world. This is the place to work and observe.

Undated, May 1943

Robert Frost is able to evaluate the present through the experience of the past and through a slight tint of originality give freshness to his experience. And that is exactly what I have been doing. Taking present experiences, I color them with the past, weave the old experiences about them, enrich them as it were and fertilize them with background and then if there is anything new that might come out of all this reworking, then that is what gives it freshness and present worthwhileness. He reminds me of myself. He is a poet and I write in prose but our methods are the same and someday I will be recognized as he is recognized.

October 1943[10]

The Importance of Knowing

Whenever I get down in the mouth, whenever I feel as though there was nothing worth living for anymore, then I have lost touch with the important part of my life. I have forgotten what really counts. Yesterday up on Basswood, pacing back and forth in front of the blind, I was suddenly very happy for I knew that I had the answer. THE IMPORTANT THING FOR ME WAS LIVING CLOSE TO THE WOODS AND WRITING. NOTHING ELSE MATTERED. WARS COULD COME AND GO, CATASTROPHES STRIKE MY FAMILY OR THE WORLD AND STILL ALL OF IMPORTANCE WOULD BE TO WRITE AND LIVE CLOSE TO THE THINGS I LOVE.

Fame or accomplishment mean nothing to me, but taking a walk as I did yesterday from Pete's to Camp was something, standing in the doorway watching the snow come down, lying on my bunk watching the moonlight try to penetrate the storm and the black spruce and the aspen there outside the window. Seeing those three squaw ducks[11] dive into the storm, riding the waves coming down Fall Lake, the vision of rice point in the storm, of the dog swimming out to get that duck, or decoys off the narrows, that little fire back against the balsams, the sense of coziness, coming home to a shower after that ride down the lake. Those things count with me.

I like soft music with my meals, like to eat in a grand dining room, like to watch people come and go. I like to go into a museum, an art gallery, like a good show and colorful crowds, but not for long. The real joy comes up here when I am alone. This is the real thing for me.

This I know. There is no question anymore. I am 45 and know my mind and the sooner you change the better you are off.[12] This year should then be the last. You have been in this work 25 years, a quarter of a century, are still young, know now the reasons for things and the answer to your problem.

And you must not get discouraged if the first few months you earn nothing, get nowhere. Give yourself a year and then you will know. Many things can happen if you have nothing to do but this. You have waited long enough.

November 8, 1943

Duck hunting over the weekend in dear old Back Bay the real answer came to me, the answer to all of my worryings, the answer that supersedes all other conclusions and here it is.

To write so that others will see what you see, to live and tell of your living in a way that will give joy and real satisfaction to others, to give them the understanding and joy that is yours, that is the real purpose of your life. It is not the army or the Navy or the Marines or the Deanship or the Border Lakes or any other consideration. Your job is to write, nothing but that. That is your mission in life, that is your big job, that and that alone. All other things are secondary. That has been the main theme of your life for twenty years and will never change. That is the reason everything goes haywire when you forget your dream, why you plunge into the depths of despondency as soon as you think of leaving it.

If this job seems inconsequential, think of it only as a crutch. The other is all that counts and if you keep working away at it, you will regain your peace of mind. What you need more than anything else is to know that your job is the biggest thing for you in the world. Nothing is bigger, nothing more important, nothing more worthwhile. If you make a fortune all well and good. If you don't it is still worthwhile.

What makes you desperate, merely the feeling that you have not time to write. If you could work things now so that you could put in all of your time on your writing, then you would be close to happiness.

The only thing that matters to me is writing up the woods and wildlife as I have wanted to do all of my life. The only thing of importance is living out of doors. Army life would be terrible to me, so would all the other forms of mass activity. I am an individualist and would die with crowds and orders regulating my life. I must be alone where I can think and cogitate.

My real happiness comes when I have written something beautiful and worthwhile. The sooner I can reach that goal, the happier I shall be.

Vision of a cabin on a day like this, the snow coming down, a good warm fire, the teakettle on and a big table before a window with me working away. Books to read and E for companionship. We will have that someday. And that will turn out to be the happiest time of our whole life.

This is coming.

December 12, 1943

Write so beautifully of your out of doors, so feelingly of the Isabella, that it will mean more than anything else you might do. Write a story called "The Isabella," make it such a moving thing that whoever reads it will weep for the sheer beauty of it, will want to read it again and again. Bring into it all of the joy, all of the beauty, everything that you have known there. For the Isabella is much more than a trout stream—it is a rendezvous with love and companionship, it brings in all of the joy of youth, all the serenity of maturity.[13]

The stuff within you surges for expression. It must come out and when it does, you will be content and feel that you have done what you are supposed to do.

January 24, 1944

A great question raised itself last night a question that might settle the old one of what to do to live a happy and more or less contented life.

Falls of the Isabella River, 1921. Photograph by Arthur H. Carhart, Forest History Society, Durham, North Carolina.

The thought of traveling through the east came up after talking to Laura and Oliver and at once the thought flashed into mind that I could enjoy no travel, no going places, no having just fun without the continual ogre with me of feeling that it was all froth, unreal, that I did not have the right to do it until I had done what I was supposed to do. This old feeling has been with me for many years and has ruined many good times and occasions. I have felt unable to throw myself wholesouledly into anything but have always gone in with reservations, half heartedly, as though I was an outcast, a foreigner, one who did not belong, but more than that one who had not the right to play the game. Right now I would not enjoy a trip with anyone because underneath would be that haunting realization that I was wasting my time, that I should be at work, that life is slipping by, that I am playing only, that I have missed the boat.

Which brings the real question. Why, if that is how you feel, don't you do something about it. Obviously as long as you stay on here and do the kind of work you have been doing, you will never get anywhere as far as escape from the old idea is concerned.

February 2, 1944
The thing to do is ask for a leave in April, a leave for the duration. That will leave an anchor to windward.[14]

Another thing is to keep the old home going and keep it waiting for Bob and Jr. We cannot fail them no matter what happens.

Comments of others should bolster your courage — Cleaves — "I expected great things of you" — Whipple — "the finest outdoor writer of his type in America" — Bob M. "Your stuff is authentic, has the faculty of making the real outdoors live" — Jack Hanley — "You could make the *Post* like a damn." Walters "Some day Sig O will be one of the most famous outdoor writers in America" — Adams "One of the finest of its kind I have ever read."

In other words I have had some signs that my stuff is passable. Here is the great chance, here the opportunity to do what all your life you had hoped to do. All you care about is writing, no other job in the world appeals to you at all, not a single one that you can think of, governor of a S. Sea island, manager of a game refuge, head of wilderness area commission, chief game warden, Pres of a college or Univ, Commander of Armies, they are all as so much sawdust. I have only one objective, to describe the way a pool looks in the evening when the mayflies are out, how a loon sounds on a wilderness lake, how a storm appears on McIntyre, how mallards come into a blind, how frost looks on the stubble, only one dream, to make myself the greatest creator of outdoor pictures in the world. With that will come lectures and other things. That is all that counts and knowing that even should the years ahead be hard, I should rest content.

To know at last that I am doing what I was intended to do should fill the ache, should make me content. Knowing that no other life will give me contentment should be enough. There can be no other life whatever. I am too much of a poet to relish too much of the physical, too much in love with the scene, the beauty of earth about me to indulge entirely my love of action.

I must have activity however and a chance to be out of doors. I must set up a regime of half and half out perhaps in the mornings back in the afternoons, reading and talking at night. There must be no halfway measures or happenstance. After breakfast start out across the hills or perhaps it would be better to write each morning until noon or thereabouts and then hike or paddle or work in the garden or go somewhere with E. Build up your library work up your reading habits, have your stuff in order so that you can work in peace, be master of your time.

You can spend a couple of months down on the farm if you wish or you can travel south to be near Bob or Jr. or you can go to Florida when the war is over or Mexico. You can really begin to live.

You have always wanted to know the answer to contentment. One of the big obstacles has always been the fact that you could not decide what you wanted to do with your life. Now it is settled without a single wavering thought. I know of nothing in the wide world that would appeal to me at all outside of writing or sketching. The ministry is not enough — no teaching job — no administrative job or conservation job of any kind but what would find me sitting back wishing for time of my own to write in. For twenty years or since 1924 approximately I have worked on this idea. Now it is definitely settled and eat or starve we are going into it full tilt.

If you have hard sledding for the first two years or so, be not alarmed unduly—it will take a little time to get under way. In time you will be writing for some of the bigger mags and that will take care of the slack.

There will be books, books that you might even illustrate yourself with your own sketching. I keep thinking of Seton's work in Animals I have Known, the fringe sketches he did all the way through.[15] I might if I work hard enough and consistently enough at it, work into something like that.

The war was merely an escape to get rid of the old jobs and to find myself or die.[16] I have found myself and the war is out. I can contribute more to human happiness through my writing than in any other way, can give to the boys who are longing for the out of doors and who may never see it again a touch of the wild they have known. Through my eyes they might live again, to see and feel a trout stream at dawn, ducks whistling down out of the blue, the crash of a mallard in the rice, the sound of a rapids, rain on the pavement, the smell of powder, the crack of rifles in November, a thousand things that they have known. That is something.

February 14, 1944

E and I talked things over last night and we feel that when Bob goes the thing to do is make an objective and work ourselves to the bone for it.[17] It will of course be my writing. If we both work at that, both of us think of nothing else than the success to be achieved there and the new horizons opening up for us, then we will not have time to become morose and discouraged.

If we think of nothing else, do nothing else, plan for nothing else than that, look upon my writing as a mission — an interpreting of the out of doors to nature hungry people, a means to give happiness to others, immerse myself in it to the exclusion of all else, then something might come.

With success will come fame and lecturing, new contacts, new friends, new ideas. Life will begin to open up as never before. The boys will be proud and happy. We can visit Sam and Giny, the Cunninghams, the Reids, Ken and Mickey, the Farm, people in the east and west, go up and spend a week or a month with Ober — it will be a different life.

And I will have my freedom to come and go. E and I can take a cabin on Basswood during the coloring in the fall and stay as long as we wish. I will of course go into outdoor photography in a manner never approached before — must get me a good camera and possibly movies —

it will be an interesting exciting profession to get into and we will have to throw ourselves into it lock stock and barrel so to speak, give it so much that we will not have time to brood or get morose no matter what happens.

That compared to playing bridge or lunk and eating turkey and sitting around night after night talking about nothing. I am proud of E being revolted at that, shows she has more than the average, will play along with me, be a partner all the way through.

We will become more and more dependent on each other but it will be fun. Up to this point we have lived for Bob and Jr., but now we have turned the leaves to a new chapter and will I feel find it entirely new and if nothing else adventurous.[18]

But we must have faith and enthusiasm that what we are doing is worthwhile. That we have and we must maintain it. It is going to be an exciting thing to do—but worthwhile. I want to lose myself entirely in contemplation of and interpretation of the out of doors, want to think of nothing else but that. That is my whole life, what I have been trending toward. My preparation now seems complete.

We are young have at least 20 more years of activity ahead of us, as long as the time we have been in Ely. These last twenty years should be as much fun or more than the first.

March 29, 1944

My column stuff, Hours Afield should give me many ideas to work into stories. In fact it should be possible to work up many like I did "The Spring Hole" — fishing episodes like those on bass flies or trout, canoe trip stuff. There is a great fund of information there.

But now suppose the *Atlantic* or *Collier's* come across and I find that stuff will sell. That will be success and from then on, I must try and repeat and repeat. To be able to land there would be enough perhaps, enough to be remembered for.

If they don't sell, then bundle up the bunch and send them in to an agent and let her worry.

Medium Again

April 1944–November 1946

THE UNTIMELY END OF "America Out of Doors" left Sigurd once again confronting the dilemma of medium. Should he write fiction? Nonfiction articles? Essays? By now he saw fiction as nearly hopeless; he just didn't have the gift for it. As for nonfiction, he was bored of writing hunting and fishing features for the outdoor magazines. He wanted to write essays, and his "America Out of Doors" column had given him lots of material he could expand into short essays to submit to magazines and eventually gather into books.

But he was not done with struggling over the issue. As 1944 came to an end, he sent a batch of essays off to another literary agent, Anita Diamant of Writers Workshop Inc. in New York. She was not impressed, calling them "rather discursive and even verbose at times." After Sigurd did some reworking, she said they were "beautifully done," but the market was "extremely limited." She wanted Sigurd to try short story fiction. He gave in, and during the summer and fall of 1945 wrote nine short stories. Diamant's feedback was brutal: "It's difficult to get through them and we found ourselves exerting effort to keep on with the story in each case. . . . If you really want to sell stories, Mr. Olson, you simply must accelerate the action."[1]

Sigurd at a wilderness campsite, 1940s. Wisconsin Historical Society Collection, 74070.

273

The last of those stories he wrote while overseas. With the war drawing to a close in 1945, the army couldn't simply bring back all three million American soldiers stationed in Europe at one time, so it created the American Army University to let them begin college course work while they waited their turn to come home. Kenneth Olson was selected for an administrative position, and he invited Sigurd to teach zoology and geology to the troops in Shrivenham, England. Sigurd arrived in July and taught through the fall. He then spent several months touring Europe with the Army's Lecture Bureau, visiting troops in France, Germany, Austria, and Italy. Finally, he became an observer for the U.S. State Department and the U.S. Army at the Nuremberg trials in March 1946. In preparation, he toured twenty-two concentration camps, beginning with Dachau on March 8. He would wake occasionally from nightmares for the rest of his life.[2]

He also found a new source of support and encouragement, an elderly woman named Ellinor Grogan. Sigurd spent time at her gray stone manor full of the works of famous artists and writers, many of whom had stayed there. She had known well one of Sigurd's favorite authors, W. H. Hudson, and showed Sigurd the desk Hudson had worked at and letters he had written her. Sigurd told her all about his own dream and struggles, and she encouraged him not to give up.

These experiences overseas helped Sigurd grow in his resolve to write what he knew he *had* to write, rather than write simply for the market. In this chapter's final entry, Sigurd is back in Ely, dreaming of books of essays illustrated by his friend Francis Lee Jaques. This dream would come true in another ten years, but first he had to handle another plot twist or two.

* * * *

April 10, 1944

Walking last night milling over the old question of medium, I came to the conclusion that there is only one thing I can write, an interpretation of what I know of the out of doors, something along the order of what I have been doing for the column. I like to write on things like The Esker, Pines, Birches, Running Water because I know and understand them.

If I can write so beautifully about any outdoor topic that editors cannot pass it up, then I have what I want to do. The world is full of fiction writers but there are very few who have the feeling for things that I have.

Take "The Stone Wall" for instance. If I can write on building a stone wall so beautifully, so poetically, so charmingly that anyone would like to read about it, if I can write about an esker the same way, or about a fishing trip, giving my own interpretation in such a way that others will look for it to enjoy then I have done something.

What has been wrong to date — that is hard to define, but it is something. Next winter I must try and find out, rework the book, put the writer into a character other than mine. Perhaps that is the secret—to build up a character that will actually have all of my reactions for that after all that is all writing is....

But I cannot write of character. Characters frighten me. All I can write of and all I should write of is what I know and feel. If I do that well enough, the world will listen. Surely I love people. I love young people, children, all people who are unaffected. I love laughter and joy and play and hard work but I cannot picture or portray the character of another. I cannot even portray my own. In fact I do not know myself. And to me it is unimportant what others do and think. <u>To me the only thing worthwhile is a new interpretation of the earth</u>. If I can do that one thing, then I have done more than enough. That is task big enough for any one man—my personal and poetic feelings about the earth and all its life and man's relationship to it.

October 10, 1944

If you can capture in a brief descriptive essay the poetry you know and feel so that others can catch it, feel it as though they were walking with me, making them so beautiful that anyone who reads will feel for the moment as though they had lived for a moment beside me, poetry in prose without the stultifying limiting effect of rhyme. Working along the path of the column writing about anything you see, anything you think about. That I believe is your medium as it has been for five years or more.

This winter rework some of the old stuff, ship out a flock of them to various magazines, reworking them, such things as "Moonlight" —

"Birthday on the Baptism" — The Esker, Drumming of the Grouse, Blue Jay, Clear Ice, The Stone Wall, Flagstone Walk, The Smell of Pines, Snowstorm, The Bluebills, Coloring of Leaves. Pussy Willows.[3]

Rework them to 1000 words each, work and rework them until they are letter perfect until they are so finished and complete that words cannot be added or taken away. Make them prose sonnets, so unearthly beautiful and lovely that everyone will want to save them. Start soon and see what you can do. Keep a dozen of them going around.

If you find a market for them, then your problem is solved because one man cannot hope to do more than that in his lifetime. That is what you want to do, that is what you can do and what you can always be happy in doing. That perhaps is your real mission in life.

Can you imagine anything more satisfying to your soul than to sit down and work on things like that. They are your poems, they are everything you ever dreamed of or wanted to do. They are the things you would do for nothing.

Short stories or long articles are possible but work, writing about others unimportant unless I catch that elusive something that shows in the short articles above.

This may be the answer to my years of dreaming and wondering — do them so beautifully, put so much feeling and picturing into them, so much understanding and beauty that no one can resist them. You might work up something really worthwhile here and totally your own.

December 22, 1944

If something happens this winter so that I can make a go of my writing, then all will be well. Give up the Border Lakes and school and concentrate only on my writing. Devote the rest of my life to the achievement of that one goal. Put in the last twenty years doing nothing but that, writing, living in the woods, doing the sort of thing I have always dreamed of doing.

Even should Diamant come back and say no, there still is hope.[4] Those bits could stand revision and improvement but not very much.

January 22, 1945

The blow has fallen. Diamant has come back with thumbs down on everything.

My sketches will have no sale. They are too indirect, vague, lack drive and directness, wander off from the point, too nebulous and fantastic. No market for anything like that. Even the *Atlantic* and *Harper's* and others are more direct and to the point. Beautiful writing, beautiful descriptions and passages all through but that is all.

Suggests that I go on with my article writing, that I do what I know how to do or try short stories. She thought I might really do something there.

I had thought that I had something different here, something strictly my own, had gone on the premise that if I wrote how I felt about things that the world would come to my door but Diamant says no. Write the sort of thing you want to write and what you would want to read but again she says no.

Well, the point is I must find a way out somewhere. This is not the end of my writing. I must find my medium and the hour is late....

I cannot do short stories and never will. That is out. I can write articles however and sell them. I have done it before and can now and that is what I must do this winter. Though I will not be able to strike out by myself, I can write and keep at least on a level keel as far as my writing need is concerned.

I don't want to write stories anymore on trout fishing or hunting. I want to do articles bringing in what I have started in the column and attempted to do above. That is my field from now on and that is what I must perfect. When I get my form down then I can plan but not before. At least I know what I want to do and work with. I like to write on picture windows and cabins and stones and blue jays but I must do it excitedly and personally. I must work out how to bring in joy and excitement and interest for everyone. Get away from the dead and prosaic. Your mission in life is to glamorize the common out of doors and if you accomplish that, then you are set. Take a balsam, a blue jay, a wild goose, a mallard, a stone wall or a spruce tree or moonlight, or brook trout. You have a job but if you win, it will be wonderful.

January 29, 1945

Have redone "Moon Magic" and "Wild Goose,"[5] have written them like any article, a swift concise introduction then a swiftly moving story with not an item that doesn't relate itself to the main idea, then a conclusion that ties the knot. Believe now I have discovered the secret. How could I be so stupid before as to think that anything I wrote down would sell. Imagery is not enough. There must be a story and a swift vivid one.

Found out also that free of interruptions I can work. Saturday a.m. rewrote "Wild Goose" in two hours, much of it original. It was fun, too, the ideas flowed and I enjoyed every moment of it. The same with Moon Magic. Shows what I can do when I am free.

If I have the key now to future work, then I have accomplished enough this winter. My future work will be only more of the same. Swiftly moving stories or articles about ideas, not over 2000 words in length but each one giving an interpretive slant. Then someday the book will come. I will develop the market I wish. What a joy it will be when I find my medium—no worry about plot, no worry about character, no worry about length or how to go about it anymore. Your only worry to think of interesting and vital subjects.

Your old dream to write vividly about the out of doors so vividly that others would see it as you do may come true. Then and when it does, any ordinary job will not bother you. Your goal will be set. That is enough for one man to do. If you do not do more than a dozen a year, it will be enough.

The whole thing will then be that you have reached your goal that is you have discovered after twenty odd years what it is that you want to do. No more will I lay awake and worry about my medium. It will be this sort of thing.

As Burroughs said, "Get down to the quick of your mind. Blow off the froth and the unessential. Vibrate when you write." I know what that means now. Be alive, vibrant, excited when you compose, revise at leisure. You were alive Sat morning. Never try to write when you are tired. Be so full of your subject that when you sit down you can write swiftly and without effort.

February 5, 1945

I have sent in to Diamant four revamped articles, "Moon Magic," "Stones Have Personality," "Trees Remind Me of People," and "Wild Goose."

I have a feeling about these four that I have done the impossible and worked my pet ideas into salable form. What makes me sure of this is that you start out with a major premise and do not vary from it an iota, the same as your regular articles. Of course it does mean a sacrifice of pure fantasy and most philosophical ideas but I see that they can be worked in only where you have a vehicle to carry them. People hate straightforward philosophy or intangible ideas.

Take "Moon Magic" — the idea is the effect of moonlight on animals and straight through I have given examples that would substantiate that premise. Instead of starting with a fanciful walk such as in the original I plunge into my premise. The same with "Stones Have Personality." Instead of letting the reader guess at my idea I come out with it and build it up through the article. The same with "Trees Remind Me of People" and also "Wild Goose."

February 9, 1945

Last night I finished "Forest Pool,"[6] now "The Story of a Pool" and believe I have done something worthwhile. The former was loosely built, had no swift chronological sequence. It had lovely pictures but not definite or concrete. There was something nebulous about it. Now it is short, concise, to the point and clear cut. Anyone who is interested in the out of doors should like it.

It took me nine hours to do it, nine hours of hard work, but my thinking about it and planning it out in my mind made it possible. It shows me for the fifth time that it is possible to use this material in articles without being fanciful or shadowy. With a definite premise or an idea and with everything built around it, any article can be interesting. That makes five revised. What frightened me first was the impossibility of the task of revision. I thought it could not be done and what seems queer now is the thought I had that I could write and sell any of my imaginings without a definite structure. It was a nice dream while it lasted but it is more satisfying to know that I am whipping a medium into shape that may be the answer to my years of floundering. If as a result of this winter's work that medium is a reality, no matter if I do not do another bit of work, then I should be satisfied.

That means that after a time, there will be a book, a collection of these articles or essays, or a series of these books. There is no end to them or no end to the articles.

I can pick out any subject under the sun and after mulling it over, thinking about it, reading and getting my mind surcharged, sit down to write and from the quick of my mind always.

My field is to interpret the out of doors, to see ordinary outdoor things or happenings in a new light, to dramatize them, color them with knowledge and imagination and understanding so that they will mean more. As in "Forest Pool" take an ordinary swamp hole in the center of a field and tell its story—that gives it meaning.

And so you can take anything, firewood, portages, campsites, cradle knolls, ski trails, trout fishing, exploring, almost anything and build up something exciting about them. They must be exciting to someone. They must have beauty and concreteness and organization, must get away from the nebulous or mysterious or the philosophical, be down to earth.

March 14, 1945

You sometimes feel cheated by the war—but this is your work. The joy in rocks and birds and trees means more than anything else to you. There is my real life. There is the real fruit of all my thought. That is what counts and always will. No matter if the rest come home covered with glory, you have this and always will know what counts with you, stones and rocks and bird songs, and trout fishing and campfires and evenings when thrushes sing, and sunsets and moonlit ski trails. This is all important to you. This means more than adventure and death and warfare and the companionship of men in battle. You have a companionship of men in the things that mean most to you. There is the companionship of love and devotion to things of the spirit.

March 15, 1945

The Ides of March once more and a worrisome time it is. Sig I am afraid of what will happen there and Bob worries us too. Such a time for all folks like us. There is no glory to war.

The income tax is in and a terrible time doing something that is against all of my nature. Imagine a poet doing an income tax, posting books.

April 3, 1945

Another 12 minutes and my 45th year will be up, a strange year at best. Thought this winter would settle the question of medium but I am still working and experimenting but feel that I have run down the weaknesses of my interpretive essays to the point where they might work.

I feel that I am on the right track and that once I master the form it will not be so difficult and impossible. That much for some expert advice.

Get into the meat of your idea, no preliminary introductory thoughts, no nebulous and fanciful paragraphs. Start with your action at once and when you carry it through to the end, wind up swiftly.

Watch your sentence structure and pack your thoughts into as small a space as possible. Your essays may not run to more than 1500 words which is what you decided originally was about right. In fact you thought of 1000 words an enlargement of your first 500 word length. Three times that length is perhaps enough and you will still be close enough to your dream of a swift interpretive sketch with a wallop at the end. Cut out too much of your own sentiment and emotionalism. That is evidently out. If it must come in then do it subtly. Bring in your feelings through action and not through flat statement. That itself is a lesson.

No short stories though they think I can do them. I am not a story teller. But if I can this winter whip my medium into shape, then the winter will have been a tremendous success and I can wish for nothing more. I shall work over "Stones," "Wild Goose," "Forest Pool," and possibly "Trees" as test types. "Moon Magic" they didn't like, or "Pools of the Isabella." They are different types. If I can whip those four into shape and I will this weekend, then perhaps I have done as much as I can do. If they sell, then I can handle any number of others in similar fashion.

April 9, 1945

Have the material off again to Diamant, "Pictures in Stone," "Tree Personalities," "Wild Goose," "Pools of the Isabella" and "Forest Pool." All cut down to 15 to 1800 words, no introductions and brief windups. "Birthday on the Baptism" went to *Outdoor Life*, "Moon Magic" to *Nature Magazine*, "Wilderness Canoe Trips" to *Northwest Life* and a collection of column stuff to *Minnesota Conservationist* — "Tree Flowers," "Spawning of the Eelpout," "Frog Chorus," "On Trimming Trees." So that hurdle is over with again.

Last week was a trial being faced on my return to Ely from the farm with the package of mss. Then Tuesday, Wednesday, Thursday and Friday working them over. I can see now what it was that was wrong. Reading *Coronet* and seeing the stuff by Jim Kjelgaard[7] on the Horned Owl, Old Dr. Nature, etc, I found that they take stuff of 1000 words. No doubt many of the small magazines used material of between 1000 and 2000 words. My stuff is better than his, perhaps not so factual or realistic but more exciting. Take my "Pictures in Stone" or "Wild Goose" or "Forest Pool." If I can build up a steady market for that type of material then I will have done what I set out to do.

I have the new introduction for "We Need Wilderness" to do and then guess my writing for the winter will be almost over.[8] It has been an interesting winter and my facility has increased and my knowledge of the market I am trying to reach. If I crack that puzzle wide open then I am on the road. I see that Diamant has the Jim Kjelgaard pattern in front of her, wants my stuff to be without sentiment or fantasy or feeling, purely factual and realistic. If it comes to that then I am through. I do not write to disseminate facts but to portray feelings and sentiment, man's emotional reaction to the out of doors with the factual merely as a thread running through.

May 17, 1945

Heard today from Anita Diamant and she said that she would try to market the five articles I sent in, "Forest Pool," "Pools of the Isabella," "Wild Goose," "Pictures in Stone," and "Tree Personalities." She said she was interested in seeing if they would sell and what reaction there would be to them. At least she is now willing to try them which is something. She must be good or she wouldn't want them in proper shape.

Now a wait of a month or so to see what happens. I can only hope and pray. This may be the turning point but I am afraid that there will be no market for any of that type of material, that I will have to work on short stories or my old outdoor articles for next year. Thank God I am too busy to take it too seriously now.

July 23, 1945

On the trail of Medium:[9]

If I can find what I am looking for, then everything will be OK and any delays, any frustrations will be nothing. If I can spend this winter finding that and discovering my field, then it will be well worthwhile. Then any sacrifice is worthwhile now or in the future.

What is the most successful thing I have done?

No short stories — not even counting Papette —

Of the articles, "Confessions of a Duck Hunter"

"The Spring Hole"

"Wilderness Shortcuts"

"Packs and Paddles"

How to do it stuff seems to be uppermost, how to take a canoe trip — perhaps that is the answer but it is not what I want to do. I feel the spiritual slant is my very own but there has been no response whatever to anything I have done.

I know vaguely what it is I want to do but cannot find it. I want to put into words what I feel. I came very close to it in "Easter on the Prairie," that brought tears to my eyes, as did "Grandmother's Trout." One other thing I wrote brought tears to Mom's eyes, "Pussy Willows" and also "Pools on the Isabella." That is what I want to do. That is the sort of thing that will make me feel that I have done something, brought a real sentimental twinge of deep feeling. That was real success to me.

I cannot be humorous or light without seeming facetious. What I really want to do is paint some of the deep almost tragic feeling I have, make things so beautiful that it makes me want to weep myself. That to me will be real art. Anything else is just sawing wood. I am more sensitive than most. If I can picture for others what I feel then any medium is all right. Then pay and work and surroundings are secondary.

Why do you want to cry when you go in a cathedral? What did the loon call do to you last night? What does saying goodbye to New York mean. What does a moonlight ski mean (Sig's coming back to tell me to come). What does the Rock Pool mean (Glenn's last trout fishing).

If you can write the sort of thing that will give anyone who reads a heart throb, then you are made. If it makes me choke up, it will make anyone choke up with the sheer beauty of it.

"The Railing" — Picture what each boy thought as he carved his name — Wisconsin, Minnesota, California, Ohio, Texas.

Short little articles, essays, pictures in words. The happiest days were those in which I worked on the column, America Out of Doors. Why, because I hit the little ideas of day by day. It was the closest I ever came to really arriving.

I can't describe animals and birds. It must be how I feel about everything.

February 10, 1946

The old dream inspired by Emerson's essay on Inspiration — A cabin or a writing place down by the River or in the pines where for 4 hours I can be undisturbed — quiet — the trees — the river — the birds & squirrels — a good table — typewriter — paper — sunlight my pipe — 4 hours a day alone to work — & muse — think what I could do & think what a joy it would be — that would be it.[10]

February 12, 1946

Midnight

It is hard to sleep & I think about my future.

Resign J.C. — do the impossible & write as you have always wanted to. Work on until July — your date & make $4000 this year —

How can you go back —

Adkins — Assemblies

Zoo or Bot lecture

Catalog — Rotary

No I can't do it.

Have courage for once — You have 20 years — Now is the time to make the break —

November 25, 1946

The long ride back from Willmar gave me time to think — looking over the unrolling stretches of Minnesota countryside gave me a chance to weigh values — meeting with Jaques and Kilgore at the museum gave me perspective.[11] "Your visits are always inspirational, they give me a feeling that what we are trying to do is justified, give me a boost so to speak." In other words we are on common ground.

"Moose at Wood's Edge" by Francis Lee Jaques, circa 1956, published in *The Singing Wilderness*. Bell Museum Collection, University of Minnesota.

My conclusions — that in something like that lies my future, not sitting at Deans meetings with Davis, Moe, Maelin, Shumway et al, talking over tiresome problems of curricula. I am not interested in those problems or others, only in the realization of my dream. I am that selfish. I shall write books, many of them, books of short sketches, "Blue Flame," beautifully illustrated, small, with covers of the woods, gift books, each item a painting in words of some small event, some picture of a high spot, a vision, some unforgettable happening injected with my philosophy, my sense of the dramatic, the kind of books outdoorsmen, sportsmen, lovers of wildlife and Thoreau will like. Blue Flame — Red Socks and Moccasins — Wilderness — The Breaking — Grandmother's Trout — Each one with perhaps fifty sketches in it, all more or less related, each one a beauty, each one a thrill to read. That is and always has been your dream, now it must come true for that is the best you can do, that is the cream of your thought and experience. That is the best and that will live.

There might easily be longer articles and short stories, perhaps other books too but the above will be the main goal. Give myself two years and see. Remember that two years means nothing even at no salary, even at the cost of your savings. Two years, ten years, twenty mean nothing only time. That came to me too. Suppose someone asked you to give five years and to accomplish your end. What would you do. You would take it, would you not.

That is my whole life, to be able to produce so that I can merit the adulation and appreciation of friends such as Breck,[12] Lee, Kilgore and a host of others. There is where I belong and only by going ahead will I ever be more than just a promise. I must produce. I must be welcomed by them with more than tolerance. I must be considered an equal. And you will never do it by just being passive.

And I know that I am the sort of individual who cannot go halfway. I want only this. Any other activity is just treadmill, marking time. Only when I put full time in on it will the surge come.

Now treat each one — Make each one about 500 to 750 words in length. Not too long to be tiresome, not too short to impoverish the effect. For each one either a picture, a colored photograph or a sketch by Jaques. Black and white might be the answer. Photos I could do myself — each one so vivid a picture — such a poem in prose — so exciting emotionally — and so philosophically basic, that the book would be worth any one of the group.

Short stories might pay the bill but here is my life's work, here the essence of my living. Why not whip together enough for one book and see what comes out of it. The calendar idea is trite. Not more than perhaps fifty all told, each one a gem, each with its picture, each one complete in itself.

Take the breaking — there is a story, a novel, a complete unit, the same with rose quartz, make each one a gem.[13]

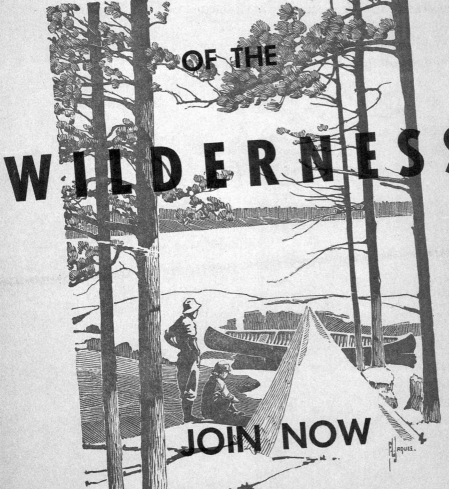

FRIENDS
OF THE
WILDERNESS

JOIN NOW

HELP SAVE THE CANOE COUNTRY

Friends of the Wilderness

P. O. BOX 935
HIBBING, MINNESOTA

FREE PRESS

A New Life in
Conservation

December 1946–October 1947

AFTER HIS YEAR OVERSEAS, returning to his old routine as dean of Ely Junior College seemed like torture to Sigurd. Making matters worse, roughly 90 of the 150 students in the fall of 1946 were former soldiers who were returning to civilian life with a lot more self-possession than the inexperienced students of earlier years. Former officers gave Sigurd unsolicited advice on how to run the college; others took up gambling in the college lounge. "Whatever happens, this is the last year and I wish it could end NOW," Sigurd wrote on December 2, 1946.

Perhaps that extra stress did it. In early January 1947 Sigurd began burning bridges, telling people he was going to resign at the end of the school year. He publicized it so that he would have the strength to follow through. After putting himself through three more months of agonizing over his decision, he finally took the step he had contemplated for many years. On April 14, 1947, he turned in his resignation to the school board. He was forty-eight years old, his hair had turned silver, and he wondered if it might be too late.

That summer and fall he put himself under a lot of pressure to get enough material published to make up for the lost income. He knew he

Poster for Friends of the Wilderness, produced in the late 1940s, with artwork by Francis Lee Jaques. Minnesota Historical Society Collection.

could easily sell hunting and fishing articles to the outdoor magazines, but they paid around $100, $150 at the most. To make up the $3,000 he made as dean, he would have to sell twenty to thirty such articles a year, an impossible feat. He had never sold more than six articles in any twelve-month period. And he knew his essays—which he saw as his true calling—were almost impossible to sell.

That meant trying fiction one last time. He tried converting essay material into short story fiction, reworked previously rejected fiction, and sent five new pieces to a new literary agent and to a colleague of his brother Kenneth. The painful feedback convinced Sigurd to focus on the kind of writing that gave him joy and best used his gifts. One of his final pieces of fiction, "Rainbow Forty," found a publisher in the *Toronto Star Weekly* on October 2, 1948. It marked the end of Sigurd's short story career.

But how would he make enough money to support himself and Elizabeth? In the fall of 1947, as Sigurd struggled, he was approached by a group of conservationists who hoped he would be willing to spearhead the campaign to ban flying over the canoe country wilderness. Sigurd had been involved in earlier campaigns over roads and dams, and two years earlier had brought national attention to this new issue with a September 1945 article in *Sports Afield*, called "Flying In." He was known as a passionate, inspirational speaker as well as writer, so he was a logical person to become the face of the Quetico–Superior movement. He might have said yes in any case, but financial concerns no doubt made the decision easier. On December 3, 1947, he took the position.[1]

On the one hand, it meant yet again putting off writing the essays he felt called to create. On the other hand, it relieved the anxiety of losing most of his income. And in the long run, this new job gave him the contacts and prominence that, seven years later, led a prominent publisher to ask Sigurd about the possibility of writing a book.

* * * *

December 2, 1946

By going to the farm I would escape the pull of local and community affairs. I could write with no interference, could engage entirely and utterly in the one activity I should be engaged in. As far as stimulus is concerned, I would need none but that — and expenses would be very light comparatively speaking.

I would withdraw—and do the thing that I alone want to do. No tourist business, no community activity, just concentrate on this alone.

Stories, essays, books, there is plenty. For Lib my companionship and knowing I am doing at last what I want to do. Friends would come. We could travel and do things together. We could come up here and spend some time.

Whatever happens, this is the last year and I wish it could end NOW.

Paint the picture of wilderness, of simple farm living, of naturalness, of the communion of man with the earth and the universe. Some stories of the farm.

December 9, 1946

Ed Shave in his introduction said, "Sig Olson used to run a feature column in the *Minneapolis Star Journal* and wrote one of the finest bits of description I've ever read, Balm of Gilead, taking a small crooked little tree and making it mean something."

Evidence again that this sort of thing might be worthwhile.

If I can write that sort of thing and make people remember over the years then I have done something worth more than fiction, more than anything else.

I still believe that this is my forte.

Undated, January 1947

What would happen if I gave up Border Lakes management, my writing and speaking and just tended to my JC job and let that suffice.

Forget my writing entirely and have fun the rest of your life, hunt and fish and read and enjoy myself and E and my friends.

Would that be running out on my dreams. I guess it would. F says it would be cheating.

Just think of one thing, your teaching, your counseling, your jobs in town. Come home at night happy and free. Have the summers to look forward to, fishing guiding and cruising.

Forget about the writing entirely be human and free. Forget about conservation battles. Don't fret any more.

You can have the teaching if you wish which would be better per-haps than the Deanship anyway.

The writing frightens me terribly. No income. Nothing. Just work, steady hard terrible work all of the time.

You could go trout fishing on the Baptism, the Isabella, the Cascade. You could get an Olds, you could have a cabin. You could put on the porch. You could in short have fun and feel free.

But if you do then you have forgotten the dream and you have re-signed yourself forever to happiness but mediocrity.

January 6, 1947

I am telling everyone that I am resigning in June, burning my bridges behind me so to speak. Strengthening my hand. I look ahead to a year of writing and doing what I wish. I wonder if it will be the answer. I ap-proach it with fear and misgiving at times, wonder what I should write, if I can sell, if I am justified in not working for the Border Lakes.

There is this much about it. Unless I take that year and devote myself entirely to it, I will never know. The sacrifice is worth it. I can always manage the Border Lakes and make about $3000 per year and then write in the winter time. Perhaps that is best after all. It is not as though I had nothing to come back to.

The writing—short stories, essays, books, articles, anything that comes to mind. Writing steadily four hours to six hours per day, six days a week should produce something.

Libby has had a tough time, if she could only feel that at last I had settled down, that I was contented and satisfied her life would be differ-ent. Instead she is in a constant turmoil.

What do I want?

Sometimes I wonder if I know. My mind is such a hodgepodge of desires. I dream of living way up in the woods, dread the monotony the chance of being lonesome — Thomas Lake, Basswood, Knife, writing up there — being gone for weeks and months at a time. No, in spite of the fact that I love solitude and the woods, it is not that much.

Perhaps I have it right here, writing at home, making jaunts out and coming back.

Sigurd puts canoes into Brent Lake during the U.S. Forest Service's American Forest Trail Riders canoe trip to Quetico Provincial Park, 1948. Photograph by Leland J. Prater, U.S. Forest Service Records, National Archives.

January 10, 1947

What do I want?

I want more than anything else to write I guess, just to have my days free — or is this an old illusion that I have come to believe through constant repetition?

I have never cared about conventions, have shied at the thought of going somewhere and taking part, could have been national president of the League if I had so wished,[2] could have gone places nationally but have fought it.

I have changed the last few years. The idea of lectures does not excite me either but what frightens me now is the thought of actually being at the turning point where I have to write to make good. As long as there was a chance of continuing I could play with the idea but now it is here and I am scared.

Do I want to head into the woods and write every day. I wonder if I shall ever know what I want.

This much is true — I have given up children, I have given up fame and position, a doctor's degree, I have given up contacts, everything for the possible realization of the dream. Now the time has come to make good. If I do not, then I die, then all has been for naught.

In other words this is the payoff. I must make good my dreams, the things I have denied. I must do the things I have always said I would, all the things I have vowed didn't mean anything to me I must renounce forever. I would rather write than be head of the Park Service, the Forest Service, a great university, head of a department. All I have ever wanted is to sit down and write.

I know now that none of these jobs would ever satisfy me. All the time the old dream would be in the background. I must make good. I cannot fail....

This is the payoff, animal stories, essays, sketches, books, fiction, keep a continual stream going and coming.

But I know this, if I stay here on the job, I will die inside. This is the end of all of this coming and going. This is the end of frustration. If I make barely enough to live on the first two years, still the gamble is worthwhile.

Canoeing on Basswood Lake, 1948. Photograph by Leland J. Prater, U.S. Forest Service Records, National Archives.

January 13, 1947

John Burroughs again after all these years. Last night reading over his religious essays I found that he believes in no God of old, that his God is nature, the power and the energy back of all things, a stupendous belief that defies imagination.

He does not say anything about the fact that God may be Good, that God is love, God is kindness and humility, tolerance and seated primarily within the human spirit. That is where he failed.

There is no personal God according to him, but all good is with nature, all vice and evil against it. Still what do the stars have with good, what do they have with evil. There is a tremendous power there, the power of the atom and its connotations.

Is it not possible to combine his belief with mine. God is Good, God is Love, the great undercurrents of life and the fact that Nature in all its ramifications can be the background even of that. Still the inexorability of impersonal natural laws has nothing to do with humans. All that counts with us as men is love and beauty and humanity. What has that to do with the stars and the universe, with geology and its processes. Nothing.

Heaven and hell are out of the picture, the old biblical beliefs and in their stead are the greater concepts of Christianity, God is Love.

Put yourself in harmony with the great life stream, with universal forces, with Christianity if one would be happy. God is Love, the great power which surges through all of humanity or God is Good.

Or God IS THE GREAT GOOD * OR GOD IS BEAUTY

Is not that enough. There is no personal God. Nature abhors vice. Man is a biological accident is therefore humble, realizing that to be man capable of love takes away egotism, makes it imperative that he live as Christ would have him live, that he himself does not count except as he gives and loves others. Fame is nothing, money nothing. GOD ALONE IS GOOD.

Thoreau, Emerson, all the great thinkers believe that God is within ourselves. "Look within," heaven lives within you, also hell, happiness is based on love and giving. The human spirit is the highest development of nature, bigger than the stars, bigger than atoms, bigger than the laws of the solar system. If all of this evolved from a primitive cosmos or unfeeling and impersonal savagery, so much more wonderful is this development. The spirit of man is the flowering of nature, greater than any other phenomenon, greater than the whirling spheres, greater than space, infinity.

Think of the vast swirling gaseous masses, the suns, the moons, the stars, the dead planets. Think of the infinitude of space, the play between atoms, the laws of chemistry and physics, the rise and fall of oceans and mountains — the inexorable laws governing everything, the long road of evolution, the birth of mind and reason, spirit and soul and at last the concept of goodness, love and beauty. Man is the only creature in all this vast and complicated universe that has this concept. He alone can feel and think and contemplate. He alone can think of God and wonder.

Therefore man is the greatest thing in all creation, therefore man's highest thoughts are the most important, his aspirations and dreams when they approach our concept of godliness above and beyond a solar system in achievement. When man says, "Seek the highest and the best," that is evidence of having arrived for only man can conceive of anything approaching greatness of soul. When man speaks as Christ did of love, then he is voicing man's noblest achievement spiritually. Christ knew and spoke only as he did because of the ignorance of his listeners.

The grandest search of man is the search for an understanding of God. Nothing is more important and if he should find it, then his work is to impart to others the secret of his achievement.

Getting back to Burroughs once more, Burroughs says God is Nature. We are of nature, therefore part of God. God is the all controlling energy and order and system. Nature is against vice and evil and for good, which I doubt — but — — — —

My premise that granting all that, that we are a part of a great inexorable system, the fact remains that we being a part of nature have gone a step farther than anything else has ever gone by the development of reason, conscience, the concept of good and love and tolerance and beauty, not natural beauty but beauty of spirit. If we must have a God to worship, then why not worship this new spirit, this awakened consciousness, this awareness. Life itself is evidence of immortality, the life plasm, the stream of protoplasm — no different however than a solar system, the same laws the same marvelous interrelations — that will go on for untold millenniums as it always has, but this flowering of soul is something above and beyond all of that something growing out of all the other and precious beyond price.

This the grandest development in nature is the end of all things —
GOD IS GOOD THE ALL GOOD GOD IS LOVE HEAVEN IS WITHIN YOU LIVE
ONLY FOR THE SPIRIT PRECEPTS GRANDER THAN THE SOLAR SYSTEM.

Granted all of that the fact remains that the solar system must have
started somewhere. I understand the system, I understand evolution, I
understand all physical processes, I understand Nature itself. But it is a
cold impersonal nature and would get on without man as well as with
him. Millions of years before man developed the solar system whirled
on. By some accidental alchemy he was born and then through the aeons
came to be what he is today. Then the God was a God of force and power,
ruthless and relentless. Then slowly the concept of love was born and
developed, the highest achievement of nature.

My work should be to bring this message to others, to crack the old
fetishes and give men a picture of God as he really is. That might be
the answer. How, through short stories, parables, essays, books. If I can
weave into my writing somehow this belief without preaching, if I can
give the masses something to hold onto in everything I write. Even with
the short sketches, beauty of nature is not enough, interpretation not
enough either unless you bring out this premise:

THAT MAN THINKING APPRECIATING LOVING UNDERSTANDING

THAT MAN BEING ABLE TO PROJECT HIS OWN PERSONALITY INTO IN-
ANIMATE NATURE

THAT MAN WITH HIS CAPACITY FOR LOVE AND GOODNESS HAS PRO-
GRESSED FAR BEYOND ALL ELSE

IS THEREFORE SO IMPORTANT SPIRITUALLY, IS SO HIGH A DEVELOP-
MENT THAT ANYTHING HE SAYS OR DOES IS VITAL.

THAT HIS CONCEPT OF GOD AS GOODNESS AND LOVE BEING THE
GREATEST ACHIEVEMENT OF THE UNIVERSE AND THAT THE EVIDENCE OF
THIS REALIZATION THE PINNACLE OF PERFECTION IT WOULD BEHOOVE
A MAN TO STRIVE TOWARD NO OTHER GOAL THAN ITS REALIZATION IN
HIMSELF.

Therefore when you write a sketch bring into it into each one somehow a thread of your belief. Never write anything that does not bolster
your stand, nothing that does not leave the reader with a sense of having
gotten something to hold onto.

A short story or a series of them might be the medium, but short interpretive sketches possibly better.

January 23, 1947

What worries me now is my loss of enthusiasm for simple things. At the moment I do not think I could write about such subjects as coloring of leaves, the esker, spring morning. It is all meaningless to me. This however will pass when I get away from my present situation.

The hopelessness comes from the thought that life is over. The boys will be gone, the old jobs will be gone, the old incentives. I look forward to years of no accomplishment, no one great dream to realize.

But don't you think that once you have begun writing, once you have dedicated your life, the old joy will return. It has always worked out so in the past and it surely will again. In June set yourself a regular writing schedule and stick with it. Think of nothing but your work, of nothing but the things you want to write about. Forget business, forget speeches, forget outfitting and teaching. Think only of stories, essays, the glory of the woods, the joys of creation. Unless I am mistaken it will all come back.

No lecturing next year either. I want next winter to do nothing but write. Then another winter it might be different but if I branch off on long lecturing trips, it will be the same thing all over again. Wait for lectures to come to you.

Duck season, deer season, skiing — I am sick at heart. It seems I cannot quite face it again without the old days. But surely it will all come back, the joy and the verve I once knew. Libby will help me. We will work together, live for each other.

But now I see nothing—not even if I arrive. Only 20 years—is it that I feel the long hand of death reaching through the mists? Am I dying now?

January 30, 1947

So the die is cast and I am resigning after all of these years, burning my bridges behind me. I think it had to come to some sort of a pass such as this to force the issue. Now I know that nothing is worthwhile sacrificing my peace of mind for, a job, prestige, nothing. That if I continue, I will be lost forever. It has come to the parting of the ways and I am taking the hard way, something I should have done ages ago.

As Libby said, perhaps you haven't been ready, perhaps nothing has been quite set. Now it is time and everything seems to be in order. If I have courage and go through with it.

I must have faith that I can do what I think I can do. I feel that once I make the break I shall generate enthusiasm and feel equal to any task. My writing will make a new man of me and there will be no tiredness.

Well, I am ready now and I shall sink or swim by my own efforts. Next year at this time I shall know. This is the payoff.

"Enjoy yourself, it is later than you think."

Sometimes I wonder if it is too late.

April 10, 1947

Have just been reading over the old diary from 1941-1944 and guess the issue is clear. Drop the Border Lakes, resign from the Deanship, feel free to write and that only.

Self analysis has certainly shown me that there is nothing else to do if I am ever to be happy or satisfied. Six weeks more and then it will be all over. This summer every morning I will work away and in the afternoons do what I have always planned on doing.

This year of 1947 will be the beginning of my real era of living and production. Not that I haven't lived in the past but it has been a postponement of what I really wanted to do. Now comes the showdown, a time when I shall live for nothing but my writing, that and that alone. It might be hard financially but I know it will go all right.

There is no longer any debate on what to do. This time I am at the end of decision. This time I shall do what for many years I have planned. 1947 is the beginning of a new life.

Approach it with joy and hope and abandon fear. Money means nothing, just the fact that I am at last on the road.

April 14, 1947

Today I resigned. It doesn't seem possible. I am frightened at the consequences of my act even though I have contemplated it for many years. Now it is a fact and there is no turning back. I am a free man and in another six weeks I will be all through.

I HAVE RESIGNED AS DEAN OF ELY JUNIOR COLLEGE. I cannot believe it. It does not seem possible.

But now that it is done I must begin to work out my salvation. I must write as I have never written before. I must remake my life. I must make good for E's sake. We must have fun. I must get every possible kind of writing under way that I know. This is the payoff.

This is the beginning of a new life. April and May and part of June and I am through. It will take time before the full realization hits me but the important thing is that it is done.

Now with the coming of summer, I am going to start to write and write fast and hard. Every single morning, every day of the week, a definite stint. I am going to live the stuff I am writing. I am going to do the thing that for twenty years I have dreamed of doing. From now on I shall be free as the wind, free to come and go and free to work. Now I am going to prove to myself that I have what it takes. I am going to be a different man, a different person entirely.

There is no limit to where I can go and what I can do. I should have done it long ago as there is no longer any joy in teaching for me. The old punch is gone. This is just marking time. I might have gone on, teaching zoo, botany, geology for years or until I got my pension, 48, 49, 50, 51, 52, 53, 54, 55 but it would merely have been a repetition of the same old story. The only thing the pension but that is so small there is little hope of anything coming of that. Thirty years.

I could have written the same as I have been doing but that would not have amounted to anything either.

April 17, 1947

The deed is done and I have resigned and the thought is frightening. The thought of $300 per month, ten dollars per day frightens me. Of course that has been the old bugbear for years. This may make it possible to equal or surpass that easily.

But it may take time and it will take courage. I suppose I would have felt the same way no matter when it had happened.

I read my diary for 1936-37 last night, a very well written section of the book and over and over again the old refrain. I want no other kind of work. They all pall. All I want to do is to write. Nothing could possibly be clearer than that. No other jobs interest me in the slightest no matter with what agency, no matter in what country. All I want to do is write. I have always wanted to know. Now I do know and there is no question about it.

As I read back over the old diaries there is the old dread, the old sense of futility, the old hopelessness and drudgery through it all and above all the feeling that time is slipping by, that if I only had time I could do something, that time was beyond price. Three hundred, five hundred a thousand dollars a month mean nothing if I am not doing what I want to do and that is what I must remember now. There is hardly a break in the impression any year. Sometimes I find a little joy, but teaching advising deaning, all the multiplicities of duties have always left me cold.

I thought last night if I could only resign myself to JC. If I could throw myself into it with enthusiasm and accept the fact that writing is just incidental, couldn't I be happy. I tried to do that for twenty years and was unsuccessful. I found I couldn't write after school or in school or weekends, that I wanted to put in full time.

I know after reading them all that peace will come when I can lose myself in my job, think of nothing else, do nothing else, that writing is more important than hunting or fishing or cruising or anything I can think of, that it is my life.

That man is content and finds peace who loses himself utterly in some work he wants to do, who does not count the hours, who does not want holidays or a chance to lay around, who greets each day with joy for it means more work, who regrets the end of each day because it means a cessation of his work. That man is content who does the thing best that he wants to do and is able to do. With me it is interpretive writing. I have a different slant than most people, I owe it to others to get what I feel.

Next year it will be interesting to see how economically we can live. With care we should cut it down to perhaps $100.00 per month. Certainly that will be something. At that rate we can live several years on what we have without difficulty. As it is now I spend about $300 per month so the $200 per month wouldn't be missed. It will be exciting to see if I can make enough to pay expenses which seems to be all we ever could do. If we went along as we do now, it wouldn't make any difference if it was $100 or $400 per month. It is all gone anyway.

I am trying desperately to justify my move. When I think of the Olds we might have had, of the addition to the house, of trips, perhaps abroad, I get panicky. This should be the payoff, instead it is the beginning of privation.

April 17, 1947

For twenty years I have written, "If I could have such a morning as this to myself to begin work on something worthwhile I would be happy."

Time and again I have said something like that and now the time approaches and I am frightened at the prospect of not having a paycheck.

The die is cast and I must make good. I must come through or die and I shall of that I am certain. If I write steadily every single day my production ought to be something I can surely pound off enough stuff to keep me going. Every single day of my life, write, write, write, harder work than I have ever done but I might find peace and contentment.

If that is the goal I find it before me and I should be glad. To think that next year I can do what I have always wanted to do, each and every day. Hike and write and think and dream and work until I am dog tired. I mustn't falter even though nothing comes in for a full year. In this year or two I will know what the score is. My stuff will appear in *The Post*, in *Colliers, Liberty* and there will be at least two books and lecture dates will be forthcoming.

And above all I will know the score. I will know that I am doing what I always intended to do but never had the courage to do.

I think it is time I left, time I tried once and for all.

April 17, 1947

Lady Grogan[3] says, "I think you must have a very happy home. Your Elizabeth seems to understand so completely that you must follow the way you see before you—even if it is not the beaten track—as though you ever had a beaten track.

"The roads into the country of Shelley and Keats were never that way. She will see more of you perhaps than before if you write in your home, but you will become absorbed in your work and live more in that world."

How true in her insight. My life never did follow a beaten track and from now on will not. I have broken away from the old conventional trail definitely and at the moment it seems terribly hard.

Now that I come to the end, I know I shall miss the Zoo and the Botany and Geology, my contacts with classes and students in activities. Of course it is not all habit or routine, I would be inhuman if there wasn't more than that. What there is to remember is that time will heal the scars as it always does, that from now on life will be completely different, that I must work along and become completely absorbed, completely lost in my dream of creation. That must be the answer and that alone.

Sigurd with Ellinor Grogan at her home near Dorchester, 1945. Olson Family Collection. Courtesy of David Backes.

No money coming in will seem frightening. But we can live for a year or two and by then I will know the score. Work, work, work, keep going come what may. This will take guts, plain and ordinary. I've got to make good and I will.

I will make more money in a year than ever before. Will get my satisfaction and peace of mind at last. If I can get over the heart rending of parting with all this. Then I shall be all right I think.

This means a new era for me. This is the beginning of a long period of productivity. For twenty years now I will continue.

April 21, 1947

April 21st and the day is drawing close. This morning I went out in the shack and sat down, had a swift vision of what it would mean to go out there and get to work as I shall do next year. Quiet and peace and the joy of getting at something. I was almost overcome with the joy of it. I wonder if it will be a joy like that, if I can greet each morn with joy and excitement when I am at my work.

At times I am terribly upset. Dean Olson Resigns scream the headlines and I look at that and ask myself if it is I, if I have done something terrible. If I have sacrificed my family and home and future happiness for a wild dream. When I think of the money I am sick at heart.

Then times come when like this morning I see what it will be and joy wells up inside me.

Last night in bed thinking of the book the thought came to me. Why not write a book embodying all the things you feel, your love of simple things, of life in the open, of good books and music, of closeness to the earth, bringing in perhaps some of the philosophy you are so fond of, some of the observations which are now a part of the sketch book. You see all of this feeling around is merely an effort to find a medium in which I can use what I have written. As a sketch book it evidently will not go far.

If I can figure out a book that all sportsmen will want so that it will sell 1,000,000 copies then I will have nothing more to worry about. If I can write a Must book for all outdoorsmen, one that they simply must have, that they will clamor for and want reprints of, a real howling success then all of my worries will be over. And I can write at my leisure only the things I wish.

But what will it be — evidently not a book such as I tried or Peattie tried or all of the other sketch and short story books. They are not enough.

If it is to be a must it has to have a powerful appeal, not as a story or a novel which is swiftly forgotten but something which has meat in it.

If I write on hunting and fishing and outdoor enjoyment generally, it must appeal to Cease and Vic and Wilson and Sig and Joe and Hub[4] and all the sportsmen I know. It cannot be too serious, perhaps might have a happy exhilaration to it, an excitement, some humor and much laughter just for the joy of living, a militant sense of doing something worthwhile for the fun of it.

Chicago attorney Frank "Hub" Hubachek, 1930s. A passionate voice for the canoe country, Hubachek established the Quetico–Superior Wilderness Research Center at Basswood Lake. Minnesota Historical Society Collection.

There is enough sorrow in the world, enough seriousness, let this book give a man a lift, make him happy, in love with the earth and all things, no preaching, no moralizing but weave through it your old premise that this is what counts, this is the real thing, the old idea of being at home in the universe.

Perhaps you have something here, I do not know. It will bear some thought and work, but it might be the answer to many things.

April 22, 1947

These days I have to bolster my resolve and I do it by reading and re-reading the old chapters of years ago. It doesn't make any difference how far back I go 1930, 1934 or 1940, they are all the same — wishing hoping and praying that I can get at my work of writing, bemoaning the loss of time, facing each day with sorrow and despair, even the so called happy years when I was young and things seemed to be going well it was the same. There is no let up, a sameness about the whole thing that is positively appalling.

And now I have resigned and I have days of doubt and fear wondering if I did the right thing. I think of the money I am losing of the prestige, of a thousand and one other things but none of them make any difference when compared to the real issue my freedom and escape from the dead days of the past. And the days were dead. I am 48 now, middle age. Do I want to continue with more of the same? Do I want to face ten or twenty years of the same identical deadness or do I want to take a chance for once and do what I have always wanted to do.

Reason says, stay with it, be safe and secure, but my past rises up with a loud roar and says, "You have done the right thing at last, do not waver or change it now. Somehow everything will come out all right. You must take this chance. You must try it or die."

This is the showdown. It is hard desperately hard but I feel that once it is over that we will all be happy. I must be brave and face the music. I cannot go back now and do not wish to go back. One story for the Post at $750 or $800 is almost $250 per month for three months. That is something to shoot at isn't it. Then if I reach the $1000 mark it will be $300 per month for three months. Then books and short articles for the Outdoor Mags. It will never be sure but that is the price, but I will be free and I will have my dreams and somehow we will live.

I want to laugh and have fun once more. I want to be my old swash-buckling self again. This is my chance. This what I have been waiting for. I could stay with teaching another couple of years and save as much as we are doing now which is nothing and then resign but then it is the old story. Much better make the break now while I at least have a fighting chance.

April 30, 1947

This summer I can surely make $200 per month instead of $300 by writing 1 story for the outdoor mags each month. At the B.L. I'd make $300 but my days would be lost in packs, grub, lists etc. By Sept — June — July — Aug I'd be on my way — Even if I make only half of that I'll be better off.

My neck is out—way out—I've got to write & make a go of it—no question—I've got to produce or go under & I will —

Last night — a flare of confidence, of such a feeling of sureness & command.

May 7, 1947

Suggestions of early history, Captain Trezona and others leave me cold as they would Thoreau, Burroughs, Muir and the type.

All I am interested in writing about is my own reactions. I still feel that if I can write a book masculine, appealing, depicting a man's love for the wild, for the woods, for hunting and fishing and outdoors generally, something that any outdoorsman would want to carry with him then I have done something.

Ducks — a man's love for marshes and gales and ducks coming in. What would Cease want to read, Glenn, Bill Croze, Fred W., Ernie H., Frank R., Ken Reid, the whole gamut of outdoorsmen. How could I write it.

Short stories? Showing what men feel?

May 18, 1947

This is to the good:

1. The peace of mind that will come from knowing at last you are trying to realize your capabilities.

2. By doing only one thing will eliminate all other distractions. (A man can only do one thing well.)

3. Time will be entirely different — time will be endless once the schedule is gone —

4. Forget about Commercial Club[5] — conservation, church & club activities & concentrate all time and energy on one endeavor —

5. The satisfaction that comes from knowing you are on the road.

6. Having freedom of movement to come and go at will.

7. The joy of each day being able to sit down at my typewriter & work without interruption.

8. The feeling of confidence & fulfillment if I win out.

9. The fun of being a <u>free lance</u> — saying you are a writer at last.

10. The tremendous lift of knowing at last all is settled.

This is to the bad:

1. No money

2. Loss of position in town

3. Failure to help Sig, Bob & E

4. Lack of contact with youth —

5. Loss of all background —

Note —

All the above means largely money and position. I have not enjoyed youth or my work. The good so far over balances the bad that there is nothing to worry about.

May 19, 1947

As the time approaches for the big move I find myself thinking more and more of how to work, what medium, what way to revamp my old articles or essays. The more I think the more sure I am that if I can work up a distinctive type of short story based on my articles I might have the answer.

Agents have told me time and again, if I can work in a plot of some kind into my writing, that I will have something, that all my stuff needed was a plot, suspense, action. Well — why not make each little episode an adventure of the spirit, give each one a narrative hook so to speak, a build up with suspense at each turn and a final dramatic climax that will leave the reader feeling that this was good and satisfying. If you can do that then your field is unlimited and you have accomplished what you have always wanted to do, dramatize and make vital and important the little adventures of the outdoors.

You don't need heavy, blood and thunder themes. All you need is to make your stuff so exciting and important in themselves that they will be as important as tremendous emotional conflicts. Let others do that. These things will be purely of the spirit and will give the out of doors a different slant.

July 2, 1947

Last night I thought of the old problem how to weave my stuff into short stories and for an instant I had a clue.

Make each one of them a short story with a narrative hook, background and atmosphere and expository material with suspense and plenty of incidents, then a surprise windup or ending that will give the reader something to chew on.

Undated, early August 1947

Yesterday's letter from Litten was a terrible blow.[6] Evidently it means that I can't write that sort of thing, that I should stick to what I can do, the type of story typified by "Birthday on the Baptism," perhaps "Grandmother's Trout." That sort of thing I can do.

Perhaps it is the book and not short stories at all. Perhaps it is an elaboration of things like "The Breaking," "Easter on the Prairie," "Kings Point," a different kind of short story than the purely plotted adventure type.

Blassingame is not so pessimistic as Litten.[7] He should know his markets better than Litten, should know what will sell. At least don't get too down-hearted all at once. You might surprise Litten entirely if some of those things sell.

And don't worry too much if this year is a flop. Take this year and see what you can do. You would never be satisfied if you didn't. School starts soon, forget it and concentrate on what you must do. This is what you have been planning for all of your life. To come out here in the morning and really go to work has been your ambition for a long time. Now it is here. Make the most of it.

Litten says cut out the refinements of language in the bluebird and the time lapse. Also cut the abrupt transitions in Rendezvous, also make the story of the Gilmore party Jack Russell's story. Make him share the brunt, make the problem his. I wonder about that. Song of the Bush is definitely out, an impossible situation entirely.

Well — I must expect this but it is hard not to get any encouragement when this is a matter of life and death. By the end of the year I will make something and then we shall see.

Undated, summer–fall 1947

To write my little sketches with heat and enthusiasm, writing at white heat pouring out the best that is in me. Write "Grandmother's Trout" at one sitting, "Easter on the Prairie" at one sitting, "Saganaga" at one sitting, making each one so different, so whole souled, so burning with passion that they will be different than anything that has been written. This is the sort of thing you quit to do, this the stuff that the world might be waiting for. It is not cold fiction or cold analytical articles but the sort of thing only you can do. You can't be funny. You can't be entertaining and so you must write with passion and do the thing that you alone can do.

You have suffered, you have suffered greatly for this ideal. Only by writing what you feel you must can your sacrifice be warranted.

You do not have to have a love element in your stuff. You can describe your own reactions in such a way that outdoorsmen all over will want to carry it with them. Write a book that everyone in the Arrowhead will want to read, that everyone in Minn will want to carry with them. A hundred thousand, a million might be your goal.

It cannot be too light or too frittery. There must be meat in it, plenty of meat, the result of the years of your thinking and study. Write about portages as you alone understand them. Write about campsites as you see them, about islands, about rapids, about deer hunting and duck hunting without going too poetic about them. Write from a mature man's point of view, the sort of thing that men will understand and love.

To find that approach is your problem. That is what you must do. Short stories I do not know.

The portage at Curtain Falls between Crooked and Iron Lakes, 1948. Listening Point Foundation Archives.

Undated, October 1947

What can I write or what do I think is worthwhile in writing? Only this — my interpretation as always of what I see and have done. Others' feelings don't count with me whatever, others' adventures — but cannot you put your ideas into the minds of your characters and so bring them out rather than in the form of a diary or introspection. Perhaps but there is so little room here. I grew up in the tradition of Thoreau and Burroughs and they I want to emulate. It isn't enough to write a short story or a novel —

I want to write of simple things, portages and logging roads and campsites and rocks and flowers and weave my interpretation about them. Florence J.[8] does it in a sense, why can't I do it who have lived so much more of this thing than she has.

I shall never be happy until I do this. If I don't do it I shall die.

Sitting in church this morning mulling over titles

Snow Comes to the Arrowhead

Arrowhead Winter

By

Sig Olson

Chapters on log cabins on snow and on sunsets and trees and ice fishing and skiing and logging trails written in such a way that anyone reading them would be charmed and amused and delighted with the new slant. I would rather write of logging roads and make them charming, of skiing and make them charming and delightful, of birds and log cabins and the coming of the snow.

Winter sunsets — Don't get sentimental or try to paint, but write on how they make you feel.

Litten thinks, "Don't bury the high talent that is yours. Don't ever be discouraged but carry on. Someday the world will recognize you."

Perhaps he is right, but I don't know. Actually it would have been fun and exciting to have written "Dead Man's Secret" and I could have done it. The pay, plus the prestige. He says you could have written it with higher emotional depth, perhaps. In this story, he felt for the wilderness much as I feel.

"You wouldn't trade the open sky for a warm room."

* * * *

But getting back to the old trouble — I want to write the sort of book that *Canadian Spring* is,[9] a running commentary of and how I feel about little things, about ducks and deer and sunsets and spring water and flowers and muskrats and swamps.

About trappers cabins.

I want to write a book that will really sell, that will establish me as the outstanding interpreter of the out of doors. I must do it in a different way. I can't do it with short stories or novels. It must be as I have tried to do it.

Write as you talk — you thought of that in church, write easily smoothly. Now take that cabin on Snowbank. It isn't much a cabin to look at just tucked back in the spruces but [typed portion of page ends; what follows is handwritten]

"What I've learned in the Wilderness"
"Wilderness"
"Wilderness Days"
"On Cabins"

THE Singing Wilderness

By SIGURD F. OLSON

A vibrant book of discovery that re-creates the sights and sounds of the Quetico-Superior country and explores with deep insight the permanent values of a great wilderness area

ILLUSTRATED BY FRANCIS LEE JAQUES

THE SINGING
WILDERNESS

April 1949–February 1954

THE YEAR 1947 was the last in which Sigurd wrote more than a few
journal entries. Once he began his new job campaigning for the
wilderness canoe country, he was busier than at any other time in his
life, making frequent trips to Chicago, Washington, D.C., and Toronto,
meeting with government agency officials and politicians, meeting with
other conservation leaders, and writing articles for national distribution
in outdoor and conservation magazines. He also wrote, directed, and
starred in a documentary film meant to build support for the campaign
to ban flying over the Superior National Forest Roadless Areas.[1]

But busyness doesn't entirely explain the demise of his journal. For
the first time in Sigurd's life, he felt he was doing something important,
was making all kinds of new connections and friendships, and was gaining national attention. He was getting the kind of recognition that had
always eluded him. And, as is clear in the first entry of this chapter, written on his fiftieth birthday, he was content.

Sigurd's efforts in the precedent-setting ban on airplanes flying into
the wilderness canoe country placed him in demand among national
conservation organizations. The National Parks Association recruited

Cover of *The Singing Wilderness*, published by Alfred Knopf in 1956. Olson Family
Collection. Courtesy of David Backes.

him first, naming him its vice president in 1951, and its president in 1953. During that period he wrote most of the entries in this chapter.

Notice that the content and tone are different than in the past. Technically, these no longer qualify as journal entries. Instead, they are notes to himself to guide his work as he tries to put together a book of essays. I include them here to show the contrast. He wrote similar types of notes to himself when working on his later books, too. Sigurd's journal, then, effectively ended in 1947. Once he resigned from the junior college and became a nationally known conservation leader, his feelings about himself and his work greatly improved. But there was one thing still missing: success in his deeper calling of writing about nature and the human spirit.

One final plot twist took care of that. As president of the National Parks Association, in November 1954 Sigurd gave a keynote speech in New York to the leaders of a couple of dozen conservation organizations. In the audience was Alfred A. Knopf. The famous publisher was so struck by Sigurd's words, he sent him a letter, asking, "I am wondering if you are not going to have a book for us one of these days?"[2] And so began Sigurd's career as an author, beginning with the best-selling The Singing Wilderness in 1956 and extending through eight more books to Of Time and Place, published shortly after his death on January 13, 1982.

* * * *

April 4, 1949

Birthday — 50 — 4/4/49

I have made the break and new horizons have opened up — a fuller life — more realization — more and bigger objectives.

I have found fame and friends and encouragement. When I write now it will be with a new & bigger audience. No short stories of adventure or love — It will be books of my feelings & probings on life and nature and mankind.

The Philosophy of a Wilderness Man

Wilderness Man

The story of how primitiveness has always been important to me — statement of objectives woven through everything I write or see. The fascination of primitive things — soil — black dirt — rocks — geology —

protoplasm — frog songs — flowers — the cabin — The theme is primitiveness — all the way through — The search & finding of the value of
primitiveness all the way through —

Church — the Druid stories

Cathedral — great groves —

Trout fishing

Hunting — 5 a.m. — not so much the hunting
    as what goes with it —

Not a return to the primitive but an awareness of what we are losing.

Undated, January 1950

The only reason you want to write is to tell your story —

1. Make men feel close to nature & joy

2. Show that God is love —

3. Show that God is spirit —

4. That the primitive is past — that man is now a spiritual animal —

Nature is cruel — implacable — harsh —
Man through his insight changes things —

1. What & how do you want to write?
        You wish to impart some truth universal such as you would
    want to find in your own search? You must write from a divine
    slant — giving good answers — so simply that all who read will
    enjoy them & benefit —

2. Try something — one little paragraph — "Farewell to Saganaga" —

Timelessness — perspective —
We were windbound — we sat & whittled pot hooks — "Time is the
stream I go fishing in"
    Why don't you speak as a sage, as a Thoreau or Burroughs — You are
wise, you are old and experienced — you can speak words of wisdom —
Do it. Why apologize — why wait — you are the sage....
    This is what you want to do — write beautifully & give a message
— a truth — something that will make people want to read & carry the

book with them. Write so charmingly about all things that hordes will read on & on —

One after the other — no novels or fiction or children's books but books for mature people — books they will love —

July 6, 1952

<u>Idea for the book</u>

It suddenly came to me last night that what I might write is a description of the sort of enjoyment all of us get, the joy in the moonlight between the islands, the flickering of the northern lights, the smooth dip and flow of the canoe beating before the waves, the smell of cedar, the sharp sweet smell of Sweet Gale as it was bruised by the canoe, "a thousand million open pores spilling out the fragrance."

All of these things are part of the old idea of writing on outdoor enjoyment and interpretation — only now you are older — the stuff will not be cloying — this is real and important and maybe the contribution you have toyed with over the years.

The million joys we have — picking of cranberries in the bog, blueberries — trout fishing, sparkling snow, music at sunset, meals before the fire, sunrises and Thoreau, the look of rocks — goldfinches, ducks against the sunset, the sound of bluebills, mallards quacking in the rice.

What you are trying to say is that if you can bring these things out in a book preferably you may have something. You have something different — no one in your acquaintance feels as you do — no one at all. If you can get this love and joy, this wonder and enthusiasm down on paper you will have it. Your job this summer is to try and write a chapter of the book. If you can get started then all problems will iron out.

The reason it looks good to me now is that the above thoughts are merely elaborations of the old theme, which makes it seem as though the old theme has merit.

You could call it — Keys to a Countryside — How to Enjoy the Out of Doors — Secrets of Enjoyment — <u>Wilderness Fun</u> — [added by hand: The Search]

What is the matter with fun — the many ways to enjoy the out of doors — clean campsites — vistas, berry picking, rocks and birds — hunting and fishing — the little cabin. The title "Wilderness Fun" can be elaborated a thousand ways. Write the introduction first and then go on with a hundred different chapters, telling why and how you and others have found the secret to enjoyment. What makes you different is exactly your capacity to enjoy. What has always made you different from your partners, exactly that. "Smell the morning," a ritual to start the day — bringing in all the smells that you know — balsam, bay — wet sand,

"Sounds" — bird songs, waves — wind through the trees —

WF can be happy and gay and give others a real sense of enjoyment — no preaching here but a joyous account of such things as last night the moonlight trip to the island. You can bring in the feeling of oneness, of peace, of accord and amity, of God, of universality. But in this it must be easily done, never forced. Perhaps another book. Wilder. Peace as you thought of long ago.

August 8, 1952

What will it be — as much of a puzzle as ever but there are glimmerings. Last night reading *Time*, under Religion a French priest says in America there <u>is no close feeling for the land</u> — in short <u>no at homeness</u> — no communion. He meant that in Europe where people have lived a long time, there is this feeling of oneness and understanding. Here <u>we are still tourists</u>.

It is much the same as I have been thinking about that what I must put across is the feeling of oneness ala Thoreau. Sig's[3] feeling and mine for the canoe country. If I can bring into my writing this feeling of communion, at homeness or whatever you want to call it then I have done something.

August 11, 1952

To catch perhaps the joy that we all have in natural things in sunsets in the opening of a flower in running water, the wind in the pines, a thousand things. The joy that makes each little adventure exciting, the thing that makes life thrilling and away from the prosaic. To capture that and bring it into your writings, eternity in a grain of sand, the story of rocks and swamps and trees — that is the sort of thing that if you can bring into your writing will make it worthwhile for everyone.

Attached herewith a clipping which points up just this. Compared to the natural wonders all other things are unimportant.[4]

Keep this in mind when you start as well as that sense of oneness and communion Father Breckberger of France talked about when he said Americans are not as yet wedded to their earth — they cannot as yet take their pleasure with her, cannot feel that oneness that perhaps Sig and I have with the out of doors.

America is footloose and unattached. We must try to capture that feeling of at one-homeness to dispel the sensation that towns are refuges from the wild. We are part of it now. Until we capture that we are still a people without roots.[5]

October 11, 1952

Why not make use of the many things you have written. You have enough material for a book right now if it is organized and put in some sort of a sequence, have <u>some sort of thread</u> running through it. Through all of your stuff is the search for the primitive the joy in simple things the fight against convention. Bring through it all too your feeling of <u>the simple, the love of God, communion with all things</u>, make that the lifeline. Such a collection of essays might be all right if there is that line running through them, some coordinating influence through which you can pour all of your knowledge and all of your feeling.

Work up the Trappers Cabin idea for the first. Then follow with <u>Why Wilderness</u>.

I have just finished the Snowbank Cabin about 1000 words and have brought out the sense of naturalness, oneness with environment and animals, the harking back to aeons to living in primitive shelters, the need for renewing old earth associations, of returning to the ancient awarenesses.

The next one will also be a trial — perhaps The Search.

December 1, 1952

I have called this book "The Search" because that is exactly what it is, a lifetime spent in trying to find the answers to my particular type of longing, the longing for the wild, for naturalness, for cleanness, and beauty. The search has gone on for half a century, is still going on but I am beginning to find some of the answers. In short in the words of Thoreau:

"I long ago lost a hound, a bay horse, and a turtle dove and am still on their trail. Many are the travelers I have spoken to concerning them, describing their tracks and what calls they answered to. I have met one or two who have heard the hound and the tramp of the horse, and even seen the dove disappear behind a cloud, and they seemed as anxious to recover them as if they had lost them themselves."

It is the same type of search that I have been going through most of my life, the same type that many people go through much of their lives. It is the recognition of these moments, these episodes that make the search worthwhile. Now looking back over half a century these moments stand out. I find I have forgotten the times when I found nothing, that the highlights stand out. It is impossible to record them all but I shall attempt to set down in this volume the moments that really count.

What is the matter of this search. How recognize the gain when it does come. It is necessary to know what one is looking for in order to find it.

The first impressions of childhood are still vivid but are important only insofar as they have contributed to the goal. As a child there was of course no recognition but now with maturer insight, I look back and find that even then there was something of the search going on.

In the hope that others who have been aware of unrest and futility will find in the reading of the record of my search I have written this little book.

What am I going to find — peace — silence, beauty, the wild cleanness, smells, sounds, but mostly the primitive, why because the primitive is the embodiment of what we as a race have lost. It is this search for something lost that keeps us going, the finding of bits of it that makes the search worthwhile.

"Something lost behind the ranges, something lost and waiting for you." Kipling.

Undated, circa 1953

This book may be the answer if I do not stray and make it a book on the woods as such. It must be spiritual, have more than information, must be the reaction of a man to the real meaning of wilderness.

Therefore such a chapter as <u>Silence</u> might be the key and set the tone. Work up such a chapter and see how it comes out — each chapter must be 2000 to 3000 words long — an essay type however different because of its spiritual appeal. This chapter might be the answer to all of your searching. If you can do one beautiful chapter, making it the sort of thing that all would like to read, beautifully written, beautiful descriptions but more than that, real feeling, real intuition, real contribution, then you might have something.

Silence — start out with a paddle at night — Izaak Walton's Study to be Quiet — the quiet center — coming out of a cabin on Basswood, standing there breathless alone and in absolute quiet.

You should not have to quote, although it would help. But it would take an awful lot of study. If you don't quote, then it is all your own and that is what counts. This will be hard work, the hardest thing you have ever done. It will take prayer and thought. Perhaps this is what you have lived for all of these years. Perhaps this is the sort of thing you can do indefinitely once you begin. This will challenge all you have, every bit of brains and insight and idealism you possess. This is the most important thing you've ever tried. This is the answer.

January 4, 1954

How does all this affect my writing, simply in this way, that what Hudson had I have, the sense of mystery, of animism. It was as vivid in me as in him, note Northwest Corner, Sister Bay, a thousand other instances, surviving in me in spite of all distractions. This sense of mystery, of close communion with all of nature, this sense of seeing more than appears at the surface, this continuance of the sense of wonder and awe, this delight in all natural phenomena is perhaps the most precious thing you have.

If you can incorporate into each of your essays and make it the continuing thread of all your writing, the thing to look for, then you need not be concerned about purpose. These chapters then are part of a whole, the unveiling of this sense of animism as seen through a mature mind.

In <u>The Cabin</u> you find it in the feeling of oneness with the trees, the white footed mouse, the squirrel, in all of the natural little shelters. More than description they give this feeling.

Sigurd at Quetico Provincial Park, circa 1950s. Wisconsin Historical Society Collection, 74065.

In <u>Fish House</u>, you become one with the waving fronds of eel grass in the water, the sense of being a part of the aquatic scene.

In <u>Moon Magic</u> it is the old response to moonlight, the joy and exuberance of all living things in the light of the full moon, not just the play habits of animals but the other.

In <u>Forest Pool</u> the sense of the pool being a part of the primeval picture.

The <u>Spring Hole</u> — again a primitive picture, perfection, untouched, America as it was, the sense of being part of it.

<u>Smell of the Morning</u> — the delight of smells, primitive smells, the wonder the awe the associations, clean natural earthy things.

<u>Northern Lights</u> — stroke stroke stroke — the sense of mystery and beauty again the old animism.

<u>Pine Knots</u> part of the sunshine of hundreds of years ago, gazing into a fire, primeval pictures when the world was young.

<u>Skyline Trail</u> — the sense of the vastness of wilderness, of part of the glacial river, the esker, part of the great spruce swamp — the contrast with people in town who did not know.

<u>Flying In</u> — Again being a part of the terrain, part of the muskeg the water the portages, the wind and rain.

All of these things show the delight, the sense of oneness, the animism that most people have lost. They can find it in all of these things in different ways. I must write with that one object in view to give my work continuity.

<u>Wilderness Music</u> — Somewhere Hudson says, scientific expeditions go in to study native tribes to find this thing they have lost. All animals have it, some humans close to the earth.

Undated, February 1954

Suggestions for <u>Pipes of Pan</u>

In reading *The Beaver* last night coming down on the train I ran across the following from an article on the American Indian.[6]

"The Indian was probably more mature psychologically than the white frontiersman who confronted him. Certainly he was more tolerant. He never doubted but that the white man had a soul as well as the buffalo. Enjoying a tranquil sense of oneness with the universe around him, not unlike that expressed in the poems of Wordsworth, he regarded harmony rather than conflict as the law of life, though he was too practical not to train his young warriors to defend themselves. He drew spiritual sustenance, as the isolated white man could not, from the age old society of his own people, finding deep satisfaction in their religious ritual, their songs, their thanksgiving dances, and their intricate web of social duties. He owned private property, though not real estate. He could never bring himself, even after centuries of contact with white men, to look upon his 'mother' the earth (from whom he had come and to whom he would return) as a chattel. He was generous and hospitable, sharing his possessions with anyone who needed them and doing it cheerfully although in the act he might seem to be impoverishing himself. He was an individualist and fought well when he had to but by nature was peaceable.

"The white man's greatest mistake was his open contempt, his willful insensitiveness to the beauty and the spiritual power of many of the Indian's beliefs."[7]

From this you can draw strength for your own beliefs and especially the note you want to strike in the book. The Pipes of Pan must have this sense of oneness with the earth, the source of all tranquility — the sense of drawing spiritual sustenance from his rituals, songs, dances, the looking upon mother earth not as a chattel, not as something to own and exploit but rather in the true sense of belonging.

Study Wordsworth, catch his sense of oneness — Thoreau the same — have this theme running all the way through. Here is the source of all goodness, all peace. Masefield has it too in the greater life in a sense which really means that he is becoming a part of the universality which the Indians also sensed. All sensitive souls strive for this. The Indians had it and felt it strongly. If you can bring it in, then you have the hard core of belief you want.

February 23, 1954

Note on Pipes of Pan

Your interpretation of Pipes of Pan was too narrow. It is more than the mystical, sense of union and oneness, more than the awe and the sense of wonderment. It is the joy that we all get from doing simple natural things, the joy of movement, the joy in any expedition, picking berries or pine knots, or fishing or hunting. When you listen to the Pipes of Pan you devote yourself to such simple joys. By such devotion you listen to the deeper tones but it is the Pipes just the same.

With this knowledge you can broaden your selection. You must however keep out of it as essays all killing, all essays that do not carry the theme, the thought, the main idea. This rules out the Killers, it rules out The Last Mallard and the Wild Goose. You must remain true to the thought, be consistent all the way through. You cannot vary an iota from the main purpose of your choice.

Have just redone Pine Knots and I think I have captured it there, the joy in finding the knots, simple primitive joy of hunting, finding and burning them, their meaning and interpretation. Have also rewritten Northern Lights — there is definitely The Pipes again. In working over all the rest you can use them all if you adhere to this idea.

February 26, 1954

The Pipes of Pan

Get down to the quick of your mind, say important things. So much of the time you are mouthing words for the sound of them, do not say what you really want to say. Write at white heat get your best thoughts down and into what you are writing about. Without that your materials will have no significance or incidentally importance. Your thoughts are as important as anyone else's. Do not be apologetic. Get them down. What you feel deeply about, your analysis, your grasp of first principles. Those are the things that count.

Epilogue

1963–1972

JUST AS SIGURD OLSON'S CONSERVATION WORK led to the connections that made possible his books of essays, so it also made him so busy that he lost much precious time that he could have spent writing. He served on the National Park Service's advisory board, was an adviser to the Park Service and to the secretary of the interior, scouted out lands all over the country for potential inclusion as protected areas under Park Service jurisdiction, and served as vice president and then president of the Wilderness Society. Every now and then during the 1960s and 1970s, he felt compelled to write notes that echoed those of the 1930s and 1940s. Throughout those early years Sigurd often wrote his darkest journal entries when daily events kept him away from his writing. All he needed to get out of his worst moods was time behind the typewriter. That never changed. Despite the fulfillment his conservation work brought him, at heart he remained a writer. Writing was his true calling, as he saw it. And getting pulled away from it too often or for too long at a time was, for Sigurd, anything but natural.

* * * *

Undated, January 1963

This work here palls and I see no future and certainly not a return.[1] After the hitch this year, I am through and can see the end coming. All I want to do is get back to my writing and thinking. That is my forte, nothing else. The days even though I have been here only a month seem endless and I am doing nothing constructive.

I can picture myself at home heading out to the cabin or the bush and the shack getting these things done, taking a few speaking

Sigurd speaks at a Boy Scouts of America meeting in Ely, 1965. Courtesy of the Charles L. Sommers Alumni Association.

engagements, but being absolutely free of all practical conservation problems.

It is the same old stalemate I have been up against before, back thirty years when I used to pound off a few paragraphs every morning and dream and hope for release. Never again shall I be caught in such an impasse.

July 5, 1963

Am getting so involved in many projects, I seem to be completely engulfed with my writing behind me.[2]

The important thing now is my health, my shoulder, my face and general attitude.[3] If I can get out of this morass this fall feeling more serene and steady and working on the book that is all. If I can forget problems for a while and responsibilities I can come back and live naturally.

A time of rest at home, no more travel, the yard, the Point, the Shack, getting things in order out of all the accumulated confusion.

Yesterday's hike felt good. Would soon swing into the pattern. This noon I'll take a walk over the ridge instead of staying in for lunch just to get a final whiff of McKinley — This I did and it felt good. I lay down at the far end of the trail beyond sight and sound of the camp and looked over the valley.

The Sauna, dusk and night sounds.

Olaus and the look in his eyes as he followed the flight of the bald eagle.[4] He is solely in his world of dreams — his sweet reaction to my account of the golden plover.

Again for the thousandth time I sit and listen and wonder what I am doing here when I should be playing my old role entirely. Next April 4th I'll be 65 the magic year when I may resign and devote the next ten years to writing and speaking and living as I think I should live. How can I get back into the old groove? I should try to gain perspective and make the next ten years count for both of us. They could be happy ones.

The feeling I am wasting my time is perhaps the toughest at affairs such as this, days of sitting, talking, rushing, travel. What gives me a sense of completion only working thinking quietly. This is the road to contentment. You will find satisfaction only by getting back to writing.

The answer then is easy, the road clear, the objectives plain. Life can be good.

Sigurd with Sierra Club president Dick Leonard (*left*) and Wilderness Society president Olaus Murie (*center*), 1953. Olson Family Collection. Courtesy of David Backes.

Am getting more and more weary and more and more convinced of the rightness of my stand.

The answer is simply to cut out what you can, possibly the Allagash and above all begin work on one chapter, or the introduction to the book.[5] The Intro as usual sets the tone. You can explain how all men travel a trail of Echoes, though dim they influence our souls and they reverberate in our minds affecting all we do.

"We are the Music Makers
We are the makers of Dreams."
Arthur O'Shaughnessy

January 27, 1964

All of this leaves me cold, all the hemming-hawing on terminology, all this about areas, makes me wonder what I am doing here[6] —

It will be impossible to do any writing or thinking — the cabin — my poetry & philosophy — the beauty — this is all important for me —

The time is coming when I will have to make the big decision. Perhaps in April will be the time — 4/4/64. Resign from the Councilor and from all committees & devote myself entirely to writing — what has all this officialdom to do with "The Pipes of Pan," the mystery, poetry, beauty of the wilderness.

All through this is going to be frustration, the same as has always dogged my life....

Reading on Citizens Committee on Natural Resources — the same — I should not be bothering myself with all this. Just marking time.

The point of it all is simply this: — Once it meant a lot but no longer. I am now on the fringes — must sooner or later ease out of it — and devote myself to what I can do best, writing & cruising around on my own —

The Allagash Area: — All these figures seem unimportant now. There was a day but no more. Others should do this not me. Wilderness preservation will go on but it engrosses me less & less. Others can carry the fight.

What I want to do is get away from all this — make a clean break — I must. It is imperative and only when I return to write & begin working will my balance return. This fall was bad. It must never happen again.

I must make a decision soon an irrevocable one like the one in 1947 a clean break — money will not count. I've got 10 years left, I should put them into the best and not feel frustrated or fighting or feel torn — It is the feeling of being torn every which way that I hate.

I will not miss it. I'm done & seen enough —

My writing is poetry

Why waste it?

January 13, 1971

McGraw Hill Book[7]

It took 6 years to do Open Horizons from the publishing of Runes, Sept 1963. The reason: the continued and growing conservation effort, masses of correspondence, Wilderness Society work, lectures, consultancy. All this has pyramided to the point where the effort to do Northern Waterways seems impossible.

Five years from now will make me 77. This will be the very last after the Anthology which is in the works now.[8] It is not worth the effort. Few Canadians will read it and the effort to save the last rivers is all theirs.

E and I deserve a break for the next five years and we will not get it if we are hounded to death with historical research and data. It will be another Lonely Land one plus all the rest of the rivers.

The $7500 is important or rather $10,000 but this is not the overriding figure. If it were possible to get away entirely, I might do it but not with all my obligations now.

All of the philosophical material you gathered before Runes and during the writing possibly could be used for a final philosophical tome I believe sort of thing. This looms as far more important than anything else. It could be a summary of belief.

October 10, 1972

The same perennial idea as of former years, possibly 25 all told.[9] Here I sit out of place as always, wasting time hours & days & months and years when I should be writing. I am 73 a few years left — Have I any right to do any more —

CHRONOLOGY

1899   Sigurd Ferdinand Olson is born in Humboldt Park, Chicago, on April 4.

1906   Family moves to Sister Bay, Wisconsin, on the rugged Door County Peninsula.

1909   Family moves to Prentice, a logging town in north-central Wisconsin.

1912   Family moves to Ashland, Wisconsin.

1916–18   Sigurd attends Northland College in Ashland; works during the summers at a farm in Seeley, Wisconsin, owned by Soren Uhrenholdt.

1918–20   Sigurd attends the University of Wisconsin in Madison; earns undergraduate degree in agriculture.

1920–22   Sigurd teaches animal husbandry, agricultural botany, and geology in the high schools of the neighboring northern Minnesota towns of Nashwauk and Keewatin.

1921   Sigurd takes his first canoe trip in June; marries Elizabeth Dorothy Uhrenholdt on August 8. Their honeymoon is a three-week canoe trip. Eight days before the wedding, on July 31, the *Milwaukee Journal* publishes Sigurd's first article, an account of his June canoe trip.

1922   Sigurd starts graduate program in geology at the University of Wisconsin in Madison; Elizabeth helps with finances by teaching elementary school in Hayward, Wisconsin.

1923   In January, Elizabeth learns she is pregnant; Sigurd drops out of school and lands a job teaching high school biology in Ely,

Paper birch at Nine Mile Lake, Superior National Forest, 1967. Photograph by Leland J. Prater, U.S. Forest Service Records, National Archives.

Minnesota, at the edge of the canoe country wilderness. They move there in February. During the summer, Sigurd finds work as a canoe trip guide, which he continues every summer throughout the 1920s. Sigurd and Elizabeth become parents on September 15, when Sigurd Thorne Olson is born.

1925 Robert Keith Olson is born on December 23. Sigurd is involved in the first battle over the canoe country wilderness, a conflict over proposals to build roads into previously inaccessible areas.

1926 In September, the U.S. secretary of agriculture ends the current canoe country conflict by allowing two major roads to be built and by creating three wilderness areas within Superior National Forest. Sigurd begins splitting his teaching duties between Ely High School and Ely Junior College. At the junior college, he teaches animal biology and human physiology.

1927 In November, Field and Stream publishes Sigurd's first magazine article, "Fishin' Jewelry."

1929 Sigurd and two other men found the Border Lakes Outfitting Company. As manager, Sigurd spends less of his time guiding than in the past. He manages the company until the mid-1940s and maintains partial ownership until 1951.

1931–32 In the fall of 1931, the Olsons move to Champaign, Illinois, so Sigurd can earn a master's degree in zoology at the University of Illinois. He works under Victor Shelford, the nation's leading animal ecologist. He earns his degree in June 1932, after completing a thesis—the first of its kind—on the timber wolf. The Olsons move back to Ely, and Sigurd begins teaching full-time at Ely Junior College.

1932 In May and June, Sports Afield publishes Sigurd's two-part article "Search for the Wild," his first writing fully devoted to wilderness philosophy.

1936 Sigurd becomes dean of Ely Junior College.

1938   In September, *American Forests* publishes Sigurd's article "Why Wilderness?" Superior National Forest's three wilderness areas, recently enlarged, are renamed the Superior Roadless Areas.

1941   Sigurd begins a syndicated newspaper column, "America Out of Doors." It lasts until 1944; then, like many syndicated columns of the time, it ends as government wartime restrictions on newsprint force newspapers to cut back.

1945   Sigurd heads to Europe for a year as a civilian employee of the army. He teaches GIs waiting to be shipped back to America and is an official observer at the Nuremberg trials.

1947   Sigurd resigns as dean of Ely Junior College to devote full time to his writing.

1948–49 Sigurd spearheads the fight to ban airplanes from the wilderness canoe country near his home. It is a precedent-setting, successful battle and brings him national recognition in conservation circles.

1951   Sigurd becomes vice president of the National Parks Association.

1953   Sigurd becomes president of the National Parks Association.

1955   Sigurd signs his first book contract, with Alfred A. Knopf. In the summer, Sigurd and a group of prominent Canadian friends spend several weeks paddling the wild Churchill River in Saskatchewan, one of a handful of rugged trips they would take together.

1956   *The Singing Wilderness* is published in April, shortly after Sigurd's fifty-seventh birthday. It becomes a *New York Times* bestseller. In the summer, the Wilderness Society elects Sigurd to its governing council. He is among the conservation leaders working on drafts of a bill to establish a national wilderness preservation system.

1958   *Listening Point* is published. The Superior Roadless Areas are renamed the Boundary Waters Canoe Area.

1959   Sigurd resigns as president of the National Parks Association and joins the advisory board of the National Park Service. He remains on the board until 1966.

1961   *The Lonely Land* is published.

1962   Sigurd becomes a consultant on wilderness and national park matters for Secretary of the Interior Stewart Udall.

1963   *Runes of the North* is published. Sigurd becomes vice president of the Wilderness Society.

1964   In July, Sigurd, at age sixty-five, embarks on his last major canoe expedition, a voyage from Lake Winnipeg to Hudson Bay along the Nelson and Hayes Rivers. In September, President Lyndon B. Johnson signs the Wilderness Act, establishing the national wilderness preservation system.

1965   Sigurd is part of a National Park Service task force that recommends preserving nearly eighty million acres of land in Alaska. Fearing a political firestorm, the agency buries the report, but the work behind it ultimately bears fruit in the Alaska National Interest Lands and Conservation Act of 1980.

1968   Sigurd becomes president of the Wilderness Society. In November, he suffers a major heart attack during the society's annual meeting at Sanibel Island, Florida.

1969   *Open Horizons* and *The Hidden Forest* are published.

1971   Sigurd resigns as president of the Wilderness Society, citing his health and desire to write. President Richard M. Nixon signs into law the act establishing Voyageurs National Park in northern Minnesota; Sigurd had played an important role as an advocate of the park since the early 1960s, and he also gave the park its name. A new elementary school in the Minneapolis suburb of Golden Valley is named after Sigurd.

1972   *Wilderness Days* is published. The Sigurd Olson Environmental Institute is established at Northland College in Ashland, Wisconsin.

1974   The highest honor in nature writing, the John Burroughs Medal, is presented to Sigurd.

1976   *Reflections from the North Country* is published.

1977   Sigurd is hanged in effigy in his hometown of Ely during debates about the status of the Boundary Waters Canoe Area.

1978   President Jimmy Carter signs the law granting full wilderness status to the Boundary Waters Canoe Area Wilderness, more than fifty years after Sigurd Olson's first efforts to protect it.

1979   In December, Sigurd undergoes successful surgery for colon cancer, but he never fully regains his strength.

1982   On January 13, Sigurd dies of a heart attack while snow-shoeing near his home. *Of Time and Place* is published.

1994   Elizabeth Olson dies of heart failure on August 23, at the age of ninety-six.

1998   The Listening Point Foundation is established.

NOTES

Introduction

1. Sigurd appeared in the December 22, 1961, issue of *Life* magazine, a special issue devoted to the outdoors and America's conservation leaders. His 1969 book *Open Horizons* used the iconic photograph on its dust jacket, as did my biography, *A Wilderness Within: The Life of Sigurd F. Olson* (Minneapolis: University of Minnesota Press, 1997). The Eisenstaedt quotation has been widely reprinted; I do not know its original source.
2. The "ambassador without portfolio" moniker was given by U.S. Assistant Secretary of the Interior Ross Leffler. See Backes, *Wilderness Within*, 301.
3. Wayburn called Sigurd "the personification of the wilderness defender" on April 8, 1972, while presenting him with an honorary life membership in the Sierra Club.
4. George Marshall to Elizabeth Olson, January 26, 1982. See Backes, *Wilderness Within*, 316.
5. Sigurd F. Olson, *The Singing Wilderness* (New York: Alfred A. Knopf, 1956), 8.
6. Backes, *Wilderness Within*, 13.

The Winter of Renewal

1. Handwritten at an abandoned cabin on Grassy Lake.
2. Here and throughout this collection, an ampersand indicates a handwritten entry. When typing, he always spelled out the word *and*.
3. The Student Volunteers was American Protestantism's most important missionary organization, and Sigurd was elected president of its chapter at the University of Wisconsin in Madison. For more, see Backes, *Wilderness Within*, 33–35.
4. He is referring to the university's YMCA at 740 Langdon Street, where he lived as a student.
5. After graduating from the University of Wisconsin in June 1920, Sigurd took a job teaching animal husbandry, agricultural botany, and geology at the high schools in the neighboring northern Minnesota towns of Nashwauk and Keewatin.
6. Published on July 31, 1921, as "Canoe Tourist Finds Joys of the Great Outdoors through the Vast Watered Wilderness of the North."
7. He is referring not to his undergraduate degree there but his brief period as a graduate student in geology, from September 1922 to January 1923.
8. Samuel Scoville Jr. (1872–1950) was an attorney, naturalist, and writer of adventure stories for young readers.
9. "Reflections of a Guide," *Field and Stream*, June 1928.
10. Here and throughout the collection, I have underlined words and phrases that Sigurd underlined in the originals. He nearly always did this by hand

and not necessarily when he wrote the entry. He regularly went back and read old entries and could have underlined his comments months or years later. I suspect that he did most of the underlining during later readings.

11. Alvin Cahn was a University of Illinois zoologist whom Sigurd had guided through the Quetico–Superior wilderness for six weeks in 1928. They became friends, and Cahn took Sigurd under his wing and began persuading him to come to the University of Illinois for a graduate degree in ecology.

12. Naturalist and author William Henry Hudson (1841–1922).

13. This experience is recalled in one of his best-known essays, "Silence," in Olson, Singing Wilderness, 130–31.

14. Sigurd and two other men founded the Border Lakes Outfitting Company on January 1, 1929 (see "Quiet Desperation," this volume).

15. This is the trail he writes about in the essay "The Skyline Trail," Olson, Singing Wilderness, 225–30.

16. "Snow Wings," Boys' Life, March 1928.

Quiet Desperation

1. In his darkest moods Sigurd tended to describe himself as "desperate" or "panicky." Anxiety seems likely to have played an important role in his moments of despair. Out of well over six hundred journal entries, nine contain clear references to current suicidal thoughts. A handful of others mention having had such thoughts in the past. There is no clear pattern in other entries from those periods that would point to depression. I discuss this in detail in Backes, Wilderness Within, 143–44.

2. The Border Lakes Outfitting Company.

3. Lanier (1842–1881), raised in Georgia, pursued his passion for poetry and music with little success, spending years working jobs that didn't satisfy him but paid the bills. During the Civil War he fought for the Macon Volunteers, was captured, and contracted tuberculosis in a Union prison. The disease forced frequent moves in search of a tolerable climate and ultimately killed him. His wife, Mary Day, edited the posthumous volume of poetry that Sigurd read.

4. The "spring work" refers to all the queries and reservations coming into the Border Lakes Outfitting Company, and the summer work he dreaded was managing the outfitting company's day-to-day operations. He missed his years of spending most of the summertime out in the wilderness as a guide. Now he had to stay in town and run things.

5. "Duck Heaven," Outdoor Life, October 1930; and "Confessions of a Duck Hunter," Sports Afield, October 1930. These were his first published articles since 1928.

6. Uzzell was a New York literary agent. For more about this first submission, see Backes, Wilderness Within, 76.

7. Ralph T. King was a University of Minnesota ecologist whom Sigurd had guided in 1930.

8. Elizabeth Olson. Throughout his journal Sigurd refers to Elizabeth as "E" or "Libby."

9. Oliver L. Austin Jr. had just started working for the Bureau of Biological Survey in Minnesota at the start of an illustrious career. Most likely Austin had been in the canoe party the previous summer with King and Sigurd.

Reluctant Ecologist

1. Aldo Leopold, wildlife ecologist at the University of Wisconsin.
2. Sigurd caught a cold in December, and several days after Christmas it developed into pneumonia. He and Elizabeth were at her childhood home in Seeley, Wisconsin, at the time. Sigurd spent days under an oxygen mask, sedated with morphine. For more, see Backes, *Wilderness Within*, 81–82.
3. He is in Champaign, Illinois.
4. Arthur Vestal was a botanist at the University of Illinois.
5. Sigurd tended to project his age forward, referring to the age he would turn on his next birthday.
6. He is in Ann Arbor during the semester break, checking out the University of Michigan and visiting relatives.
7. Victor E. Shelford was a renowned plant ecologist and Sigurd's major professor.
8. Charles Kenneth Leith was perhaps the nation's top geologist of his time when Sigurd attended graduate school at the University of Wisconsin in the fall of 1922.
9. The University of Michigan in Ann Arbor.
10. He spent part of the day at the Detroit Museum of Art. He came away inspired and more convinced he was no scientist, but rather a writer who captures with words on paper the kinds of emotions artists capture with paint on canvas. He even spent some time over the next year or so considering taking up painting as a vocation, reading several books about it.

Unsettled in Ely

1. Aldo Leopold, *A Sand County Almanac, and Sketches Here and There* (New York: Oxford University Press, 1949). For more on Leopold's offer to Sigurd, see Backes, *Wilderness Within*, 96–98.
2. Peterson Fishing Camp was owned by M. W. Peterson, one of Sigurd's partners in the Border Lakes Outfitting Company. Emil "Ogima" Anderson was a fellow canoe country guide and freelance writer.
3. Herbert Ravenel Sass (1884–1958) was a naturalist, artist, poet, novelist, historian, and an iconic "Southern gentleman" from Charleston, South Carolina. Samuel Scoville Jr. (1872–1950), a grandson of Henry Ward Beecher, was a lawyer, naturalist, and author of nature-related fiction. Archibald Rutledge (1883–1973) was South Carolina's first poet laureate, and the author of more than fifty books.
4. James Oliver Curwood (1878-1927) wrote adventure stories, the most popular of which were set in Alaska or the Yukon. I have not been able to identify the writer named Poindexter.
5. *Field and Stream* published "Let's Go Exploring" four years later, in June 1937.
6. Sigurd enclosed this paragraph in a bracket to signify its importance.

7. International Boundary Commission.
8. Ernest Oberholtzer, the leading spokesperson at the time for preserving the Quetico–Superior wilderness of Minnesota and Ontario, would in 1935 join with seven other men in founding the Wilderness Society. He and Sigurd had exchanged letters as early as December 1930 and had met in the fall of 1932. After Sigurd's testimony in Minneapolis, they began to visit with each other on occasion and work together on conservation issues. Olin Kaupanger was secretary of the Minnesota division of the Izaak Walton League of America.
9. Once again, he is thinking ahead to his next birthday.
10. "A New Policy Needed for the Superior," *Minnesota Conservationist*, May 1934. The title refers to Superior National Forest. "Roads or Planes in the Superior," *Minnesota Waltonian*, April 1934. "Let's Go Exploring," *Field and Stream*, June 1937. "Cruising in the Arrowhead," *Outdoors*, May 1934.
11. Paul K. Whipple was the editor. I have not located a published copy of "En Roulant." "May We Come Along?" was published by *Field and Stream* in January 1938 under the title "Taking Us, Dad?"
12. Indecipherable word.
13. Ernest Oberholtzer.

Farewell to Saganaga

1. When Sigurd refers to "stories," he means short story fiction.
2. He is referring to character development for short story fiction.
3. The lake is about fifteen miles southwest of Ely.
4. Evidently a biological survey of Yosemite National Park.
5. "Tobatik" (TOE-bah-tick) was the local pronunciation for the Totogatik River in northwestern Wisconsin.
6. *Minnesota Conservationist* published it in May 1935.
7. The Olson family took a summer vacation in the West.
8. Indecipherable word.
9. He had been thinking about becoming a summer naturalist for the National Park Service.

The Dean

1. Back Bay is part of Basswood Lake.
2. "Culture and Happiness" is chapter 6 in John Cowper Powys's masterwork, *The Meaning of Culture* (New York: W. W. Norton & Co., 1929). Powys (1872–1963) was a British novelist, philosopher, poet, and literary critic.
3. "Ober" is Ernest Oberholtzer; "Pete" is Mervin W. Peterson, partner in the Border Lakes Outfitting Company as well as neighbor and friend to the Olsons; "Florence" is Pete's wife; "E" is Elizabeth; "Ken" is Sigurd's older brother. Bob Marshall was the principal founder of the Wilderness Society. Sigurd had met him in the summer of 1935 when Marshall visited northern Minnesota, and they quickly bonded.
4. All three were short story fiction turned down by premier magazines but picked up by his friend Robert C. Mueller, managing editor of *Sports Afield*.

For more on their relationship, see Backes, *Wilderness Within*, 128–30. Mueller published "Papette" in the January-February 1932 issue, and "Trail's End" in the October 1933 issue. I have not located a copy of "En Roulant."

5. Julius Santo, dean of Ely Junior College and close friend of Sigurd.

6. Sigurd often wrote his journal entries while at the junior college.

7. Sigurd drew a bracket around the left side of this paragraph.

8. Just one of the magazine articles was published in 1936, "The Romance of Portages," *Minnesota Conservationist*, April 1936. *Field and Stream* published "Let's Go Exploring" in June 1937. For the scientific journal articles, see "Organization and Range of the Pack," *Ecology*, January 1938, and "A Study in Predatory Relationship with Particular Reference to the Wolf," *Scientific Monthly*, April 1938.

9. Ray Hoefler was secretary of the Ely Commercial Club. Kermit Wick befriended Sigurd during several hunting and fishing trips to northern Minnesota in the early 1930s.

10. He attended the University of Illinois in 1931–32, not 1930–31.

11. "Why Wilderness," *American Forests*, September 1938. Included in Sigurd F. Olson, *The Meaning of Wilderness: Essential Articles and Speeches*, ed. David Backes (Minneapolis: University of Minnesota Press, 2001).

12. Edward Weeks, *This Trade of Writing* (New York: Little, Brown and Co., 1936).

13. "Virginia" is the nearby Iron Range city, not the state.

14. Sigurd's older brother had just become dean of Northwestern University's Medill School of Journalism.

15. Da Costa was a successful writer of short stories for national magazines such as the *Saturday Evening Post*. Sigurd had guided Da Costa on canoe trips, and they became friends. Da Costa was a source of encouragement for Sigurd, and a guide to the writing market.

Grandmother's Trout

1. The duck story probably is "Mallards Are Different," *Field and Stream*, November 1938. Robert K. Olson especially recalled "Beauchard's Beaver," a short story about a multigenerational French family that trapped in the north and saved a beaver colony from various calamities. "He worked on it and worked on it," Robert said, "and the whole family got involved, we all had to discuss it—he'd read it to us, so we couldn't back off being involved. And then he sent it off, and it came back rejected—once, twice, thrice." See Backes, *Wilderness Within*, 140. For more about his writing struggles during this period, see 138–43.

2. He means *American Forests*.

3. Lin Yutang (1895–1976) was a Chinese philosopher, writer, and translator whose books often became bestsellers in the West. Sigurd may be referring to Yutang's popular 1937 book *The Importance of Living* (New York: John Day/Reynal and Hitchcock), which was about positive thinking and relieving anxiety. When I went through Sigurd's collection of books in the fall of 1990, however, the sole volume by Lin Yutang was a 1943 edition of his *Between Tears and Laughter* (New York: John Day).

4. "Sciurus" is the scientific term for a member of the genus of bushy-tailed creatures we know as squirrels.
5. Winfred Rhoades was a psychologist who wrote popular self-help books from the 1930s through the 1950s.
6. "Why Wilderness?," *American Forests*, September 1938. Included in Olson, *The Meaning of Wilderness*.
7. *Field and Stream* published "Fireside Pictures" in March 1940.
8. This day is his thirty-ninth birthday.
9. "The Mallards of Back Bay," *Sports Afield*, October 1939.
10. Don Hough, a Minnesota native, was another successful writer Sigurd had become friends with through summertime guiding. In the 1930s Hough worked for *Collier's* and the *Saturday Evening Post*. A humorist, he wrote several film scripts in the 1940s, and seven books from 1943 to 1960.
11. "Shift of the Wind" eventually was accepted by *Sports Afield* and published in December 1944.
12. Most of these either became or were incorporated into essays in Sigurd's books. "Easter on the Prairie," "Grandmother's Trout," "Saganaga," and "Muskeg" (renamed "Forest Pool") became part of his first book, *The Singing Wilderness*. "King's Point" was featured in his second book, *Listening Point* (New York: Alfred A. Knopf, 1958). "Northwest Corner" was adapted into part of his fifth book, *Open Horizons* (New York: Alfred A. Knopf, 1969).
13. Sigurd drew a bracket around the left side of this paragraph.
14. He is looking back to the summer of 1917, which he spent working on the Uhrenholdt farm in Seeley, Wisconsin, north of Hayward. It is here he met Elizabeth, and where in 1921 they married, with Sigurd's father, L. J. Olson, a Swedish Baptist minister, leading the ceremony. Chris Uhrenholdt was one of Elizabeth's brothers. Jack Thompson was a logger who hunted with Sigurd and regaled him with bunkhouse songs and stories of the old days.

We Used to Sing
1. He will turn forty on April 4.
2. Jane Hardy and A. L. Fierst were literary agents in New York.
3. Don Hough.
4. The Uhrenholdt farm in Seeley, Wisconsin.
5. In this case "Kings Point" was short story fiction. Sigurd was entering a brief phase of trying to turn some of his rejected essays into fiction.
6. Elmo was another literary agent in New York.
7. Hardy wrote to Sigurd on May 8, 1939, "You write charmingly, but you will never sell until you learn to put your perfectly lovely writing around a real plot." See Backes, *Wilderness Within*, 160.
8. Ann Elmo's June 1 letter said, "They are all exceedingly well handled, but ... there is practically no market for this type of thing. I do think it would be advisable for you to incorporate these experiences in fiction." See Backes, *Wilderness Within*, 160.
9. Most likely Sigurd is referring to Stanley Vestal, widely known for his books on the old American West, who also wrote advice for writers.

10. Sigurd drew a thick vertical line along the left side of each of these three paragraphs, in addition to the underlining shown here.
11. In 1938 the Olsons hired a maid to do the cooking and cleaning.
12. Sigurd earlier identified him as "Mr. R.D. Handy of Duluth."
13. In the original Sigurd accidentally typed "January 45, 1940."
14. By "school" he means "college." Sigurd Jr. was sixteen, and Bob was fourteen.
15. Sam Campbell was a popular Wisconsin nature writer, photographer, and speaker who was a good friend of Sigurd. See Steven Yahr, *Letters from the Sanctuary: The Sam Campbell Story* (Ithaca, Mich.: A. B. Publishing, 2019).
16. Likely a reference to Bob Mueller, editor of *Sports Afield*.
17. "The Last Mallard," *Sports Afield*, November 1940; "Gold in Them Hills," *Sports Afield*, July 1944; "Shift of the Wind," *Sports Afield*, December 1944.
18. "The annual" is likely the yearbook of Ely Junior College.
19. Sigurd triple-underlined the final four words, "not in this life."
20. Russia had invaded Finland three months earlier, on November 30, 1939.

Big Brother's Big Idea
1. "Fireside Pictures" was the title of an article of Sigurd's just then making its appearance in the March issue of *Field and Stream*.
2. A former student of Olson's at Ely Junior College, Bill Rom (1917–2008) founded Canoe Country Outfitters in 1946. At the time it was said to have been the largest canoe outfitter in the world and served generations of visitors to Quetico Provincial Park and the Superior National Forest.
3. Dr. Sidney J. Knowles was a Chicago dentist who Sigurd befriended on early guiding trips near Ely.
4. Sigurd added to the left of this paragraph a potential title to a syndicated column: "Wood Notes."
5. Stewart Edward White, *Wild Geese Calling* (New York: Doubleday, Doran and Co., 1940).
6. James Hilton (1900–1954), the English novelist and author of *Lost Horizon* (New York: Macmillan, 1933).
7. Kenneth Reid was the new director of the Izaak Walton League of America. He worked closely with Sigurd on canoe country issues throughout the 1940s.
8. Elsie Robinson (1883–1956) was a popular newspaper columnist whose syndicated column "Listen World" reached twenty million readers.
9. "Stuffy" was the nickname of Basil L. Walters, one of America's prominent journalists and editors of the era. Sigurd probably established contact through his brother Ken, whose own journalism career overlapped with that of Walters at the *Milwaukee Journal* in the early 1920s. Walters currently was managing editor at the *Des Moines Register* but (in a stroke of good timing for Sigurd) was about to move to Minnesota as executive editor of the *Minneapolis Star-Journal*. Paul Meyers managed the North American Sportsman's Bureau in Chicago, which syndicated the "America Out of Doors" newspaper column and published an annual *Sportsman's Guide and Directory*. Sigurd had written for Meyers on occasion since 1937 and had served on the bureau's advisory board.

10. Bill Wenstrom was one of the guides Sigurd learned from during his summers with Wilderness Outfitters during the 1920s. "It was Big Bill Wenstrom who taught me how to throw on a canoe," Sigurd recalled four decades later. "He didn't tell me, but I noticed the ease with which he did it, the balancing on his thighs, the short kick of the hips, the twist of the arms as the canoe went overhead. It took many tries before I could drop one neatly on my shoulders, but when I was finally able to do so, it was the easiest way of all." See Olson, *Open Horizons*, 97.
11. Actually, he is forty-one.
12. Nickname of Ken's wife, Mildred.
13. Izaak Walton League of America.

America Out of Doors

1. Walters quoted in Backes, *Wilderness Within*, 164. The series began on March 23.
2. For more on Sigurd's experience with "America Out of Doors," see *Wilderness Within*, 167–68, 171–72, 189, 205.
3. Wildlife painter Francis Lee Jaques (1887–1969) illustrated Sigurd's first three books.
4. Basil L. "Stuffy" Walters. Perhaps "Tubby" was another nickname of his, for Sigurd used it multiple times, but I have not seen it used in other sources.
5. Ray P. Holland, a *Field and Stream* editor Sigurd knew.
6. The *Star-Journal* published "The Bohemians" the next day, March 23.
7. The paper gave it the title "First Spring Flower."
8. Patterson was the editor at Meyer's syndicate.
9. Boots was a male blond cocker spaniel Sigurd had gotten in 1940 as a hunting dog.

Casualty of War

1. See the entry for July 23, 1945, in the next chapter.
2. Reid was executive director of the Izaak Walton League of America.
3. Sigurd added the last two sentences by hand in this otherwise typed entry.
4. John Kieran, *John Kieran's Nature Notes* (New York: Doubleday, 1941).
5. James G. Needham, *About Ourselves: A Survey of Human Nature from the Zoological Viewpoint* (Lancaster, Pa.: Cattell Press, 1941).
6. See Backes, *Wilderness Within*, 38–39.
7. Ibid., 44.
8. This story is related in Hendrik Willem van Loon, *The Arts* (New York: Simon and Schuster, 1937), 4–6.
9. Sigurd drew a bracket around the left side of this paragraph.
10. Sigurd recorded the month but not the day.
11. Long-tailed ducks. "Squaw" is now a pejorative term.
12. As so often, he is thinking ahead to his next birthday.
13. This idea eventually developed into one of his most memorable essays, "Pools of the Isabella," in Olson, *Singing Wilderness*.
14. Important context: Elizabeth wrote to her sister Johanne this month, "Sig has ulcers so badly that I doubt he can go on with school next year. He has

tried hard to hide it—feels humiliated for some reason. He's in serious
condition and I think the only thing that can help him will be a year without
school work." See Backes, *Wilderness Within*, 172–73.

15. Ernest Thompson Seton, *Wild Animals I Have Known* (New York: Charles
Scribner's Sons, 1898).

16. He is referring to his hope of entering the military during World War II,
despite his age. No doubt he is right about the escapist aspect, but there was
more, too. He always regretted just missing out on World War I and living
his romanticized ideas about military service. See Backes, *Wilderness Within*,
28–33.

17. Robert K. Olson had recently turned eighteen and enlisted with the Army
Air Corps. The war ended before he completed training, so he never saw
combat. His older brother, Sigurd Jr., left home in March 1943 to train with
the Eighty-Sixth Infantry. He led a platoon in the ski troops of the Tenth
Mountain Division and helped open the northern Apennines in Italy to
Allied forces. His unit suffered a 75 percent casualty rate.

18. Sigurd drew a curved line in the left margin to highlight this paragraph.

Medium Again
1. See Backes, *Wilderness Within*, 175–76.
2. This period of his life is covered in Backes, *Wilderness Within*, 173–80.
3. Some of these titles will sound familiar to readers of Sigurd's books, for they
are early versions of later essays, such as "Moon Magic," "Birthday on the
Manitou," and "The Stone Wall," from Olson, *Singing Wilderness*; and "Pussy
Willow," from Olson, *Listening Point*. Note that he originally placed the
location of the birthday story on the Baptism River and later changed it to
the Manitou. While a simple correction of a faulty memory is possible (the
two rivers are close to each other), he may well have changed it for narrative
purposes. He cared less about factual details than the overall message and
feeling he was trying to convey.
4. He was just beginning to send essays to Anita Diamant of Writer's Workshop Inc. in New York.
5. Both of these eventually made their way into *The Singing Wilderness*, with the
latter taking the plural form, "Wild Geese."
6. This, too, made it into *The Singing Wilderness*.
7. Jim Kjelgaard (1910–1959) was an author of young adult fiction whose books
were primarily about dogs and wild animals.
8. Sigurd Olson, "We Need Wilderness," *National Parks Magazine*,
January–March 1946. Reprinted in Olson, *Meaning of Wilderness*, 58–68.
9. He is in England as he writes. He set sail from New York on July 5.
10. He is in Heidelberg, Germany, as he writes this entry and the next.
11. William Kilgore Jr. (1879–1953) was a curator at the Bell Museum of Natural
History.
12. Walter J. Breckenridge (1903–2003), director of the Bell Museum from 1946
to 1970.
13. "The Breaking" was the title of an essay in *Listening Point*. But it would be
nearly a decade before Sigurd found and purchased that property. Here, he

is probably referring to his summer 1917 experience working on the Uhren-holdt farm in Seeley, Wisconsin. His major task was clearing and plowing a marshy plot of land. See Backes, Wilderness Within, 22–25; and Olson, Open Horizons, 43–47. "Rose Quartz" is also the title of an essay in Listening Point.

A New Life in Conservation

1. For more on this and on the campaign, see Backes, Wilderness Within, 190–207.
2. Izaak Walton League of America.
3. See the introduction to "Medium Again" for more on Ellinor Grogan.
4. Frank "Hub" Hubachek (1894–1986), a Harvard-educated attorney from Chicago, was active in the formation of the Quetico–Superior Council in 1925 and creator of the Wilderness Research Center on Basswood Lake, now on Fall Lake and under the ownership of the University of Minnesota.
5. Ely Commercial Club.
6. Frederic Litten was a colleague of Kenneth Olson at Northwestern University. Sigurd knew his fiction was weak but feared he wouldn't make enough income to support himself and Elizabeth unless he could sell short stories, so he sent Litten five short stories he had previously sent to Anita Diamant. Litten's response on August 7 was much like Diamant's. "The writing is not adequate," he said. "The cliche and the trite (word and phrase) are too often found. Errors of technique harm the effect; the transitions are abrupt." See Backes, Wilderness Within, 188.
7. Sigurd had given up on Anita Diamant and started working with Lurton Blassingame, another New York literary agent. He, too, criticized Sigurd's short stories, saying that they were wordy and sentimental and that Sigurd made punctuation and other errors "that irritate editors." See Backes, Wilderness Within, 188.
8. Florence Page Jaques, author and spouse of artist Francis Lee Jaques.
9. Florence Page Jaques, Canadian Spring (New York: Harper & Brothers, 1947).

The Singing Wilderness

1. The film Wilderness Canoe Country was produced by the President's Quetico–Superior Committee. It is held at the Minnesota History Center in St. Paul.
2. For Knopf quotation, see Backes, Wilderness Within, 242. Sigurd served as the National Parks Association president until 1959.
3. His older son.
4. The article Sigurd attached was "The Mystery," by Lee Hastings Bristol Jr. It starts out with William Blake:
     To see the world in a grain of sand,
     And a heaven in a wild flower;
     Hold infinity in the palm of your hand,
     And eternity in an hour.
   This became one of Sigurd's favorites. He typed it on an index card and hung it in his writing shack near his typewriter.
5. Sigurd drew a vertical line along the left side of this paragraph.

6. *The Beaver* was a magazine of Canadian history started by the Hudson's Bay Company in 1920. In 2010 it was renamed *Canada's History*.
7. Sigurd drew two vertical lines along the left side of this paragraph.

Epilogue

1. Writing from Washington, D.C., he is referring to his work as a consultant to the National Park Service and the secretary of the interior, which began in 1957 and continued at least until 1971.
2. He is in Denali National Park, Alaska, with the National Park Service's advisory board. He served on the board from 1959 to 1966.
3. Sigurd was recovering from an accident in which he tore ligaments and chipped a bone in his right shoulder. His facial twitch, meanwhile, got bad enough as he aged (becoming not just a twitch but a shaking of his head) that many people assumed he had Parkinson's disease. But he didn't. Elizabeth Olson told me that it began as an eye twitch during his final year as dean of Ely Junior College, and that doctors said it was stress induced. He tried to control it but eventually simply lived with it as best he could.
4. Olaus Murie, Sigurd's friend and fellow wilderness advocate, was in poor health and would die on October 21, 1963.
5. He is referring to *Open Horizons*, which took him six more years to complete.
6. He is back in Washington, D.C., again, doing his consultant work with the National Park Service and Department of the Interior.
7. Sigurd had contracted with McGraw-Hill on October 26, 1965, for a book on northern waterways. He was supposed to deliver it by January 1969. Now that the book is two years overdue, the publisher wants him to return the $2,500 advance or give a firm date of delivery. Sigurd realizes he must focus on the manuscript that will become *Reflections from the North Country* (New York: Alfred A. Knopf, 1976).
8. Sigurd F. Olson, *Sigurd F. Olson's Wilderness Days* (New York: Alfred A. Knopf, 1972).
9. Sigurd writes during the annual meeting of the Wilderness Society's governing council. He served on the council from 1956 to 1974. He also served as the group's vice president from 1963 to 1968, and as its president from 1968 to 1971.

Sigurd F. Olson (1899–1982) was a writer, wilderness guide, and one of America's foremost conservationists. For much of his career he fought to keep roads and dams out of the northern wilderness of Superior National Forest and Quetico Provincial Park. He served as an ecologist for the Izaak Walton League of America and vice president and president of both the National Parks Association and the Wilderness Society. His advocacy for the Quetico–Superior region was crucial in securing protected wilderness status for the Boundary Waters Canoe Area and Voyageurs National Park. In 1974, he earned the John Burroughs Medal, the highest honor in nature writing. His many best-selling books include *The Singing Wilderness*, *Listening Point*, *The Lonely Land*, and *Runes of the North*, all published by the University of Minnesota Press.

David Backes is author of A *Wilderness Within: The Life of Sigurd F. Olson*, published by the University of Minnesota Press and winner of the Small Press Book Award for biography. His other books include *The Meaning of Wilderness*, a collection of Sigurd Olson's essays and speeches, and *Spirit of the North: The Quotable Sigurd F. Olson*. He was a professor at the University of Wisconsin–Milwaukee.